*Figure 1* Frontispiece, Jonathan Swift (1718), by Charles Jervas.

# Jonathan Swift's
# *Gulliver's Travels*

Jonathan Swift's *Gulliver's Travels* (1726) ranks as one of the most biting satires of British and European society ever published. Since first publication, reactions to the book have varied from delight to disgust, but Swift's powerful treatment of the issues of power, morality, colonization, social conventions and human nature seldom fails to engage and challenge his readers.

Taking the form of a sourcebook, this guide to Swift's controversial novel offers:

- extensive introductory comment on the contexts and many interpretations of the text, from publication to the present
- annotated extracts from key contextual documents, reviews, critical works and the text itself
- cross-references between documents and sections of the guide, in order to suggest links between texts, contexts and criticism
- suggestions for further reading.

Part of the *Routledge Guides to Literature* series, this volume is essential reading for all those beginning detailed study of *Gulliver's Travels* and seeking not only a guide to the novel, but also a way through the wealth of contextual and critical material that surrounds Swift's text.

**Roger D. Lund** is Fallon Professor of English at Le Moyne University, USA. He has published widely on eighteenth-century literature.

# Routledge Guides to Literature*

**Editorial Advisory Board:** Richard Bradford (University of Ulster at Coleraine), Jan Jedrzejewski (University of Ulster at Coleraine), Duncan Wu (St. Catherine's College, University of Oxford)

**Routledge Guides to Literature** offer clear introductions to the most widely studied authors and literary texts.

Each book engages with texts, contexts and criticism, highlighting the range of critical views and contextual factors that need to be taken into consideration in advanced studies of literary works. The series encourages informed but independent readings of texts by ranging as widely as possible across the contextual and critical issues relevant to the works examined and highlighting areas of debate as well as those of critical consensus. Alongside general guides to texts and authors, the series includes 'sourcebooks', which allow access to reprinted contextual and critical materials as well as annotated extracts of primary text.

**Available in this series:**

* Some books in this series were originally published in the Routledge Literary Sourcebooks series, edited by Duncan Wu, or the Complete Critical Guide to English Literature series, edited by Richard Bradford and Jan Jedrzejewski.

# Jonathan Swift's
# *Gulliver's Travels*
## A Sourcebook

*Edited by Roger D. Lund*

Routledge
Taylor & Francis Group

NEW YORK AND LONDON

First published 2006 by Routledge
270 Madison Avenue, New York, NY 10016

Simultaneously published in the UK
by Routledge
2 Milton Park, Abingdon, Oxon, OX14 4RN

*Routledge is an imprint of the Taylor & Francis Group, an informa business*

© 2006 Roger D. Lund

Typeset in Sabon and Gill Sans by RefineCatch Limited, Bungay, Suffolk
Printed and bound in Great Britain by TJ International Ltd, Padstow, Cornwall

*Library of Congress Cataloging in Publication Data*
Jonathan Swift's Gulliver's Travels : a sourcebook / edited by Roger D. Lund
        p. cm.—(Routledge guides to literature)
Includes bibliographical references and index.
1. Swift, Jonathan, 1667–1745. Gulliver's Travels    2. Voyages, Imaginary—History and
criticism.    3. Satire, English—History and criticism.    4. Imaginary societies in
literature.    5. Travelers in literature.    I. Lund, Roger D., 1949–    .    II. Series.
PR3724.G8L86 2006
823'5—dc22                                                          2005031484

*British Library Cataloguing in Publication Data*
A catalogue record for this book is available from the British Library.

ISBN10: 0–415–70020–5 (hbk)
ISBN10: 0–415–70021–3 (pbk)

ISBN13: 9–78–0–415–70020–7 (hbk)
ISBN13: 9–78–0–415–70021–4 (pbk)

**For David and Sarah**

# Contents

# 2: Interpretations

# 3: Key Passages

## Introduction

## Key Passages

# 4: Further Reading

# Illustrations

# Annotation and Footnotes

Annotation is a key feature of this series. Both the original notes from reprinted texts and new annotations by the editor appear at the bottom of the relevant page. The reprinted notes are prefaced by the author's name in square brackets, e.g. [Robinson's note].

# Acknowledgements

I would like to thank my students in ENG 218 for reminding me just how difficult first encounters with Gulliver can be. I would also like to thank Dr Raegan Russell of Manlius Pebble Hill School, DeWitt, NY for loaning me her Advanced Placement Literature class. Liz Thompson, Kate Parker, Polly Dodson and Duncan Wu have been unfailingly generous with their advice. I am grateful to Roger Eliot Stoddard of the Houghton Library, to Riley Illustrations, and to the National Portrait Gallery, London, for permission to reprint illustrations. I am indebted as well to the Le Moyne College Committee on Faculty Development and Research, and the research fund of the Francis Fallon Professorship. As usual, my wife Sheila Murphy has been more patient than I deserve. I thank her for that. Finally, I would like to acknowledge the importance of my two favourite students, Sarah and David Lund, to whom this book is dedicated, in the hope that as their tastes mature, they, too, will discover the charms of Swift's 'wonderful Book'.

Thanks also to the following, for permission to reproduce materials.

Extracts from *The Correspondence of Jonathan Swift: Volume III, 1724–1731* (1963) edited by Harold Williams. By Permission of Oxford University Press.

Extracts from 'Swift's Struddlebugs, Progress and the Analogy of History' by William Freedman, *Studies in English Literature*, Issue 3, vol. 35 (1995), pp. 458–60, 464–6. Reproduced by kind permission of the editor.

Extracts from 'The Hairy Maid at the Harpsichord: Some Speculations on the Meaning of Gulliver's Travels' by Dennis Todd, from *Texas Studies in Literature and Language* vol. 32, no. 2, pp. 239–83. Copyright © 1992 the University of Texas Press. All right reserved. Reproduced by permission of the author and publisher.

Extracts from 'The Unity of Gulliver's Travels' by Clarence Tracy in *Queens Quarterly*, vol. 68, no. 4, 1962. Reprinted by permission of the publisher.

Excerpt from Frank Brady, 'Vexations and Diversions: Three Problems in "Gulliver's Travels" ', *Modern Philology*, vol. 75, no. 4, 1978, pp. 346–7. Copyright © 1978 The University of Chicago Press. Reproduced by kind permission of the publisher.

Laura Brown. 'Reading Race and Gender: Jonathan Swift', *Eighteenth-Century Studies* vol. 23, no. 4 (summer 1990), 433–6. Copyright © American Society for Eighteenth-Century Studies. Reprinted with permission of the Johns Hopkins University Press.

'The Pride of Lemuel Gulliver' by Samuel H. Monk, first published in the *Sewanee Review*, vol. 63, no. 1, winter 1955. Copyright © 1955 University of the South. Reprinted with the permission of the editor.

Extracts from *Gulliver and the Gentle Reader*, by Claude Rawson (Amherst, NY: Humanity Books). Copyright © 1991 by Claude Rawson. Reprinted with permission.

Robert Phiddian, 'A Hopeless Project': Gulliver Inside the Languages of Science in Book III', in *Eighteenth Century Life*, vol. 22, no. 1, pp. 50–61 (excerpted pages 51–3). © 1998 The Johns Hopkins University Press. All rights reserved. Used by permission of the publisher.

Extracts from *Jonathan Swift: Political Writer* by J. A. Downie. Routledge, 1984. Reproduced by kind permission of the publisher.

Figure 1: Jonathan Swift, by Charles Jervas, 1718. Reproduced by permission of the National Portrait Gallery, London.

Figure 2: Title page from vol. III of Jonathan Swift's *Works* (Dublin: Faulker, 1735). Reproduced by permission of the Houghton Library, Harvard University.

Figure 3: 'Microsoft in Lilliput' from *The Wall Street Journal*, 4 November 2003. By permission of William Bramhall, c/o Riley Illustrations.

Figure 4: Captain Gulliver, 'Splendide Mendax', title page, Volume III of Jonathan Swift's *Works* (Dublin: Falkner, 1735). Reproduced by permission of the Houghton Library, Harvard University.

Figure 5: Map of Lilliput from Swift's *Travels into Several Remote Nations of the World* (*Gulliver's Travels*), (London: Motte, 1726). Reproduced by permission of the Houghton Library, Harvard University.

Figure 6: Map of Laputa and Balnibarbi from Swift's *Travels into Several Remote Nations of the World* (*Gulliver's Travels*), (London: Motte, 1726). Reproduced by permission of the Houghton Library, Harvard University.

Figure 7: Word Frame of Lagado from Swift's *Travels into Several Remote Nations of the World* (*Gulliver's Travels*), (London: Motte, 1726). Reproduced by permission of the Houghton Library, Harvard University.

# Introduction

From the moment of its appearance in 1726, *Gulliver's Travels* was a best seller, and it maintained its popularity throughout the eighteenth century. It has never dropped from the critical radar screen. Designed to look like a genuine travel narrative, *Travels into Several Remote Nations of the World* (the original title) offers accounts of four voyages to imaginary locations: Lilliput, a land of pygmies; Brobdingnag, a land of giants; Laputa, a flying island inhabited by mathematicians and musicians; and, finally, an island inhabited by talking horses (Houyhnhnms) and a race of bestial creatures (Yahoos) resembling humans. Although nineteenth-century critics rejected the *Travels* as the work of a misanthropic madman, largely because of Swift's suggestion that human beings might *be* Yahoos, the first two voyages (or 'Books' as they are commonly called) remained popular (sometimes in bowdlerized versions) as entertainment for children.

Because *Gulliver's Travels* is also a satire, the work has always been read with reference to the times in which it was written, and it has always generated debate as to what Swift's true intentions might have been. Swift remarks that he wrote the *Travels* to 'vex mankind', whereas Gulliver, Swift's satiric spokesman and occasional victim, insists that he wrote his account out of a desire for the '*publick Good*'. For over two centuries critics have been uncertain whether to favour Swift the moralist, determined to defend the claims of virtue and reason against the enormities of human behaviour, or to prefer Swift the writer, whose mastery of authorial indirection and stylistic ambiguity leaves the reader in doubt as to where Swift's true intentions lie. The aim of this sourcebook is to provide readers with the materials needed to explore a number of these questions on their own.

This book is divided into three main sections, each with a brief introduction and headnotes for each extract included. Throughout this sourcebook, I have cross-referenced the discussions in the critical introductions and headnotes with relevant materials elsewhere in the book. Since its original publication, readers of *Gulliver's Travels* have eagerly sought to find parallel passages in the works of Swift's contemporaries and in the works of satirists and philosophers who Swift himself had read. The first section, 'Contexts', begins with a 'Contextual Overview', linking the broader historical, political and scientific context within which Swift was writing and the extracts included in this section. A chronology is intended to help the reader understand the relationship between the main events in Swift's personal and professional life and the wider social, literary and political events of his time. 'Contemporary Documents' begins with a sampling of Swift's own letters, including comments on the composition and publication of *Gulliver's Travels*. These are followed by extracts from works which seem to have influenced Swift's stylistic or thematic choices in the *Travels* as well as excerpts from other works that Swift imitated, parodied or simply absorbed.

The second part, 'Interpretations', offers a generous sampling of the critical debate over the origins and meanings of *Gulliver's Travels*. I have included several extracts from the earliest critical responses to the *Travels*. While these brief passages introduce readers to the scope of the controversy which the work initially inspired, they also inscribe the main lines of the debate that would continue for the next two centuries and they lay the groundwork for the excerpts of twentieth-century criticism, which conclude this section. The headnotes to each of the twentieth-century essays outline the critical debate that inspired the essay and place the extract within the context of the continuing critical discussion.

The third part, 'Key Passages', consists of a series of excerpts from *Gulliver's Travels* itself, which are linked by explanatory headnotes and accompanied by annotations designed to define unfamiliar words, clarify vexed passages and provide further context for the interpretation of the extracts themselves. Both headnotes and annotations point to the continuities between passages included and provide further information on significant critical responses to individual passages and cross-references to material included elsewhere in the sourcebook. This part begins with a brief introduction outlining some of the salient features of the textual history of *Gulliver's Travels*, and explaining why the 1735 Dublin edition has been chosen as the copy text for the extracts included here. This volume concludes with a guide to further reading. This annotated list provides further information on the wider range of biographies, bibliographies and texts available for the study of the *Travels* and offers an expanded guide to the various critical and scholarly discussions of the topics around which this sourcebook has been organized.

## Note on abbreviations

The standard edition of Jonathan Swift's prose is the *Prose Works of Jonathan Swift*, ed. Herbert Davis, 14 vols (Oxford: Blackwell, 1939–68), which I have abbreviated *PW*, the standard designation among Swift scholars, *Gulliver's Travels*, vol. XI, appeared first in 1941 and again in 1959 in a revised edition. When vol. XI is quoted I have indicated which edition has been used. For Swift's Letters, I have cited *The Correspondence of Jonathan Swift*, 5 vols, ed. Harold Williams (Oxford: Clarendon Press, 1963–5), abbreviated *Corr.* throughout. Although Swift's publishers originally labelled each of the four voyages as Part One, Part Two, etc., Swift's readers have traditionally referred to the voyages as 'Books', not 'Parts', and that is how I have described them throughout this Sourcebook.

# 1

# Contexts

# Contextual Overview

Jonathan Swift's career as celebrated satirist, churchman and pamphleteer could not have had a less auspicious beginning. Several months before Swift's birth in Dublin on 30 November 1667, Swift's father had died, leaving the family penniless. Swift's mother returned to England in search of greater financial security, while Swift was abandoned in Ireland to attend school at the behest of charitable friends. This initial calamity had consequences that Swift continued to 'feel throughout the whole course of his life', telling us something, perhaps, about his ambiguous relationship towards women and his lifelong fear of abandonment (see Critical History, p. 51). The conditions of Swift's birth may also explain his lifelong ambiguity towards Ireland, the land where he was born, but where, until late in his life, he never felt entirely comfortable.

As a smart well-educated, but penniless, young man, Swift sought his fortune in much the same fashion as other young men in similar circumstances: he pursued a career in the Church. After attending Kilkenny School and Trinity College, Dublin, Swift took a position in England as Secretary to Sir William Temple, a retired courtier and statesman (and distant relative) who became Swift's mentor and inspiration. Swift was ordained a priest in the Church of Ireland (a branch of the Church of England), but he hoped that he could find preferment in England itself. Instead, Swift was given a parish in Ulster, where there were few Anglicans, but an overwhelming majority of Scottish Presbyterians whose presence only served to deepen Swift's hatred of all forms of religious nonconformity. Swift returned to England on behalf of the Church of Ireland and while there he sought, without success, to gain preferment from the ruling Whigs of the day. Swift had better luck with the Tories, and when the government changed in 1710, the Tories, unlike the Whigs, curried Swift's favour and gave him a position as the editor of *The Examiner* (1710–11), one of the government periodicals. The leaders of the government – Robert Harley, the Earl of Oxford, and Henry St. John, Viscount Bolingbroke – became Swift's friends. Their successful conclusion of the War of the Spanish Succession (1702–13) made them heroes in Swift's eyes. Both Swift's hatred of warfare and his admiration for Harley and Bolingbroke are reflected in *Gulliver's Travels*, where Gulliver's difficulties in Lilliput reflect the political fall of Harley and Bolingbroke, and his hatred of warfare is reflected in Gulliver's ironic praise of military carnage in both Books II and IV (see Key Passages, **pp. 147–8, 170–2**).

Swift expected Harley and Bolingbroke to find him a suitable position in the Church of England; instead they appointed him Dean of St Patrick's Cathedral, Dublin, a position he would hold until his death in 1745. While at first Swift felt he had been sent into exile, he gradually made his peace with Ireland, and when Ireland was threatened by the attempt to abuse the Anglican 'Ascendancy' (or the English aristocracy) in Ireland by forcing on the Irish a debased copper coinage, Swift responded with the *Drapier's Letters* (1724), pamphlets that inspired the Irish to resist 'Wood's Halfpence', and in the process turned Swift into an Irish national hero. It was during the years that he was involved in the Irish struggle with the English government and its prime minister, Sir Robert Walpole, that Swift wrote *Gulliver's Travels*. Certainly, the *Travels* reflects Swift's contempt for English politics, but it also reveals his interest in a whole series of issues that characterized the intellectual discussion of Swift's age. Specifically, *Gulliver's Travels* focuses our attention on the importance of exploration and travel in the early eighteenth century, on the rise of science and a new-found confidence in human powers of reason. All of these interests were underscored by the effort, inspired by Renaissance Humanism, to define man's place in the universe and to define the achievements of modern Europeans in the context of the great fund of ancient learning that had just been recovered by translators and scholars. These themes find their place in *Gulliver's Travels*, a work of fiction that seems in various places to be a parody of travel literature, an attack on modern politics and modern science; and perhaps even an attack on the species as a whole.

In a letter to his agent Charles Ford (14 August 1725), Swift remarked that he had finished his 'Travells' and he was now 'transcribing them; they are admirable Things, and will wonderfully mend the world' (*Corr.* III, p. 87). Here Swift seems to assume the role of satirist bent on the moral transformation of his fellows. But since Swift had remarked, in *The Battle of the Books* (1704), that satire is a kind of glass in which we recognize every face but our own, one might legitimately question just how seriously we are to take Swift's stated intention to reform the age with satire. Swift is famous for adopting the identities of those he wishes to satirize and it is always difficult to tell which of Swift's statements bespeak his genuine convictions and which are born of the role he has assumed. In *The Bickerstaff Papers* (1708–9), Swift assumes the role of Isaac Bickerstaff, publisher of an almanac that offered a series of outlandish predictions – including the death of John Partridge, a notorious London astrologer, whom Swift wished to ridicule and expose. When Partridge insisted that the date had passed and he was still very much alive, Bickerstaff responded that Partridge was mistaken. Here Swift adopts the mask of an astrologer in order to satirize a character he despised, but in the *Drapier's Letters*, Swift assumes the identity of an Irish merchant in order to convey his genuine convictions regarding England's oppression of the Irish.

Swift was a born hoaxer, and as he pointed out in a letter to Alexander Pope (29 September 1725), he preferred to 'vex the world rather than divert it' (see Letters, p. 25).[1] Where his critics are concerned Swift has provided vexation

---

1    Alexander Pope (1688–1745), pre-eminent poet of the first half of the eighteenth century and one of Swift's closest friends.

aplenty, nowhere more so than in the effort to somehow determine just what sort of book *Gulliver's Travels* is supposed to be. It is generally agreed that in broad terms *Gulliver's Travels* is meant to imitate or to parody the eighteenth-century travel narrative, but in the process the book exploits the features of a number of other genres as well. None of these forms appears in a pure state, however, and it may be useful to think of *Gulliver's Travels* as a palimpsest, a kind of manuscript that has been written over a number of times so that portions of the original texts remain and are still partially visible, a layering effect that makes it difficult to determine just how the work should be categorized.[2]

This intertextual complexity has not prevented critics from attempting to 'place' the work, however. Certainly we find precedent for the comic exuberance of *Gulliver's Travels* in the carnivalesque excess of François Rabelais's *Gargantua and Pantagruel* (1532–62), a comic masterpiece that casts a satirical eye on the foolish practices of medieval Catholicism. Rabelais's hero, Gargantua, a giant so large that when he combs his head cannon balls fall out of his hair, also provides a model for the giant Gulliver in Lilliput. Perhaps the most infamous episode in *Gargantua and Pantagruel* describes Gargantua's attempt to find a perfect substance with which to wipe his backside. After experimenting with a huge inventory of objects including pillows, nettles, and even a cat, Gargantua concludes that the best thing for the job is the downy neck of a goose. This riotously obscene kind of humour almost certainly provides a precedent for Gulliver's preoccupation with his own excrement in *Gulliver's Travels* (see Critical History, **pp. 50–1**, Modern Criticism, **pp. 93–8** and Key Passages, **p. 125**).

In addition, Swift clearly borrows from the tradition of the Philosophic or Imaginary voyage. In this form, the author's satirical criticism of modern society is couched in an imaginary voyage to non-existent or little-known countries where European behaviour and institutions are measured against the customs and traditions of strange, and often ideal, societies. For example, in *Gulliver's Travels*, scholars have detected the outlines of Thomas More's *Utopia* (1516), where the narrator's straightforward description of an ideal society serves as a corrective to the shortcomings of More's contemporaries.[3] Swift also owes obvious debts to Lucian's *True Story*, written sometime near the beginning of the second century (see **pp. 29–30**), a fantastic travel account which, in the fashion of the Glubbdubdrib episode of the *Travels*, takes the hero back to speak directly with the heroes of the ancient world, and which makes fun, in a very Swiftian fashion, of the truth claims of such narratives (see Key Passages, **pp. 161–2** and Modern Criticism, **pp. 72–6**).

Like *A True Story*, *Gulliver's Travels* has been classified as a Menippean satire, a form of satire initiated by the Greek cynic, Menippus, and developed by disciples like Lucian in the second century. According to Northrup Frye, this odd kind of satire 'deals less with people as such than with mental attitudes'; it handles 'abstract ideas and theories' embodied in characters who are 'stylized rather than naturalistic' and who serve as 'mouthpieces of all the ideas they

2   Peter Wagner, 'Swift's Great Palimpsest: Intertextuality and Travel Literature in *Gulliver's Travels*', *Dispositio*, vol. 17 (1992), pp. 107–32.
3   See John Traugott, 'A Voyage to Nowhere with Thomas More and Jonathan Swift: *Utopia* and *The Voyage to the Houyhnhnms*', *Sewanee Review*, LXIX, no. 4 (autumn, 1961), pp. 534–65.

represent'.[4] Swift also drew on more recent versions of the Philosophic Voyage like Cyrano de Bergerac's *Comical History of the States and Empires of the Worlds in the Moon and the Sun* (see Contemporary Documents **pp. 31–2**). Swift may have profited as well from 'Rational Utopias', like Gabriel de Foigny's *A New Discovery of Terra Australis, or the Southern World* (1693), a travelogue pretending to be the history of a Frenchman shipwrecked on the coast of Australia, which, he discovers, is inhabited by a whole race of entirely reasonable men who sound like the Houyhnhnms. As this sourcebook's section on further reading suggests (see Key passages **pp. 189–91**), a great deal of scholarly attention has been devoted to discovering individual 'sources' for particular episodes in the *Travels*, and because they serve as crucial 'contexts' for the *Travels*, I have reprinted excerpts from a number of them here.

## Modern Counterfeits

Merely focusing on Swift's 'sources', however, diverts our attention from the peculiar ways in which he has adopted, absorbed, parodied and transformed these texts to create something new: not simply a specimen of another genre, no matter how loosely defined, but a kind of mock-form in which the formal outlines of the imitated works are erased, but whose identity can still be detected and whose influence can still be felt by the reader. Swift's elaboration of mock-form in the *Travels* involves parody, imitation, even plagiarism, in a mischievous and self-consciously imitative exploration of what books were like in the eighteenth century, a time when publishers would resort to almost any gimmick – including idiosyncratic typography, flamboyant and misleading title pages, and endless prefatory insertions – to whet the reader's appetite. As Fredric V. Bogel suggests, the sort of 'mock' that we find in the mock-form of Augustan satirists, like Swift, signifies 'not mockery, but surrogacy, substitute or counterfeit status – like the 'mock-' in 'mock-turtle'. Such works are 'counterfeits', and 'the whole point of a counterfeit is to be at once not the real thing and virtually impossible to dis-tinguish from the real thing'.[5] The very shape and appearance of the *Travels*, with its title page advertising *Travels to Several Remote Nations of the World*, author's portrait, publisher's introduction, maps and illustrations suggests that just like *A Tale of a Tub*, whose prefatory materials and editorial intrusions threaten to engulf the text, *Gulliver's Travels* is a counterfeit travel narrative, not 'the real thing', and yet virtually impossible to distinguish 'from the real thing' (see Figures 2, 5 and 6). This judgement is implicit in Dr John Arbuthnot's report to Swift (5 November 1726) that Lord Scarborough, 'no inventor of Storys', had met a captain who said he 'was very well acquainted with Gulliver, but that the printer had Mistaken, that he lived in Wapping, & not in Rotherhith'.[6] One

---

4    Northrop Frye, *The Anatomy of Criticism* (Princeton, NJ: Princeton University Press, 1957), p. 309.
5    Fredric V. Bogel, 'Teaching Pope Today: Satire, Resistance, Theory', in *Approaches to Teaching Pope's Poetry*, ed. Wallace Jackson and R. Paul Yoder (New York: Modern Language Association, 1993), p. 68.
6    Locations on different sides of the River Thames.

suspects that Arbuthnot's tongue is planted firmly in his cheek as he teases Swift about the captain mistaking the real street address of an imaginary character. When Arbuthnot explains that he had 'lent' the *Travels* to an old gentleman who 'went immediately to his Map to search for Lilly putt' (**p. 27**) he describes the experience of the modern reader who is asked always to mediate between the real and the fanciful in the *Travels*.

## Travel Narratives

This ambiguity is a direct result of Swift's own engagement with travel literature. While he was writing *Gulliver's Travels*, Swift wrote to a friend that he had been reading 'I don't know how many diverting Books of History and Travells' (*Corr.* II, p. 430), a process reflected in Gulliver's own confession that he once took 'great Delight' in perusing 'Books of Travels'. But, says Gulliver, his experience as a traveller, particularly his experience in Houyhnhnmland, has turned that delight into a 'great Disgust against this Part of Reading, and some Indignation to see the Credulity of Mankind so impudently abused' (see Key Passages, **pp. 181–2**). Such remarks reveal how carefully Swift shapes his own counterfeit travel narrative, as he painstakingly recreates the shape and substance of the contemporary travel writing he so easily dismisses, simultaneously laughing at the 'credulity' of modern readers even as he exploits their eagerness to believe. Of course, Swift took great delight in the confusion this kind of narrative surrogacy produced in his readers. His remark to Alexander Pope (27 November 1726) that 'a Bishop here said, that Book was full of improbable lies, and for his part, he hardly believed a word of it' (see **p. 27**), leaves us wondering just which of the words we are intended to believe since, apparently, not all of them are untrue.

Like Swift, his readers were fascinated by the exciting and unusual details to be found in contemporary travel accounts. Nothing is too obscure or too trivial for comment. The title page of Lionel Wafer's *A New Voyage and Description of the Isthmus of America* (London, J. Knapton, 1729), gives some sense of the variety of information that travel writers had to offer. According to Wafer, his book provides an account of 'The *Form* and *Make* of the *Country*, the *Coasts, Hills, Rivers*, &c. Woods, *Soil, Weather*, &c. *Trees, Fruit, Beasts, Birds, Fish*, &c'. It also tells of 'the *Indian Inhabitants*, their Features, Complexion, &c. their Manners, Customs, Employments, Marriages, Feasts, Hunting, Computations, Language &c'. Like Gulliver, Wafer pays particular attention to the languages he encounters and he includes extended vocabularies of languages which readers back in England would never have occasion to use (see Key Passages, **p. 153**). Swift borrows heavily from such early travel accounts. The first brief specimen of contemporary travel writing included here, a passage from Samuel Sturmy's *Mariner's Magazine* (1669), was inserted almost verbatim in the opening paragraphs of Book II. It is William Dampier, however, with whom we may most profitably compare Gulliver as travel writer. As he suggests in his prefatory 'Letter from Capt. Gulliver to his Cousin Sympson', Gulliver had been 'prevailed upon to publish a very loose and uncorrect Account of my Travels; with Direction to hire some young Gentleman of either University to put them in Order, and correct their Style, as my Cousin *Dampier* did by my Advice, in his Book called *A Voyage* *round the World*' (see Key Passages, **pp. 120–2**). The excerpt from Dampier's *Voyage round the World* included here reveals just how much of Gulliver's fixation on circumstantial detail can be traced to Dampier's own preoccupation with style.

Because readers of travel narrative shared the same expectations, and because travel writers themselves worked with a common set of literary conventions – including claims to present material that was new, completely surprising and, above all, perfectly true – the echoes of legitimacy were easy to recapture by travel liars determined to create the illusion of truth. Swift falls into this category, but he was by no means alone. Perhaps the most notorious travel liar of the eighteenth century was a man who called himself George Psalmanazar, a European who claimed to be a native of Formosa (now Taiwan), and whose *Historical and Geographical Description of Formosa ... Giving an Account of the Religion, Customs, Manners &c. of the Inhabitants* (1704), was a complete fabrication. Nevertheless, so convincing was Psalmanazar's account that it was translated into several languages and for a time he was actually consulted as an expert on Asia. This is the kind of game that Swift is playing, achieving a high level of verisimilitude, or truth to nature, by adopting the style and mannerisms of the very writers he purported to reject. The fact that Gulliver addresses his introductory letter to his 'Cousin Sympson' suggests that Swift also self-consciously imitates a whole body of fake travel narratives – what Percy Adams has aptly called 'travel lies' – of which William Symson's A *New Voyage to the East Indies* (1715) – briefly excerpted here (**p. 33**) – is a prime example.[7]

## Gulliver's Travels and Scriblerian Satire

Travel narratives are not the only contemporary documents that Swift includes in his *Travels*. Swift also introduces a number of other satirical materials emerging from this association with what was known as the Scriblerus Club. This group of friends – Alexander Pope, Dr John Arbuthnot (Queen Anne's physician), the Irish clergyman Thomas Parnell, John Gay and Robert Harley (Prime Minister of England) and Swift – met frequently in 1713–14 to compose satires on modern 'abuses of learning and religion'. Abuses in religion tended to refer to the influence of Epicurean atomism, which argued that the world had been formed not by God, but by the accidental collision of atoms in the void. When, in Book III, Gulliver describes a language made up entirely of things and not words, the materialism of the modern Epicureans is one of his satirical targets (see Key Passages, **p. 142** below). The Scriblerians also ridicule the new popularity of Deism, a rough belief that reason was a more certain guide to moral behaviour than the teachings of the Christian church. The Houyhnhnms' addiction to reason in Book IV of *Gulliver's Travels* has been seen by some as a satirical reflection on the modern popularity of Deism.

---

7  See Percy G. Adams, *Travelers and Travel Liars 1660–1800* (Berkeley, Calif.: University of California Press, 1962).

Abuses in learning are legion, and the Scriblerians invariably ridicule bad poets, who are forced to write for bread, modern translators, who mangle classics like the *Aeneid* and the *Iliad*, and all writers who have come to depend on dictionaries, a thesaurus, how-to manuals, atlases and other short cuts to wisdom. Such abuses in modern learning were satirized in *Peri Bathous: or the Art of Sinking in Poetry* (1728), a mock how-to manual for bad poets, which parodies the poetic failures of many contemporary poets, a cast of 'Dunces', permanently enshrined in Pope's *Dunciad* (1728).[8] One of the Scriblerian projects was the creation of the memoirs of Martinus Scriblerus, an all-purpose pedant who incarnated the various forms of dullness that the Scriblerians satirized elsewhere. While the *Memoirs* were not published until 1741, long after the publication of *Gulliver's Travels* and long after Swift had returned to Ireland following his brief visit to England in 1726, they included a description of Martinus's travels, included here (see **pp. 33–4**), which provides a rough sketch of *Gulliver's Travels* as Swift produced them. It is difficult to tell whether the original outline of the *Travels* was actually produced in the meetings of the Scriblerus Club, or whether it was added after the fact to capitalize on the popularity of Swift's masterpiece.

At various points in *Gulliver's Travels* one encounters isolated satires that seem to have more to do with the Scriblerian agenda than they do with travels to foreign parts. In Book III, for example, Gulliver turns etymologist in order to explain the origins of the term '*Laputa*', a word derived from a Spanish word meaning 'the whore', a definition Gulliver completely overlooks in favour of a more pedantic explanation that '*Laputa* was *quasi outed; Lap* signifying properly the dancing of the Sun Beams in the Sea, and *outed* a Wing, which however I shall not obtrude, but submit to the judicious Reader' (III, ii, p. 202). This is nonsense, but it is clearly recognizable as the kind of nonsense that one might encounter in the textual criticism of Richard Bentley, the preeminent classicist of the early eighteenth century, famous for his correction of the errors made by translators of ancient texts by the most scrupulous, but often most pedantic, means.

The Scriblerians' war with Bentley forms part of the larger struggle between the Ancients and the Moderns which had broken out in the final decade of the seventeenth century when Swift's mentor Sir William Temple published a defence of the antiquity and authenticity of *The Epistles of Phalaris*, along with a series of arguments asserting the superiority of the Ancients over their counterparts in the modern world. When Bentley proved that the *Epistles of Phalaris* was a forgery, thereby embarrassing Temple, Swift responded with *The Battle of the Books* (1704), a satire in which all the Ancient poets in the King's library defeat their modern translators and critics in open combat. Although the issues that separated the Ancients and Moderns were often arcane, and while the Moderns often had the best arguments for why human knowledge was advancing on multiple fronts, the Scriblerians tended nonetheless to side with the Ancients (see Modern Criticism, **pp. 72–6**).

As slight as Gulliver's mock etymology of *Laputa* might seem, it forms part of a larger Scriblerian joke. In 1735 there appeared *Critical Remarks on Capt. Gulliver's Travels. By Doctor Bantley. Published from the Author's Original*

---

8   See Roger D. Lund, 'The Eel of Science: Index Learning, Scriblerian Satire, and the Rise of Information Culture', *Eighteenth-Century Life*, 22 (May 1998), pp. 18–42.

*MSS.* This parody of Bentley, often ascribed to Dr Arbuthnot, attempts to defend the accuracy of Gulliver's account of the Houyhnhnms by dredging through classical manuscripts to prove that wise talking horses had existed from the beginnings of the world. 'What can be more evident,' Bantley remarks, 'than that the *Houyhnhnm* Language was perfectly understood by the antient *Greeks*, as the *Irish* (which hath the nearest Similitude of Sound and Pronunciation to that Language) is intelligible to many curious Persons at present' (p. 28).

## Science and *Gulliver's Travels*

It is also within the context of Scriblerian satire that we can best understand Swift's attack on modern science in Book III. The third Book of *Gulliver's Travels* has always given readers difficulty. Even Dr. Arbuthnot remarked that the satire on the Academy of Lagado was 'the least brilliant', and Gay found the account of the flying island the 'least entertaining' (**pp. 27–8**). There can be no denying that for many readers Swift's antipathy to mathematics, astronomy and all forms of scientific experimentation has constituted a significant weakness of *Gulliver's Travels*. Many editors have simply omitted Book III altogether. The rise of experimental science in England, which found its focus in the Royal Society of London for the Improving of Natural Knowledge, founded by Charles II in 1662, brought with it a new confidence in the human capacity, through observation and experimentation, to conquer the mysteries of physical nature. Some modern scientists also claimed the ability to eliminate all metaphorical ambiguity through the introduction of a new style of scientific reporting. In his *History of the Royal Society* (1667) (**pp. 34–5**), Thomas Sprat urged the members of the Society to revive the 'primitive Purity' of speech when men delivered so 'many Things almost in an equal Number of Words', instructions Swift literalizes in Book III of the *Travels* where the residents of Lagado dispense with words altogether and communicate using objects alone; indeed, they are required to carry heavy packs loaded with things just to carry on a simple conversation (see Key Passages, **pp. 159–61**).

Sprat argues that modern scientists writing for the Royal Society should seek to imitate 'mathematical Plainness', preferring the 'Language of Artizans, Countrymen, and Merchants, before that of Wits, and Scholars'. This is precisely the role that Gulliver fills. He is variously a surgeon, a ship's captain and merchant, the sort of hard-headed observer to whom Sprat calls attention. But Gulliver is also a 'scientific traveler' like Dampier and others who were sent out by the Royal Society with explicit orders to report back on their discoveries. Much of Gulliver's preoccupation with specific dates, times, and measurements imitates the scientific precision of accounts sent back to the Royal Society, just as his boast that the 'sole intention' in publishing his Travels 'was the PUBLICK GOOD' (see Key Passages, **p. 182**) echoes similar claims for modern science articulated in Sprat's *History*. But this is not all. For within the guidelines established by Sprat, Gulliver's status as a merchant, a countryman and a doctor actually seems designed to lend credibility to his narrative. Sprat had argued that because such observers dealt only in 'matters of fact' rather than matters of opinion, merchants and artisans, most of whom depended on mathematical data of some kind, were therefore inherently more dependable than politicians or wits. Gulliver may argue in the end that he is incapable of lying because he has met the Houyhnhnms, but he might just as easily claim that his accounts are believable because he comes from the ranks of merchants, artisans and countrymen.[9]

This expectation may be part of the joke, for just as Gulliver's 'sea-language' copies popular accounts of sea voyages (see **p. 31**), so the things he discovers are of limited value. From Lilliput he manages to salvage some small livestock which he displays as curiosities and then sells for a profit. In fact, many of the early scientific experiments and discoveries seem to modern eyes like mere curiosities. In 1700, Swift's friend, Dr William King, published *The Transactioneer* (1700), a parody of the early scientific articles appearing in the pages of the *Philosophical Transactions* of the Royal Society, one of the first scientific journals ever published. King cites the *Transactions*, No. 233, describing a woman '*seven years bringing forth a Child Bone by Bone, and all by the Fundament*',[10] the sort of account one would now expect to find in a tabloid newspaper. This is the kind of scientific writing that Swift parodies in Book III of *Gulliver's Travels*, where with a very few tactical additions or alterations to the actual texts of selected *Philosophical Transactions* of the Royal Society, Swift was able to make the scientific enterprise seem preposterous. So, for example, in order to create the comic possibilities inherent in the effort to revive a dead dog with a pair of bellows inserted in the rectum, Swift had only to combine elements of actual accounts of Robert Hooke's experimental attempt to artificially revive a dog using a bellows and Nathaniel St. Andre's observations on reversing the processes of digestion (see **pp. 35–6**).

## The Origins of the Houyhnhnms and the Yahoos

If Book III seemed most ill constructed to Swift's early readers, and unfair in its attitude toward modern science, Book IV has proven perhaps most troublesome to Swift's readers because of its moral implications. As he said to Pope, Swift had never claimed that man was rational, only '*rationis capax*', capable of reason. It was '*vous autres* [you others] who assumed that man was *animal rationale*', a rational animal (see **pp. 25–6**). As Irvin Ehrenpreis points out, the whole question of human rationality as it is treated in the *Travels* partakes of a much larger debate over what could be said to define our humanity: is it our shape, our intelligence, or something else entirely? Swift was familiar with the argument that reason does not belong exclusively to human beings, but at the same time he was aware of the argument, popularized by René Descartes in *The Discourse on Method* (1637), that animals are purely material automatons that cannot think, whereas humans have both a body and a thinking soul. In Book II of the *Travels*,

---

9  On the truth value of merchants and artisans, see Mary Poovey, *A History of the Modern Fact* (Chicago, Ill.: University of Chicago Press, 1998), pp. 115–20.

10  By the Fundament: this child was born from the anus. See William King, *The Transactioneer* (1700), ed. Roger D. Lund (Los Angeles, Calif.: Augustan Reprint Society, 1988), p. viii. The table of contents also lists scientific descriptions of '*A Sheet of Paper from China*', '*A New way to Preserve a Maidenhead*', and '*Cows that sh—te Fire*'.

when the wise men of Brobdingnag first see Gulliver they assume that he too is an automaton, or perhaps a piece of clockwork (see Key Passages, **p. 135**). Swift also dramatizes the question, popularized in late-seventeenth-century debates between the philosopher John Locke and Benjamin Stillingfleet, Bishop of Worcester, over the question of whether humans can be said to have a 'real essence', or as Locke argued, only a 'nominal essence', a list of perceptible qualities by which we can be recognized as human beings. 'To demonstrate his lessons, Locke naturally fell back upon the traditional examples; and since he took reason and shape to be the most important properties of the nominal essence, he often paired off men with simians, showing that these two properties were not necessarily tied to one another.'[11] According to this argument,

> There are Creatures in the world that have shapes like ours, but are hairy, and want Language and Reason. There are Naturals [i.e. idiots] amongst us that have perfectly our shape, but want Reason, and some of them Language too. There are Creatures as it is said . . . that, with Language and Reason and a shape in other Things agreeing with ours, have hairy Tails; others where the Males have no Beards and the Females have. If it be asked whether these be all Men or no, all of human Species? It is plain, the question refers only to the nominal Essence. . . . Shall the difference of Hair only on the Skin be a mark of a different internal specific constitution between a Changeling [i.e an idiot] and a Drill [i.e a baboon], when they agree in Shape, and want of Reason and Speech?[12]

Such an argument may help to explain the comparison between Gulliver and the Yahoos, but why the equation between reason and horses?

For an explanation of this phenomenon one must turn to the logic textbooks that dominated the British universities during the seventeenth and eighteenth centuries, and which Swift would have encountered at Trinity College. As R. S. Crane remarks: 'No one could study elementary logic anywhere in the British Isles in the generation before Gulliver without encountering this formula [*Homo est animal rationale*], or man is a rational animal.'[13] Preeminent among these logic manuals was the *Isagoge* of the third-century neoplatonist, Porphyry. This logical taxonomy, later known as 'Porphyry's Tree', divided phenomena into animate and inanimate, rational and irrational, reaching the conclusion that only man was a truly rational animal. Porphyry's taxonomy (see **p. 36**) provided an even more specific model for the Houyhnhnms. In opposing man, as 'rational' to other irrational brutes, Porphyry chose as his example the horse. For Porphyry's followers in the seventeenth and eighteenth centuries this distinction between man and horse became a logical commonplace. According to Crane, anyone who

---

11  Irvin Ehrenpreis, 'The Meaning of Gulliver's Last Voyage', *Review of English Literature*, vol. 3 (1962), pp. 26–7. See also Rosalie L. Colie, 'Gulliver, the Locke-Stillingfleet Controversy and the Nature of Man', *History of Ideas Newsletter*, vol. 2, no. 3 (July, 1956), pp. 58–62.
12  John Locke, *An Essay Concerning Human Understanding* (1694), ed. Peter H. Nidditch (Oxford: Oxford University Press, 1975), III, vi, pp. 450–51.
13  R. S. Crane, 'The Houyhnhnms, the Yahoos, and the History of Ideas', in *Reason and the Imagination*, ed. J. A. Mazzeo (New York: Columbia University Press; London: Routledge & Kegan Paul, 1962), p. 245.

studied these logic manuals would have noted also that a further distinguishing characteristic of the horse was invariably 'given as whinnying (*facultas hinniendi*); equus, it was said again and again, *est animal hinnibile*',[14] – that is, an animal that whinnies. Ironically, this definition also applies to Gulliver, whose stay in Houyhnhnmland literally transforms him into 'an animal who whinnies'.

The origin of the Yahoos has inspired equally vigorous critical speculation. Scholars point out that there has always been a tendency to connect Swift's portraits of the Yahoos with the native Irish population. 'Early and late, then, the general English account of the Irish peasant, or the lower orders in town and city, reads pretty much like Swift's depictions of Yahoos' with emphasis on their idleness, brutality, drunkenness, odour, their perpetual howling over their dead and, a detail irresistible to Swift, the monstrous size of the female breasts'.[15] We see many of these features in the passage from *A Trip to Ireland, Being a Description of the Country, People and Manners* (see **p. 36**). Other critics have looked farther afield to find antecedents of the Yahoos in the primitive peoples described in contemporary travel accounts. Swift's portrait of the Yahoos almost certainly owes something to the descriptions of pygmies in Edward Tyson's *Orang-Outang, Sive Homo Sylvestris* (1699), a pamphlet that sets out to define the connections and similarities between apes, pygmies and Europeans. Critics have recently argued that the confusion of apes, Hottentots and native Africans provides an important context for understanding the origins of the Yahoos (see **pp. 36–7**). Selections from *Buffon's Natural History* (**pp. 36–7**) 'summarize accounts of the Negro from earlier writings in French and English', and reveal that *Gulliver's Travels* 'is pervasively connected with—indeed essentially compiled from—contemporary evidence of racial difference derived from accounts of the race that was in this period most immediately and visibly the object and human implement of mercantile capitalist expansion.'[16]

## Politics and *Gulliver's Travels*

Of all the influences, both literary and historical, that left their mark on *Gulliver's Travels*, perhaps none is more important than contemporary politics. This is only natural since Swift had been a political animal from his earliest years. Introduced to English politics as the secretary and literary editor of Sir William Temple, Swift began his career seeking preferment from the Whigs who held power during the reign of William and Mary and the first eight years of Queen Anne's reign (ca. 1689–1710). Because the Whigs refused to grant his requests either for personal preferment (specifically a church living in England) or for relief of the Church of Ireland, Swift gravitated to the orbit of such Tory ministers as Edward Harley, Earl of Oxford and Henry St John, Viscount Bolingbroke,

---

14  Ibid., p. 248.
15  Donald T. Torchiana, 'Jonathan Swift, the Irish, and the Yahoos: The Case Reconsidered', *Philological Quarterly*, 54 (1975), pp. 199ff.
16  Laura Brown, 'Reading Race and Gender: Jonathan Swift,' *Eighteenth-Century Studies*, vol. 23, no. 4 (1990), p. 436; see also Claude Rawson, *God, Gulliver, and Genocide: Barbarism and the European Imagination 1492–1945* (Oxford: Oxford University Press, 2001).

the most brilliant among Tory politicians and philosophers. When the Tories were asked to organize a government, Harley recruited Swift to write pamphlets attacking Whig war policy and eventually appointed him as editor of the *Examiner* (1710–11), the unofficial, but nonetheless authoritative voice of Tory politics. However, so closely was he identified with the ministry of Harley and Bolingbroke, that when they were impeached by a new Whig parliament for the generous terms on which the Tories had achieved peace with France in the Treaty of Utrecht (1713), Swift was afraid he would be prosecuted as well. These fears were not entirely unfounded, and it seems likely that for several years at least some of Swift's mail was opened by government inspectors.

Gulliver's discussion of the political and religious differences between High-Heels and Low-Heels in Lilliput reflects the rift between Tory and Whig that had divided England in the years when Swift was associated with the ministry of Harley and Bolingbroke. It is difficult to define Tory and Whig precisely, and indeed Swift himself never succeeded, describing himself as a Whig in politics and a Tory in religion. Certain generalizations do apply, however. The Whigs arose in the 1670s in an effort to exclude James II (a Roman Catholic) from the throne of England. They were strong supporters of the Glorious Revolution (1688) in which William and Mary were invited to replace James II on the throne of England. This move assured that British monarchs would always be Protestant, and would be limited by Parliament. Throughout the eighteenth century the Whigs remained strong advocates of religious toleration, even including such beliefs as Deism and freethinking. And because they supported the foreign wars entered into by William III, who had also been leader of the Dutch Republic, Whigs tended to encourage the growth of commerce and central banking which provided additional capital to pursue William's wars in Europe.

The Tories arose in defence of James II's right to assume the English throne, even though he was a Roman Catholic. As a result, the Tories were always suspected of a secret loyalty to the House of Stuart, and were therefore regarded as a security threat by the Whigs, who surrounded first William III, and then the Hanoverian monarchs who followed Queen Anne. The Tories also tended to be firm supporters of the Church of England and hostile to any attempts on the part of Presbyterians or other religious dissenters to gain prominence. As an ordained priest of the Church of Ireland, virtually indistinguishable from the Church of England, Swift's loyalties lay here. Finally, because they drew their strength from the country gentry whose wealth lay in land, Tories often opposed foreign wars which tended to increase the land tax. In both his political writings and in *Gulliver's Travels*, Swift is a strong opponent of Britain's wars. The issue of who constituted a Tory and who was a true Whig filled the pamphlet literature of the early eighteenth century. Swift himself contributed to the pile with *The Sentiments of a Church-of-England Man* (1708). Paul de Rapin-Thoyras (see **pp. 38–9**) is among the calmest and least polemical of these pamphleteers, and his remarks on Tory and Whig provide a close parallel with the discussion of English politics in Book I.

Although the years immediately following Swift's return to Ireland were relatively quiet, he re-emerged on the political landscape with the publication of his four *Drapier's Letters* (1724), an ironic assault on the attempt of the English Government to impose a new debased coinage on Ireland. Walpole's Government, proverbial for its corruption, had granted Wood, an English ironmonger, a patent to produce copper halfpence and farthings for the Irish, as a result of substantial bribe paid to the King's mistress, the Duchess of Kendal. Inspired in part by Swift's pamphlets, the Irish furiously resisted English attempts to impose this copper coinage and in 1725 the patent was withdrawn. Walpole's ministry was furious, and placed a bounty of £300 (more than ten times the annual earnings of a working man) for information leading to the arrest of the author of the *Drapier's Letters*. It is a measure of Swift's standing among the Irish that although his identity was widely known, no one attempted to collect the reward.

*Gulliver's Travels* is written in the middle of the struggle with Walpole's Government. Books I, II and IV were written in 1721, 1722 and 1723. Book III was written in 1725. It is not surprising, therefore, that even though his satire on political parties in *Gulliver's Travels* was fairly general, Swift was still concerned that he had 'reflected' on Walpole and his ministers in a way that would offend them. Contemporary pamphlets charged that Swift had attempted to 'interrupt the Harmony and good Understanding between the Majesty and his Subjects, and to create a Dislike in the People to those in the Administration' (see **pp. 39–40**), and Swift's correspondence with his friends reveals concern that people might take offence at his political satire. Given his long-standing hostility to Robert Walpole's ministry, Swift's fear of political reprisal is perhaps understandable, as was his fear that the printer of *Gulliver's Travels* might be prosecuted. As Swift said in a letter to Pope (29 September 1725), his *Travels* were ready for the press whenever he could find 'a Printer . . . brave enough to venture his Eares' (**p. 25**).[17]

This explains why the conditions under which the *Travels* were published seemed so mysterious. The bookseller Benjamin Motte received a letter from Richard Sympson (8 August 1726) offering the book for £200, and including a portion of the manuscript. According to Pope, Motte received the whole manuscript 'he knew not from whence, nor from whom, dropp'd at his house in the dark, from a Hackney-coach' (**p. 27**). Even after Motte published *Gulliver's Travels*, the mystification continued. Although Swift (in the guise of Richard Sympson) expressed anxiety that the *Travels* might 'be thought in one or two places to be a little Satyrical, yet it is agreed they will give no Offence' (**p. 26**). The work might have given no real offence, but it did inspire commentary. In a letter to Swift (17 November 1726) Gay correctly predicted that people would attempt to find 'particular applications' in every page and as a result 'we shall have keys published to give light into Gulliver's design' (see **p. 28**).

Not only did *Gulliver's Travels* inspire a number of keys, it also inspired a whole body of imitations and collateral satires. I have reprinted an excerpt from one of four poems on *Gulliver's Travels* written by Alexander Pope and included at the beginning of a number of copies of the 1727 edition. This epistle entitled 'Mary Gulliver to Capt. Lemuel Gulliver' (see **pp. 40–1**) provides Mrs Gulliver's ironic response to her husband's return to England. Just as the *Travels* owes debts to a number of earlier philosophic and fantastic voyages, it also provides a model for later fantasies of flight, stories in which, like Gulliver in Laputa, humans

---

17 Cropping the ears was sometimes an added punishment for those condemned to stand in the pillory.

actually fly. As the final entry in this section on 'Contemporary Documents', I have included a brief passage from *A Voyage to Cacklogallinia* (**p. 42**), a travel account published in 1727, which details the adventures of a traveller – not unlike Gulliver – cast adrift in a land inhabited by giant talking chickens who eventually transport him to the moon, much in the manner of Cyrano de Bergerac.

# VOLUME III.

Of the AUTHOR'S

# WORKS.

CONTAINING,

# TRAVELS

INTO SEVERAL

Remote Nations of the WORLD.

In Four PARTS, *viz.*

I. A Voyage to LIL-
LIPUT.

II. A Voyage to BROB-
DINGNAG.

III. A Voyage to LA-

PUTA, BALNIBARBI,
LUGGNAGG, GLUBB-
DUBDRIB and JAPAN.

IV. A Voyage to the
COUNTRY of the
HOUYHNHNMS.

By *LEMUEL GULLIVER,* firſt a Surgeon,
and then a CAPTAIN of ſeveral SHIPS.

——— ——— *Retreq;*
*Vulgus abhorret ab his.*

In this Impreſſion ſeveral Errors in the *London* and *Dublin*
Editions are corrected.

# DUBLIN:

Printed by and for GEORGE FAULKNER, Printer
and Bookſeller, in *Eſſex-Street,* oppoſite to the
Bridge. MDCCXXXV.

Figure 2 Title Page, Dublin Edition (1735).

# Chronology

Bullet points are used to denote events in Swift's life, and asterisks to denote historical and literary events.

**1667**
- 30 November, Swift born to Abigail Swift; Swift's father, Jonathan Swift, had died previously
* John Milton publishes *Paradise Lost*

**1673**
- Enters Kilkenny Grammar School, the best in Ireland

**1682**
- Admitted to Trinity College, Dublin

**1685**
* Charles II dies. James II (a Roman Catholic) assumes the throne

**1686**
- Receives BA degree from Trinity College, Dublin

**1687**
* Newton's *Principia mathematica* outlines the theory of gravity

**1688**
- Leaves Ireland
* William of Orange invited to England to replace the abdicated James II. Political unrest in Ireland

**1689**
- Becomes Secretary to Sir William Temple, at Moor Park, Surrey. Temple had served as a diplomat in the reign of Charles II. His essay *Upon Ancient and Modern Learning* served as the inspiration for Swift's *Battle of the Books*

(1704); at Moor Park he meets 'Stella' (Esther Johnson), fourteen years his junior, who would become a lifetime friend

\* Accession of William III and Mary II

**1690**

- Suffers his first bout of Ménière's Syndrome, including vertigo and deafness; returns to Ireland to regain his health
\* William III defeats James II at the Battle of the Boyne, securing English rule in Ireland
\* John Locke's *Essay Concerning Human Understanding*

**1691**

- Returns to England and the service of Temple

**1692**

- Receives MA, Oxford; publishes his first work, 'Ode to the Athenian Society'

**1694**

- Returns to Ireland; ordained a deacon in the Church of Ireland

**1695**

- Ordained priest (January), in Church of Ireland, first parish in Kilroot, Ulster

**1696**

- Returns to England and Temple's service; begins work on *A Tale of a Tub*

**1697**

- Writes *The Battle of the Books*

**1699**

- Returns to Ireland as Chaplain to the Earl of Berkeley, Lord Justice of Ireland; Sir William Temple dies; Swift publishes the first two volumes of Temple's *Correspondence*

**1700**

- Appointed Vicar of Laracor and Rathbeggan; then prebend of Dunlavan, St Patrick's Cathedral, Dublin

**1701**

- Brings Esther Johnson ('Stella') and her aunt, Mrs Dingley, to Ireland. According to tradition, Swift and 'Stella' never meet without a third party present

**1702**

- Receives Doctor of Divinity degree, Trinity College, Dublin (April); returns to England in pursuit of preferment
\* Death of William III, accession of Queen Anne; War of Spanish Succession begins

**1703**

- In England November to May

**1704**

- *A Tale of a Tub* and *The Battle of the Books* published anonymously; Swift returns to Ireland
* Isaac Newton publishes *The Opticks*

**1707**

- November 1707 to June 1709, Swift in England to lobby for the remission of the tax on clerical incomes of the Church of Ireland; the Whig Government rejects his request; Swift meets Esther Vanhomrigh ('Vanessa'), twenty years his junior, with whom he would be romantically linked; this 'relationship' forms the basis for Swift's longest poem, *Cadenus and Vanessa* (1726)

**1708**

- Publishes *The Bickerstaff Papers*, a parody of the popular almanacs of John Partridge; publishes religious pamphlets in defence of Church of England, including *An Argument Against Abolishing Christianity*; associates with Joseph Addison and Richard Steele, writers of the *Spectator*, most popular and successful periodical in England; returns to Ireland without official preferment

**1710**

- Swift returns to England on behalf of Church of Ireland; meets Robert Harley; and publishes fifth edition of *A Tale of a Tub* with an 'Apology' designed to help readers to understand it; Swift's mother dies
* Whig government falls; Harley forms new, predominantly Tory government

**1711**

- Publishes *The Conduct of the Allies*, an attack on Whig policy, serves as editor of the *Examiner*, a newspaper designed to present the government point of view

**1712**

- Publishes *A Proposal for Correcting the English Tongue*, which recommended the creation of a British academy to fix the language; Swift asked to join the 'Brother's Club' made up of notable Tories, including Dr John Arbuthnot, Queen Anne's physician, who would become Swift's lifelong friend

**1713**

- Forms the Scriblerus Club along with Alexander Pope, John Gay, Dr John Arbuthnot and Robert Harley, the Earl of Oxford and Prime Minister; appointed Dean of St Patrick's Cathedral, Dublin; returns to Ireland for investiture (June); recalled to London (September)

1714
- Publishes *The Public Spirit of the Whigs*, a slashing attack on Whig opposition to the Peace of Utrecht (1713) which ended the War of the Spanish Succession; Swift returns to Ireland; Esther Vanhomrigh follows Swift to Ireland.
* Queen Anne dies (1 August); Harley–Bolingbroke ministry falls; George I becomes King of England

1715
* Jacobite Rebellion in Scotland attempts to restore James III, 'The Old Pretender', to the throne of England

1719
* Daniel Defoe writes *Robinson Crusoe*, a work with which *Gulliver's Travels* would be compared

1721
- Swift begins working on *Gulliver's Travels*. Publishes his first great Irish pamphlet, the *Proposal for the Universal Use of Irish Manufacture*

1722
* William Wood, English ironmonger given patent to mint copper coins for Ireland, igniting protest among the Irish

1723
- Esther Vanhomrigh dies

1724
- Publishes *The Drapier's Letters* protesting the English imposition of Wood's halfpence; nearing completion of Book III of the *Travels*.

1725
- *Gulliver's Travels* completed.
* Wood's halfpence defeated.

1726
- Visits England with manuscript of *Gulliver's Travels*; returns to Ireland before the *Travels* is published (28 October 1726); returns to England one last time. Stays with Pope and Gay; helps prepare vol. III of the Pope–Swift *Miscellanies*

1727
* George II ascends the throne

1728
- Esther Johnson dies (28 January)

1729
- Publishes *A Modest Proposal*, a satire recommending that one solution to Irish poverty is to eat the infant children of the Irish Catholic population

1732
* John Gay dies

1733
* Pope publishes *An Essay on Man*

1735
* Faulkner begins publication of Swift's collected *Works* in Dublin, including a corrected version of *Gulliver's Travels*; Dr John Arbuthnot dies

1739
- Publishes *Verses on the Death of Dr. Swift* (probably written in 1731)

1742
- Seriously ill; commission *de lunatico inquirendo* (a legal body charged to determine if a person is insane) finds Swift to be 'of unsound mind and memory'
* Henry Fielding publishes *Joseph Andrews*; Walpole resigns as prime minister; first performance of Handel's *Messiah* in Dublin

1744
* Alexander Pope dies

1745
- 19 October, Swift dies; buried in St Patrick's Cathedral next to Esther Johnson; leaves money to build a mental asylum

# Contemporary Documents

## Letters to and from Jonathan Swift

The following excerpts from letters between Swift and his friends offer glimpses into the early process of composition and provide a useful sampling of the earliest responses to *Gulliver's Travels*. These excerpts have all been taken from *The Correspondence of Jonathan Swift*, ed. Harold Williams, 5 vols (Oxford: Clarendon Press, 1963–5). All subsequent citations are abbreviated *Corr.*, and include volume and page numbers.

### From **Swift to Alexander Pope (29 September 1725)**
*Corr.* III, pp. 102–3

This is perhaps Swift's clearest statement of his intentions in the *Travels*. Here he touches on questions of political satire in the work and outlines his definition of man's capacity for reason, a central issue in subsequent critical arguments that Swift was a misanthrope.

I have employd my time (besides ditching) in finishing correcting, amending, and Transcribing my Travells, in four parts Compleat newly Augmented, and intended for the press when the world shall deserve them, or rather when a Printer shall be found brave enough to venture his Eares, I like your Schemes of our meeting after Distresses and dispertions but the chief end I propose to my self in all my labors is to vex the world rather then divert it, and if I could compass that designe without hurting my own person or Fortune I would be the most Indefatigable writer you have ever seen without reading. . . . I have ever hated all Nations professions and Communityes and all my love is towards individualls for instance I hate the tribe of Lawyers, but I love Councellor such a one, Judge such a one for so with Physicians (I will not Speak of my own Trade) Soldiers, English, Scotch, French; and the rest but principally I hate and detest that animal called man, although I hartily love John, Peter, Thomas and so forth. This is the system upon which I have governed my self many years (but do not tell) and so I shall go on till I have done with them I have got Materials Towards a Treatis proving the falsity of that Definition *animal rationale*; and to show it should be only *rationis capax*. Upon this great foundation of Misanthropy (though not Timons manner) The whole building of my Travells is erected: And I never will have peace of mind till all honest men are of my Opinion: by Consequence you are to embrace it immediatly and procure that all who deserve my Esteem may do so too.

## From **'Richard Sympson' to Benjamin Motte (8 August 1726)**
*Corr.* III, pp. 152–3

Writing under the alias 'Richard Sympson', Swift sends part of the manuscript of *Gulliver Travels* to Motte, the bookseller, asking £200 for it, which was a significant sum. Throughout Swift maintains an anxious tone, as though someone were trying to discover his secret.

My Cousin M^r Lemuel Gulliver entrusted me some Years ago with a Copy of his Travells,[1] whereof that which I here send you is about a fourth part, for I shortned them very much as you will find in my Preface to the Reader. I have shewn them to several persons of great Judgment and Distinction, who are confident they will sell very well. And although some parts of this and the following Volumes may be thought in one or two places to be a little Satyrical, yet it is agreed they will give no Offence, but in that you must Judge for your self, and take the Advice of your Friends, and if they or you be of another opinion, you may let me know it when you return these Papers, which I expect shall be in three Days at furthest. The good Report I have received of you makes me put so great a trust into your Hands, which I hope you will give me no Reason to repent, and in that Confidence I require that you will never suffer these Papers to be once out of your Sight.

As the printing these Travels will probably be of great value to you, so as a Manager for my Friend and Cousin I expect you will give a due consideration for it, because I know the Author intends the Profit for the use of poor Sea-men, and I am advised to say that two Hundred pounds is the least Summ I will receive on his account, but if it shall happen that the Sale will not answer as I expect and believe, then whatever shall be thought too much even upon your own word shall be duly repaid.

## **John Arbuthnot to Swift (5 November 1726)** *Corr.* III, pp. 179–80

In this extract, Dr John Arbuthnot, one of Swift's closest friends, tells Swift what people in London are thinking about *Gulliver's Travels*. Along with Alexander

---

1 [Williams' note.] When Swift left Ireland early in March he carried with him the manuscript of *Gulliver's Travels*. This was, almost certainly, not in his hand, but a 'fair copy' for the printer. Although he was in England for five months in 1726, negotiations with a possible publisher, Benjamin Motte, occupied only a few days at the end of his visit, opening with this letter composed by Swift, but, for purposes of secrecy, copied out in the hand of Gay, with whom, at the time, he was lodging in London.

Pope, the playwright John Gay, the Irish poet Thomas Parnell and Robert Harley, Lord Treasurer and head of the Government, Arbuthnot was a member of the Scriblerus Club, which met frequently in Arbuthnot's rooms at St James's Palace, where Arbuthnot served as physician to Queen Anne. Because he was a doctor and a scientist, Arbuthnot's complaint about Book III, with its satire on science, carries special weight.

Gulliver is a happy man that at his age can write such a merry work . . . I tell yow freely the part of the projectors is the least brilliant . . . Gulliver is in every body's Hands. Lord Scarborow who is no inventor of Storys told me that he fell in company with a Master of a ship, who told him that he was very well acquainted with Gulliver, but that the printer had Mistaken, that he livd in Wapping, & not in Rotherhith.[1] I lent the Book to an old Gentleman, who went immediately to his Map to search for Lilly putt.

## Alexander Pope to Swift (16 November 1726) *Corr.* III, pp. 180–1

In this letter, Swift's close friend, Alexander Pope, congratulates him on the success of the *Travels* and tries to reassure him that no one has been truly offended by the satire.

I congratulate you first upon what you call your Couzen's wonderful Book,[1] which is *publica trita manu* [commonly in the public hands] at present, and I prophecy will be in future the admiration of all men. That countenance with which it is received by some statesmen, is delightful; I wish I could tell you how every single man looks upon it, to observe which has been my whole diversion this fortnight . . .

I find no considerable man very angry at the book: some indeed think it rather too bold, and too general a Satire: but none that I hear of accuse it of particular reflections (I mean no persons of consequence, or good judgment; the mob of Criticks, you know, always are desirous to apply Satire to those that they envy for being above them) so that you needed not to have been so secret upon this head. Motte[2] receiv'd the copy (he tells me) he knew not from whence, nor from whom, dropp'd at his house in the dark, from a Hackney-coach: by computing the time, I found it was after you left England, so for my part, I suspend my judgment.

---

1    These are London neighbourhoods on different sides of the River Thames.

1    [Williams' note.] A fictitious Richard Sympson, professing himself Gulliver's cousin, submitted secretively to Benjamin Motte the manuscript of *Gulliver's Travels*.

2    [Williams' note.] It has been suggested that these words imply that Pope may have dropped the manuscript of *Gulliver* at Motte's door; but there is not good evidence for this. A time limitation rules out Ford, who has also been suggested. A consideration of all the evidence favours Erasmus Lewis or Gay. See Harold H. Williams, *The Text of Gulliver's Travels* (Cambridge: Cambridge University Press, 1952), ed., pp. 13–19.

## John Gay to Swift (17 November 1726) *Corr.* III, pp. 182–3

In this letter Gay keeps up the pretence that no one knows Swift is the author of *Gulliver's Travels*. This letter describes in detail how different readers are responding to Swift's satire and serves to reassure Swift that no one in power is very upset with the satirical reflections on English politics.

About ten days ago a Book was publish'd here of the Travels of one Gulliver, which hath been the conversation of the whole town ever since: The whole impression sold in a week; and nothing is more diverting than to hear the different opinions people give of it, though all agree in liking it extreamly. 'Tis generally said that you are the Author, but I am told, the Bookseller declares he knows not from what hand it came. From the highest to the lowest it is universally read, from the Cabinet-council to the Nursery. The Politicians to a man agree, that it is free from particular reflections, but that the Satire on general societies of men is too severe. Not but we now and then meet with people of greater perspicuity, who are in search for particular applications in every leaf; and it is highly probable we shall have keys published to give light into Gulliver's design. Your Lord——[1] is the person who least approves it, blaming it as a design of evil consequence to depreciate human nature, at which it cannot be wondered that he takes most offence, being himself the most accomplish'd of his species, and so losing more than any other of that praise which is due both to the dignity and virtue of a man. . . . You may see by this, that you are not much injur'd by being suppos'd the Author of this piece. If you are, you have disoblig'd us, and two or three of your best friends, in not giving us the least hint of it while you were with us; and in particular Dr. Arbuthnot, who says it is ten thousand pitys he had not known it, he could have added such abundance of things upon every subject. Among Lady-critics, some have found out that Mr. Gulliver had a particular malice to maids of honour.[2] Those of them who frequent the Church, say, his design is impious, and that it is an insult on Providence, by depreciating the works of the Creator. Not-withstanding I am told the Princess hath read it with great pleasure. As to other Critics, they think the flying island[3] is the least entertaining; and so great an opinion the town have of the impossibility of Gulliver's writing at all below himself, that 'tis agreed that Part was not writ by the same Hand, tho' this hath its defenders too. It hath pass'd Lords and Commons, *nemine contradicente* [without contradiction]; and the whole town, men, women, and children are quite full of it. Perhaps I may all this time be talking to you of a Book you have never seen, and which hath not yet reach'd Ireland; if it hath not, I believe what we have said will be sufficient to recommend it to your reading, and that you order me to send it to you.

---

1   [Williams' note.] Bolingbroke.
2   The maids at Court in Book II (see Key Passages, **pp. 134–5**).
3   'The Voyage to Laputa' in Book III (see Key Passages, **p. 149**).

But it will be much better to come over your self, and read it here, where you will have the pleasure of variety of commentators, to explain the difficult passages to you.

## Swift to Alexander Pope ([27] November 1726) *Corr.* III, p. 189

In the following letter Swift pretends at first not to know the identity of the author of the *Travels*. Swift lets the mask fall, however, complaining that Motte has made alterations in the text (see Key Passages, **pp. 115–16**).

I read the Book over, and in the second volume observe several passages which appear to be patched, and altered, and the style of a different sort (unless I am much mistaken). Dr. Arbuthnot likes the Projectors least, others you tell me, the Flying island; some think it wrong to be so hard upon whole Bodies or Corporations, yet the general opinion is, that reflections on particular persons are most to be blamed: so that in these cases, I think the best method is to let censure and opinion take their course. A Bishop here said, that Book was full of improbable lies, and for his part, he hardly believed a word of it; and so much for Gulliver.

## Charles Ford to Benjamin Motte (3 January 1727) *Corr.* III, pp. 194–5

In the following letter, Swift's agent, Charles Ford (or perhaps Swift writing under Ford's name) makes a formal complaint about Motte's changes, many made out of political caution. Ford keeps up the pretence that he doesn't know the identity of the real author.

I bought here Capt$^n$ Gulliver's Travels, publish'd by you, both because I heard much Talk of it, and because of a Rumor, that a Friend of mine is suspected to be the Author. I have read this Book twice over with great care, as well as great Pleasure, & am sorry to tell you that it abounds with many gross Errors of the Press, whereof I have sent you as many as I could find, with the Corrections of them as the plain Sense must lead, and I hope you will insert them when you make another Edition.

# Sources, Influences and Imitations

From **Lucian, *A True Story*, in *Selected Satires of Lucian*** (1962) ed. and trans. Lionel Casson (New York: Norton), pp. 41–2

Lucian of Samosata (ca. AD 125–80) is best known as one of the earliest masters of the fictional travel narrative, of which *A True Story* is perhaps his best-known example. As Sir Walter Scott points out (see Early Critical Reception, **pp. 70–1**), Swift knew Lucian's work well, arguing that *A True Story* offers a precedent for episodes in *Gulliver's Travels*. Unlike Gulliver who is a liar who claims to tell the truth, the narrator of *A True Story* tells important truths but claims to be lying. Lucian was also an early master of the satiric dialogue. During the course of the journey Lucian lands in the Isle of the Blest, where he meets with all the great writers of the ancient world – from Aristippus and Epicurus to Aesop and Homer. In a passage that calls to mind Gulliver's interview with the ancients in Book III (see Key Passages, **pp. 161–2**), Lucian quizzes Homer about the legends that had grown around his works over the centuries.

I have turned to lying—but a more honest lying than all the others. The one and only truth you'll hear from me is that I am lying; by frankly admitting that there isn't a word of truth in what I say, I feel I'm avoiding the possibility of attack from any quarter.

Well, then, I'm writing about things I neither saw nor heard of from another soul, things which don't exist and couldn't possibly exist. So all readers beware: don't believe any of it.

[. . .] I made a point of asking [Homer] where his birthplace was, explaining that it was a matter people were still trying hard to settle at this late date. He told me he was aware that some thought it was Chios, others Smyrna, and most Colophon, but actually he was a Babylonian; his real name was Tigranes and he only changed it to Homer when he was sent as a hostage (*homeros*) to Greece. . . . Since he had satisfied me on these points, I then asked why he had started the *Iliad* with the words "Sing of the wrath." For no particular reason, he replied; it had just come into his head that way. I also wanted to know whether he had written the *Odyssey* before the *Iliad* as is generally held, and the answer was no. And he's not blind, as is also generally believed; I knew that immediately—I didn't have to ask; I could see it with my own eyes. I quizzed him like this on a number of occasions later on as well, whenever I saw he had time to spare, and he answered all my questions readily—particularly after his success in the lawsuit. This was an action for criminal assault brought by Thersites on the grounds that the poet had jeered at him in the *Iliad*; Homer retained Odysseus as attorney and won the case.[1]

---

1  Here Lucian laughs at the myths surrounding Homer's birthplace (many cities claimed it) and his putative blindness. Thersites, a soldier in the *Iliad* who was lame and bow-legged and whose head was shaped like a sugar loaf, was described by Homer as an unpleasant satirist and railer who abused the heroes of the *Iliad*. Here he sues Homer for defamation and as his attorney he hires Odysseus, noted for his sophistry.

From **Cyrano de Bergerac, *Histoire de la lune*. In English. *A Comical History of the States and Empires of the Worlds in the Moon and the Sun*** (1687) by A. Lovell A. M. (London: Henry Rhodes), pp. 33, 34–5

In the following passage Cyrano, like Gulliver in Brobdingnag, finds himself in a land of gigantic quadrapeds who argue about what sort of creature he might be and who conclude that he cannot be human. Just as Gulliver is displayed as a sideshow freak by the Brobdingnagian farmer (see Key Passages, **p. 140**), so Cyrano is also turned over to a local keeper of wild animals who displays him as a curiosity (see Modern Criticism, **pp. 76–9**).

When these People saw that I was so little (for most of them are Twelve Cubits long), and that I walked only upon Two Legs, they could not believe me to be a Man: For they were of opinion, that Nature having given to men as well as Beasts Two Legs and Two arms, they should both make use of them alike . . . that Juggler carried me to his House; where he taught me to Tumble, Vault, make Mouths, and shew a Hundred odd Tricks, for which in the Afternoons he received Money at the door, from those that came in to see me: But Heaven pitying my Sorrows, and vext to see the Temple of its Maker profaned, so ordered it, that one day as I was tied to a Rope, wherewith the Mountebank made me Leap and Skip to divert the People; I heard a Man's voice, who asked me what I was, in Greek.

From **Gabriel de Foigny, *A New Discovery of Terra Incognita Australis, or The Southern World*** (1693) (London: Charles Hein), pp. 76–7

In the following passage, which is reminiscent of Gulliver's discussion of his own nakedness with the Master Houyhnhnm (see Key Passages, **p. 168**), James Sadeur, a Frenchman who was shipwrecked on the coast of Australia, debates with one of the reasonable Australians on the question of why humans cover their nakedness when that is the way we were all created.

In fine, I told him, *That the weakness of the nature of either Sex was such, that there was no looking upon one that was* Naked *without* Blushing, *and* Shame, *and without being sensible of such Emotions, as* Modesty *oblig'd me to pass over in silence.*

*Is there a Consequence in all that thou has advanc'd* (said he) *and from whence can this custom come? Is not this to father upon all the world what is contrary to Nature?* We are Born Naked, *and we can't be cover'd without believing that 'tis shameful to be seen as we are* . . . Beasts continually see themselves and one another, but this sight causes no alteration in them: How then can you who believe your selves of a Superior order to them be more weak then they? or else it must be that your Sight is weaker than that of Animals, since you can't see through a single covering what is under; for there are some of them can even penetrate through a Wall; this is all that I can judge of those of thy Country, because thou tellest me they have some *Sparks of Reason*, but they are so weak, that instead of enlightening them, they only serve to conduct 'em more surely in their Error.

## From **Samuel Sturmy, *The Mariner's Magazine*** (1669) (London: E. Cotes), n.p.

> In 'The Publisher to the Reader' (not included here), Swift exploits the pseudonym Richard Sympson (meant to suggest the travel liar Richard Symson) to claim that he has cut numerous references to 'the Winds and Tides . . . together with the minute Descriptions of the Management of the Ship in Storms'. Gulliver himself acknowledges that 'some of the Sea-*Yahoos*' have 'found fault' with his 'Sea-Language' of the sort we find in the opening pages of Book II: 'Finding it was like to overblow, we took in our Sprit-sail, and stood by to hand the Fore-sail; but making foul Weather, we looked the Guns were all fast, and handed the Missen. The Ship lay very broad off, so we thought it Better spooning before the Sea, than trying or hulling. We reeft the Foresail and set him, we hawled aft the Fore-sheet; the Helm was hard a Weather. The Ship wore bravely. We belay'd the Foredown-hall; but the Sail was split, and we hawl'd down the Yard, and got the Sail into the Ship, and unbound all the things clear of it' (II, i, pp. 94–5). Part of the joke is that much of Swift's 'sea-language' is copied almost directly from the pages of *The Mariner's Magazine*, a small specimen of which is reproduced here.

It is like to over-blow; Take in your Sprit-sail, stand by to hand the Fore-sail. . . . We make foul weather, look the Guns be all fast, come hand the Mizen. The Ship lies very broad off; it is better spooning before the Sea, than trying or hulling; go reef the Fore-sail and set him; hawl aft the Fore-sheet: The Helmne is hard a weather, mind at Helmne what is said to you carefully. The Ship wears bravely steady, she is before it; belay the fore doon hall, it is done.

## From **William Dampier, *A New Voyage Round the World*** (1697) (London: James Knapton), Preface

> The following excerpt from Dampier's *New Voyage Round the World* (1697), reveals just how closely Swift had echoed Dampier's style in the Voyage to Brobdingnag. According to Gulliver, his own story would contain 'little besides common Events, without those ornamental Descriptions of strange Plants, Trees, Birds, and other Animals', a close parallel to what follows (see Key Passages, **p. 149**).

As to my Stile, it cannot be expected, that a Seaman should affect Politeness; for were I able to do it, yet I think I should be little sollicitous about it, in a work of this Nature. I have frequently indeed divested myself of Sea Phrases, to gratify the Land Reader; for which the Seamen will hardly forgive me: And yet, possibly, I shall not seem Complaisant enough to the other; because I still retain the use of so many Sea-terms. I confess I have not been at all scrupulous in this matter, either as to the one or the other of these; for I am perswaded, that if what I say be intelligible, it matters not greatly in what word it is express'd.

For the same reason I have not been curious as to the spelling of the Names of Places, Plants, Fruits, Animals, &c. which in many of these remoter parts are given at the pleasure of Travellers, and vary according to their different Humours: Neither have I confined my self to such Names as are given by Learned Authors, or so much as enquired after many of them. I write for my Countrymen; and have therefore, for the most part, used such Names as are familiar to our English seamen, and those of our Colonies abroad, yet without neglecting others, that occur'd.

## From **William Symson, *A New Voyage to the East Indies***
(1715) (London: H. Mere), pp. 35–6

> While Swift may laugh at the credulity of readers who actually believe the reports of travel liars, he is perfectly happy to borrow from their narratives when it suits him. The following extract from Symson's *A New Voyage* is copied almost verbatim into the First Book of the *Travels*, where the orthography of the Indians is projected upon the Lilliputians who also write 'aslant from one Corner of the Paper to the other, like Ladies in England' (I, vi, p. 59).

Besides the common *Indian* Language, there is another peculiar to the *Brachmans*, who are the highest Degree of *Indians*, and their learned Men, and that is the learned Language there, as *Latin* is in Europe. It is very difficult to Strangers, and call'd *Sansercel*. Their Way of Writing is not like the *Europeans*, in a Line from the Left to the Right; nor like the *Hebrews*, from the Right to the Left; nor yet like the *Chinese*, from the Top of the Paper strait down to the Bottom; but from the Left Corner down to the Right, slanting downwards.

## From **Alexander Pope, 'Of the Secession of Martinus, and Some Hint of His Travels'** (1741) Chapter XIII of the *Memoirs of the Extraordinary Life, Works, and Discoveries of Martinus Scriblerus, Works of Alexander Pope*, ed. Rev. Whitwell Elwin, and William John Courthope, 10 vols. (London: John Murray, 1871), X, pp. 337–8

> The *Memoirs of Martinus Scriblerus*, written largely by Swift's close friends Alexander Pope and John Arbuthnot, pretends to be the biography of Martinus Scriblerus, an all-purpose pedant who pursues a number of foolish adventures, including falling in love with one half of a pair of conjoined twins, searching for the seat of the soul, and undertaking the anatomical dissection of a farting corpse. Like the scientists of Lagado (see Key Passages, **pp. 157–64**), Scriblerus is also a projector and one of his projects is an account of his own travels, a proposal that closely resembles the outline of *Gulliver's Travels*.

It was in the year 1699, that Martin set out on his travels. Thou wilt certainly be very curious to know what they were. It is not yet time to inform thee. But what hints I am at liberty to give, I will.

Thou shalt know then, that in his first voyage he was carried by a prosperous storm, to a discovery of the remains of the ancient Pygmaean Empire.

That in his second, he was as happily ship-wreck'd on the land of the Giants, now the most humane people in the world.

That in the third voyage, he discovered a whole kingdom of Philosophers, who govern by the mathematicks; with whose admirable schemes and projects he returned to benefit his own dear country; but had the misfortune to find them rejected by the envious ministers of Queen Anne, and himself sent treacherously away.

And hence it is, that in his fourth voyage he discovers a vein of melancholy proceeding almost to a disgust of his species; but above all, a mortal detestation to the whole flagitious race of ministers, and a final resolution not to give in any memorial to the Secretary of State, in order to subject the lands he discovered to the crown of Great Britain.

Now, if by these hints, the reader can help himself to a farther discovery of the nature and contents of these travels, he is welcome to as much light as they afford him; I am obliged, by all the ties of honour, not to speak more openly.

But if any man shall see very extraordinary voyages, into such very extraordinary nations, which manifest the most distinguishing marks of a philosopher, a politician, and a legislator; and can imagine them to belong to a surgeon of a ship, or a captain of a merchantman, let him remain in his ignorance.

And whoever he be, that shall further observe, in every page of such a book, that cordial love of mankind, that inviolable regard to truth, that passion for his dear country, and that particular attachment to the excellent Princess Queen Anne; surely that man deserves to be pitied, if by all those visible signs and characters, he cannot distinguish and acknowledge the great Scriblerus.

## From **Thomas Sprat, *The History of the Royal Society of London for the Improving of Natural Knowledge*** (1667), third edition corrected (London: J. Knapton, 1722), p. 113

This passage describing a preference for 'things' over mere 'words' provides a precedent for the 'word machine' in Book III. It also suggests the actions of those scientists who communicate using only material objects (see Key Passages, **p. 161**).

They have therefore been more rigorous in putting in Execution the only Remedy, that can be found for this Extravagance; and that has been a constant Resolution, to reject all the Amplifications, Digressions, and Swellings of Style; to return back to the primitive Purity and Shortness, when Men deliver'd so many Things, almost in an equal Number of Words. They have exacted from all their Members, a close, naked, natural way of Speaking; positive Expressions, clear Senses; native Easiness; bringing all Things as near the mathematical Plainness as they can; and preferring the Language of Artizans, Countrymen, and Merchants, before that of Wits, and Scholars.

## From **Robert Hooke, 'An Account of a Dog Dissected'** (1667) in Thomas Sprat, *History of the Royal Society of London for Improving Natural Knowledge* third edition corrected (London: J. Knapton, 1722), p. 232

This scientific description and the one following were combined by Swift in his parody of the 'Bellows-dog' experiment in Book III (see Key Passages, **p. 158**).

In Prosecution of some Inquiries into the Nature of Respiration in several Animals; a Dog was dissected, and by means of a Pair of Bellows, and a certain Pipe thrust into the Wind-pipe of the Creature, the Heart continued beating for a very long while after all the Thorax and Belly had been open'd, nay after the Diaphragm had been in great Part cut away, and the Pericardium remov'd from the Heart. And from several Trials made, it seem'd very probable, that this Motion might have been continued, as long almost as there was any Blood left within the Vessels of the Dog; for the Motion of the Heart seem'd very little chang'd, after above an Hour's time from the first displaying the Thorax; though we found, that upon removing the Bellows, the Lungs would presently grow flaccid, and the Heart begin to have convulsive Motions; but upon removing the Motion of the Bellows, the Heart recover'd its former Motion, and the Convulsions ceased. Though I made a Ligature upon all the great Vessels that went into the lower Parts of its Body, I could not find any Alteration in the Pulse of the Heart; the Circulation, it seems, being perform'd some other Way. I cou'd not perceive any thing distinctly, whether the Air did unite and mix with the Blood; nor did in the least perceive the Heart to swell upon the Extension of the Lungs; nor did the Lungs seem to swell upon the Contraction of the Heart.

## From **Nathaniel St. Andre, 'An Account of an Extraordinary Effect of the Cholick'** (1717) in *The Philosophical Transactions,* vol. XXX, p. 580

This extract and the Hooke extract (**above**) belong together, and their relationship is briefly noted in the text box on **p. 158**.

The *Peristaltick* Motion of the Intestines[1] is by all Anatomists suppos'd the proper Motion of those Cylindrical Tubes.

---

1   The constricting and relaxing action of the intestines that move food through the digestive system.

The use of this Motion is to propel the Chyle[2] into the *vasa lactea*,[3] and to accelerate the grosser Parts of the Aliment downwards, in order to expel them, when all their nutritive Contents are extracted.

This Motion thus establish'd, it naturally seems to follow that an Inversion of it (call'd for that Reason an *Antiperistaltick Motion*)[4] shou'd force the *Aliments, Bile, pancreatic Juices*, and lastly the *Faeces* to ascend towards the Mouth.

. . . The suppos'd *Antiperistaltick Hypothesis* seems at first Sight very natural, and answers most Difficulties. For if the Vermicular Motion accelerates the Contents of the Intestins downwards; the Antivermicular,[5] by the Law of Contraries, should force them upwards towards the Mouth.

From **Porphyry, Isagoge** (1697) trans. Franco, Burgersdijck, in *Monitio Logica: or, An Abstract and Translation of Burgersdicius his Logick (London: Richard Cumberland), pp. 13–14*

According to the pioneering investigations of R. S. Crane (see Contextual Overview, **p. 14**), this description, which Swift would have learned as a university student, was a standard account of man's status as a rational animal.

Man is a Substance; but because an Angel is also a Substance; *That it may appear how* Man *differs from* an *Angel*, Substance ought to be divided into Corporeal and Incorporeal. A Man is a *Body*, an Angel *without* a *Body:* But a Stone also is a *Body:* That therefore a Man may be distinguished from a Stone, divide Bodily or Corporeal Substance into Animate and Inanimate, that is, *with or without* a *Soul*. Man is a Corporeal Substance Animate, Stone Inanimate. But Plants are also *Animate:* Let us divide therefore again Corporeal Substance Animate into *Feeling and void of Feeling*. Man feels, a Plant 'not: But a Horse *also feels*, and likewise other Beasts. Divide we therefore Animate Corporeal Feeling Substance into Rational and Irrational. Here therefore *are we to stand*, since it appears that every, and only Man *is Rational*.

From **[Anon.] A Trip to Ireland, Being a Description of the Country** (1699) (London: n.p.), pp. 1–9

This pamphlet is characteristic of the accounts of the primitive Irish which may have contributed to Swift's vision of the Yahoos. The emphasis here is on the stench of the Irish, their diet of roots and their horrible wailing (see **p. 15** and Key Passages, **pp. 154–6**).

---

2   Milky fluid consisting of proteins and fats which are combined in the lining of the intestines.
3   Thoracic duct. Part of the lymphatic system.
4   This implies that the intestines are forcing the food backwards out of the mouth.
5   Vermicular and anti-vermicular are wormlike motion of the intestines.

Their *Dwellings* or *Cabins*, I should more exactly describe if I durst have adventured oftner into them; or could have staid long enough to have Survey'd them at my being there. . . . As for the outward *Structure*, an *English Cow house* hath more *Architecture* far . . . and for *sweetness*, I have heard many affirm, that the foulest Corner about the *Bear-garden*[1] is *Musk* and *Amber* to their *sweetest Rooms*. . . . The *Beds* are upon such a firm Foundation, that nothing but an *Earthquake* can move them; Instead of *Feathers* or *Flocks*, they use *Rushes* or *Straw*, which serves them without changing till cast *Horse-litter* is a fragrant *Nosegay* to it. . . . *Sheets* they never provide, and to tell *the naked Truth* . . . they *ligg*[2] together like *Adam* and *Eve* before the *Fall*, not a *Rag* to cover them, but themselves: Which may be one reason why they so multiply; for being necessitated to keep together for warmth, they ingender as thick as *Fly-blows*, each little *Hutt* being as full of *Children*, as a *Conney-Burrough*[3] in a well stock'd *Warren* is of Rabbits. . . . Their *Women* generally are very little beholding to Nature for their *Beauty*, and less to *Art*: . . . Their *Breasts* are excepted against by some, for being the same size with their *buttocks*: and their *Hands* are so tann'd leather'd, that *Gloves* were but thrown away upon them. . . . Some Historians do speak them to be very tender and careful of their Young ones; but wherein that tenderness consists, is not readily to be found out. For their Food is not in the least degree better than they allow their Pigs, *Bonny-rowre* for the Summer, and *Potato-roots* in the Winter are their choicest Dainties. . . . But however careless they be of the *Living*, they are mightily concerned for the *Dead*, having a Custom . . . of howling when they carry any one to Burial, and screaming over the Graves, not like other Christians, but like People without Hope.

From **Edward Tyson, Orang-Outang, Sive Homo Sylvestris: Or the Anatomy of a Pygmie Compared with that of a Monkey, an Ape, and a Man** (1699) (London: Thomas Bennet & Daniel Brown), pp. 8–9

Edward Tyson, who was a fellow of the Royal College of Physicians and a member of the Royal Society of London for the Improving of Natural Knowledge, offered this pamphlet as a comparative anatomical study of pygmies, apes and men, and it is a work that Swift probably knew. Although Tyson's portrait of pygmies may seem racist, it makes more sense to view it as an early attempt to compare apes and human beings in the manner of Darwin. Tyson's pygmies with their flat noses and their lank hair provide another model for the Yahoos (see Key Passages, **pp. 165–6**).

The Hair of our *Pygmie* or *Wild Man* was of a Coal-black colour, and strait; and much more resembling the Hair of *Men* than the Furr of Brutes: For in the Furr of Brutes, besides the longer Hair, there is usually a finer and shorter *Pile* intermixt: Here 'twas all of a kind; only about the *Pubis* the hair was grayish, seemed longer,

---

1  A place where bears are kept to fight one another for entertainment.
2  Slang for sexual intercourse.
3  Slang for rabbit burrow. 'Cony' is a synonym for 'rabbit'.

and somewhat different: so on the upper Lip and Chin, there were grayish hairs like a *Beard*. . . . The Nose of our *Pygmie* was flat like an *Ape's*, not protruberant as a *Man's*; and on the outside of each *Nostril* there was a little slit turning upwards, as in *Apes*. 'Tis observed of the *Indian Blacks*, that their *Nose* is much flatter than the Europeans; which may be thought rather Natural to that Nation, than occasioned (as some would make us believe) by the Mother's tying the Infant to her Back, and so when at Work bruising and flatting it against her Shoulders; because 'tis so universal in them all.

## From **George Louis Leclerc Buffon, *Buffon's Natural History, Containing a Theory of the Earth, A General History of Man, of the Brute Creation, and of Vegetables, Minerals, etc.,*** (1792) 10 vols. (London: J. S. Barr) 9, pp. 136–7

> The description of the Hottentots provided by the French naturalist Buffon offers a version of how the public often viewed the natives of Africa. This conception of Africans also contributed to Swift's portrait of the Yahoos (see Critical History, **p. 61**). This also suggests the manner in which Gulliver is compared side by side with the Yahoos (see Key Passages, **pp. 164–6**).

To form a proper judgment between them, a savage man and an ape should be viewed together; for we have no just idea of man in a pure state of nature. The head covered with bristly hairs, or with curled wool; the face partly hid by a long beard, and still longer hairs in the front, which surround his eyes, and make them appear sunk in his head, like those of the brutes; the lips thick and projecting, the nose flat, the aspect wild or stupid; the ears, body, and limbs are covered with hair, the nails long, thick, and crooked . . . the breasts of the female long and flabby, and the skin of her belly hanging down to her knees; the children wallowing in filth, and crawling on their hands and feet; and, in short, the adults sitting on their hams, forming an hideous appearance, rendered more so by being smeared all over with stinking grease. This sketch, drawn from a savage Hottentot [a Negro], is still a flattering portrait, for there is as great distance between a man in a pure state of nature and a Hottentot, as there is between a Hottentot and us.

## From **Paul de Rapin-Thoyras, *The History of Whig and Tory; from the Conquest to the Present Time*** (1723) trans. Mr. Ozell, 4th edition (London: n.p.), pp. 57–9

> This passage provides a close parallel to Gulliver's description of the High-Heels and Low-Heels in Lilliput in Book I (see Key Passages, **pp. 130–32**).

From all that has been said in reference to the various branches of *Whigs* and *Tories*, it is easy to gather that these two Names are very obscure, and equivocal

Terms, because they do, or at least ought to carry along with them many different Ideas, according to the Occasion upon which it is used.[1]

For instance, if I hear any one say, that the *Whigs* and *Tories* are mightily enflamed against each other, this forms in my Mind an Idea which takes in all the various Branches of *Whigs* and *Tories* in general. But if I hear, that the *Tories* are for making the King absolute and independent ... or that the *Whigs* are for abolishing the Royal Power, my imagination fixes only upon the *Arbitrary State Tories*, and the *Republican Whigs*. The other *Whigs*, and the other *Tories*, would, no doubt, be offended, if such sentiments were ascribed to them.

In like manner; if I hear that the *Tories* wou'd rather bring in a *Popish King*, than be govern'd by a *Protestant King*, who shou'd favour the *Whigs*; I shou'd do Wrong to the *Tories* in general, to impute to them a Thought which takes place in the Hearts of the *Popish Tories*, and perhaps of some *arbitrary Tories* too.[2]

Lastly; if I hear, that the *Whigs* contrive the Destruction of the Church of *England*, I can conceive it no otherwise than in reference to the *Presbyterian Whigs*, since it wou'd be to the last Degree unjust to accuse the *Church Whigs*, in which Number are many Bishops, of seeking the Ruin of their own Church.[3]

Thus the names of *Whig* and *Tory* inspire certain confused Ideas, which few People are able to disintangle. But those Ideas are still more confused, when we consider that one and the same Person may be both *Whig* and *Tory* too, according to the Case before him.[4]

## From **(Anon.) *A Letter from a Clergyman to His Friend: With an Account of the Travels of Capt. Lemuel Gulliver*** (1726) (London: A. Moore), pp. 9, 11

This pamphlet charges that *Gulliver's Travels* was little better than a thinly disguised libel on the ministry of Robert Walpole, complaining that the 'artful Disguises of an Author' make it impossible to determine his true meaning, and thus avoid prosecution. (On the dangers of prosecution see **pp. 25–7** and Modern Criticism, **pp. 106–11**).

What can be viler in the Intention? What may be worse in the Consequence, than Attempt to interrupt the Harmony and good Understanding between the Majesty

---

1 Although the names 'Whig' and 'Tory' were used to describe the two political parties in England in the early eighteenth century, there was no agreement as to exactly what these terms meant or to whom they referred.
2 Because they had defended the prerogatives of the Crown in the crisis (1681–3) over whether to exclude James II from the throne because he was a Roman Catholic, the Tories were accused of favouring Roman Catholic tyranny and of making cause with Catholics in France. Because the Whigs had sought to unseat James II, they were portrayed as the enemies of monarchical government.
3 This refers to the charge made by certain Tories that the Church was 'in danger' from enemies within, mostly Whigs who tended to side with the Presbyterians or with the faction within the Church of England who wished to accommodate those who did not agree entirely with the orthodox position of the Church.
4 Swift himself had argued that he was 'inclined to be what they called a Whig in politics ... But as to religion, I confessed myself to be an High-churchman' (*PW*, vol. VIII, p. 120).

and his Subjects, and to create a Dislike in the People to those in the Administration; and especially to endeavour at this, in such a Juncture as the present?

[. . .] Besides, I conceive it, Sir, the Peoples Judgment ought to be regarded; or an ill designing Man may do much harm, with great Impunity: If in Order to, he should pretend only to amuse, and deliver himself in obstruse Terms, such as may naturally enough be apply'd to the Disadvantage of the Publick, and are so apply'd; surely in this Case he ought to be punish'd for the Detriment that ensues and for not speaking the Truth, if he meant the Truth, in plain Terms.

## From **Alexander Pope, Mary Gulliver to Captain Lemuel Gulliver** (1727) in *The Works of J. S., D. D., D.S.P.D. In Four Volumes* (Dublin: George Faulkner, 1735), vol. III, pp. 399–404

Swift's friend Alexander Pope imagines what Mary Gulliver must think when she considers her husband's bizarre behaviour, not least of which is his hesitancy to sleep with her. Here she tries to imagine what she could say or do to restore his affection, and in the process she provides a short synopsis of all his adventures, including his peeing on the palace fire in Lilliput and being used a sex-toy in Brobdingnag (see Key Passages, **pp. 133–4, 144–5**). In keeping with her own sexual frustration, Mrs Gulliver ends her lament by expressing a wistful hope that if her husband is going to behave like a horse, then the least she might hope for is that he has been endowed like one too.

> These, for some Monuments when you deign to quit,
> And (at due distance) sweet Discourse admit,
> 'Tis all my Pleasure thy past Toil to know,
> For pleas'd Remembrance builds Delight on Woe.
> At every Danger pants thy Consort's Breast,
> And gaping Infants squawle to hear the rest.
> How I tremble, when by thousands bound
> I saw thee stretch'd on *Lilliputian* Ground;
> When scaling Armies climb'd up ev'ry Part,[1]
> Each Step they trod, I felt upon my Heart.
> But when thy Torrent quench'd the dreadful Blaze,
> King, Queen and Nation, staring with Amaze,
> Full in my View how all my Husband came,
> And what extinguish'd theirs, encreas'd my Flame.[2]
> Those *Spectacles*, ordain'd thine Eyes to save,
> Were once my Present, *Love* that Armour gave.
> How did I mourn at *Bolgolam's* Decree!

---

1   Here Mary describes Gulliver bound down by the Lilliputians who crawl upon his body (see Key Passages, **pp. 123–4**).
2   This is a reference to Gulliver's extinguishing the palace fire by urinating on it (see Key Passages, 133–4).

For when he sign'd thy Death, he sentenc'd me.[3]
When folks might see thee all the Country round
For Six-pence, I'd have giv'n a thousand Pound.
Lord! When the *Giant-Babe* that Head of thine
Got in his Mouth, my Heart was up in mine!
When in the *Marrow-Bone* I see thee ramm'd;
Or on the House-top by the Monkey cramm'd;[4]
The Piteous Images renew my Pain,
And all thy Dangers I weep o'er again!
But on the *Maiden's Nipple* when you rid,
Pray Heav'n 'twas all a wanton Maiden did![5]
*Glumdalclitch* too!—with thee I mourn her Case.
Heav'n guard the gentle Girl from all Disgrace![6]
O may the King that one Neglect forgive,
And pardon her the Fault by which I live!
Was there no other Way to set him free?
My Life, alas! I fear prov'd Death to Thee!

O teach me, Dear, new Words to speak my Flame;
Teach me to wooe thee by thy best-lov'd Name!
Whether the Style of *Grildrig* please thee most,
So call'd on *Brobdingnag's* stupendous Coast,
When on the Monarch's ample Hand you sate,
And hollow'd in his Ear Intrigues of State:
Or *Quinbus Flestrin* more Endearment brings,
When like a Mountain you look'd down on Kings:
If Ducal *Nardac*, *Lilliputian* Peer,
Or *Glumglum's* humbler Title sooth thy Ear:[7]
Nay, wou'd kind *Jove* my Organs so dispose,
To hymn harmonious *Houyhnhnm* thro' the Nose,

I'd call thee *Houyhnhnm*, that high sounding Name,
Thy Children's Noses all should twang the same.
So might I find my loving Spouse of course
Endu'd with all the *Virtues* of a Horse.

---

3  In Book I, Lord Bolgolam demanded that Gulliver should be put to death as a traitor because it was treasonous to make water in the precincts of the palace.
4  This refers to Gulliver's adventures in Brobdingnag when the farmer's baby stuck Gulliver's head in her mouth, when the dwarf rammed Gulliver feet first into the centre of a beef bone, and when the Queen's monkey carried Gulliver up to a rooftop and threatened to drop him (see Key Passages, p. 138).
5  This refers to Gulliver's humiliation when the maids of honour at court stripped him naked and then played with him as if he were a sex toy (see Key Passages, pp. 144–5).
6  Mary Gulliver fears that Glumdalclitch, his Brobdingnagian nurse, will be punished because an eagle flew off with the box in which Gulliver was living.
7  These are familiar names that were applied to Gulliver. In Lilliput he was called Grildrig, and Quinbus Flestrin (Man-Mountain). He was awarded the title of Nardac.

From **Captain Samuel Brunt, A Voyage to Cacklogallinia: With a Description of the Religion, Policy, Customs and Manners of that Country** (1727) (London: J. Watson), pp. 32–4

In this imitation of the fourth book of *Gulliver's Travels* we encounter the Cacklogallinians. Like the Houyhnhnms, these large chickens have a surprising range of skills. Here we find them sitting on their rumps milking goats. And just as the Houyhnhnms can sew using their hooves, these chickens actually trim trees into topiary using their claws to hold the shears (see Key Passages, **p. 165**). One also notes the same fascination with imaginary language that one finds throughout *Gulliver's Travels*.

The Cock who was the larger the Two, coming pretty near me, tho' he discov'd in his Eyes both Fear and Astonishment, repeated the Words, *Quaw shoomaw*. The Hen, who kept a greater Distance, cried out, *Ednu sinvi*, which I since learn'd is *Whence come you?*

I was as much surprized to hear Fowls speak, as they were to see such a Monster as I appeared to be. I answer'd in her own Words, *Ednu sinvi*; upon which she ask'd me, I suppose a String of Questions, with a Loquacity common to the Sex, and then fell a cackling. Three or four Chickens came running to her, and at the Sight of me hid their Heads under their Mother's Wing, as I suppos'd her. One of them, who was a Cock not above Five Foot high, at last took Courage to peep out, and said something to his Father; and, as I guess, taking Courage from what Answer he return'd, ventured to approach me. He walk'd round me, tho' he kept some Distance, and spoke in a threatening Tone. I answer'd in a melancholy one, and in my own Language, That I was an unfortunate shipwreck'd Man. The Youngster, I suppose, thinking me a harmless Animal, ventured to strike me, and if I had not avoided the Stroke, I believe he had split my Skull, for his Spurs were about Eighteen Inches long, near Five about, and as sharp as Needles.

. . . After we had pass'd a small Copse of about a Quarter of a Mile, we came into a fine Meadow, where we saw several Hens milking Goats; they sat on their Rumps, and were as dextrous with their two Feet, as any of our Dairy Maids with their Hands. They carried two Pails a-piece with a Yoke, like our Tub-women; and indeed there are not in *Europe* who exceed this Nation in Mechanicks as far as they are useful to them. I have seen a *Cacklogallinian* (for so they call themselves) hover with a Pair of Sheers in his two Feet, and cut Trees with all the regularity imaginable.

# 2

# Interpretations

# Critical History

Gulliver's Travels is one of the few great works of English literature which has maintained its appeal to a mass audience for over two and a half centuries while continuing to inspire ongoing critical controversy. The articles excerpted in this section of the book are designed to highlight many of the most important issues in this critical debate. First, I briefly discuss the popularity of *Gulliver's Travels* as a book for children and the extent to which images and ideas drawn from Gulliver's adventures have become established features of popular culture. Next, this Critical History deals with the assertion first made by Swift's earliest critics that the violence and anger revealed in *Gulliver's Travels* could only be explained with reference to Swift's personal psychology and a reputation for misanthropy that was established by his earliest critics (see **pp. 64–8**), and which provides the focus for many twentieth-century discussions of Swift's purposes in the *Travels* (see **pp. 89–93**). For modern feminist critics, the discussion of Swift's psychology leads to a more particular focus on his relationships with and attitudes towards women (see **pp. 84–9**). Critics who were unsatisfied with personal and psychological approaches to *Gulliver's Travels* have turned instead to questions of historical origins of the work in the Ancients–Moderns controversy of the late seventeenth century (see **pp. 72–6**), in the rise of modern science (see **pp. 98–102**) and, perhaps most important, in the relationship between *Gulliver's Travels* and the novel (see **pp. 68–71, 79–84**). Other issues that are highlighted in this section include Swift's ambiguous relation to his readers (see **pp. 93–8**), his ongoing fascination with language (see **pp. 102–6**), and the political implications of the *Travels* (see **pp. 106–11**).

Looking back from the end of the eighteenth century, James Beattie remarks on the popularity of the *Travels*, and the fact that it had been 'more read, than any other publication of the present century'. According to Beattie, the secret of *Gulliver's* popularity derives from the fact that it has 'something in it to hit every taste. The statesman, the philosopher, and the critick, will admire his keenness of satire, energy of description, and vivacity of language: the vulgar, and even children, who cannot enter into these refinements, will find their account in the story, and be highly amused with it'[1]. Dr Samuel Johnson remarked of the *Travels*

---

1   James Beattie, *Dissertations Moral and Critical* (London: W. Straham and T. Cadell, 1783), p. 515.

that 'when once you have thought of big men and little men, it is very easy to do all the rest',[2] but Johnson wildly underestimated the importance of the imagery Swift added to the vocabulary of popular culture. Lilliput quickly became a metaphor for giants beset by pygmies, either moral or political, for petty politicians determined to somehow thwart the wishes of greater men. The Lilliputian metaphor still retains its explanatory power. A recent *Wall Street Journal* article (4 November 2003), entitled 'Microsoft in Lilliput', outlines the struggles between the computer software giant Microsoft and the European Union, complete with a caricature of Bill Gates, CEO of Microsoft, tied down like Gulliver, by the bureaucrats of the EU.

The process of popularization began immediately on publication of *Gulliver's Travels* in 1726: between 1726 and 1800 nearly 300 books were published that included 'Lilliput', 'Lilliputian' or 'Gulliver' in their titles. *Gulliver's Travels* inspired numerous sequels like John Arbuthnot's *An Account of the State of Learning in the Empire of Lilliput. Together with the History and Character of Bullum the Emperor's Library-Keeper* (1728), an attack on the critical practices

*Figure 3* **Microsoft in Lilliput.**

2   Quoted in Kathleen Williams, ed. *Swift: The Critical Heritage* (New York: Barnes & Noble, 1970), p. 205.

of Richard Bentley, the preeminent classical scholar of the age (see Contextual Overview, **pp. 11–12**). There is virtually no limit to the ways in which other writers exploit the conventions of Swift's *Travels*. Among these imitations one might list Henry Fielding's *The Masquerade. A Poem. . . . By Lemuel Gulliver, Poet Laureat to the King of Lilliput* (1728), or David Garrick's *Lilliput. A Dramatic Entertainment* (1757). Gulliver becomes a popular pseudonym: we find specimens like *The Censoriad. A Poem. Written Originally by Martin Gulliver* (1730), or *The Memoirs of the Court of Lilliput. Written by Captain Gulliver* (1727).

The name 'Lilliput' provides an instant hook for political pamphlets like *An Address from Lilliput, to the [Parliament] of Ireland. With a Collection of Fifty two Lilliputian Patriot Toasts. . . .* (1754). The *Travels* also provide a flexible template that can be readapted to a variety of purposes, even including porno-graphic burlesques like *A Voyage to Lethe; by Capt. Samuel Cock . . .* (1741), said to describe one of Gulliver's voyages which a wreck at sea prevented him from completing. The most visible connection between this mock-travel voyage to the Gulph of Venus – with excursions to the Temple of Dildona and the Sodomanian Idol, Paederastia – is its heavy dependence on sexual innuendo and double entendres, a practice for which Swift provides ample precedent.

One of the most influential and popular of these imitations is a series of stories said to have been told by Baron Munchausen, and transcribed by Rudolph Erich Raspe. First published in English in 1786, Baron Munchausen's *Gulliver Revived: Containing Singular Travels, Campaigns, Voyages, and Adventures in Russia, Iceland, Turkey, Egypt, Gibraltar, Up the Mediterranean, and the Atlantic Ocean: Also an Account of a Voyage Into the Moon. . . .* went through numerous editions by the end of the eighteenth century and maintained its popularity through the nineteenth century as well. The twentieth century has seen some twenty film versions of the stories of this great travel liar, most notably Terry Gilliam's *Baron Munchausen* (1988).[3]

*Gulliver's Travels*, on the other hand, has not been as well served by its film adaptations. The most recent film version of the *Travels*, one that was warmly received, presumably by those who had never read the book, is a television mini-series originally broadcast in the United States (1996) starring Ted Danson and Mary Steenburgen (as Mrs. Gulliver). In this version, Dr. Bates attempts to take over Dr. Gulliver's practice, seduce his wife and eventually commit Gulliver to Bedlam. Perhaps the most memorable film version of the *Travels* is Walt Disney's animated short subject, *Gulliver Mickey* (1934), which presents Mickey Mouse in the role of Gulliver, variously fending off Lilliputian arrows and defeating the Blefuscudian fleet.

## *Gulliver's Travels* as Children's Literature

It is perhaps only natural that Gulliver should appeal to animators, since his story has always attracted young readers. Since 1726 scores of editions and adaptations

3   Patrick Ellis, 'The Cinematic Legacy of Baron von Munchausen', <http://www.horschamp.qc.ca/new_offscreen/munchausen.html>.

specifically for children have been published. Some of them have been expurgated, some not; some have included all four books, but a good number have included only the first two. Following the example of John Newbery's *Lilliputian Magazine* (1752), which equated Lilliput with the world of childhood, a host of works not specifically related to Gulliver's adventures used the well-known equation between Lilliput and small people as a means of appealing to the young. Not surprisingly, many of these works were educational or morally instructive: *The Newtonian System of Philosophy Adapted to the Capacities of Young Gentlemen and Ladies . . . Being the Substance of Six Lectures Read to the Lilliputian Society, by Tom Telescope. . . .* (1761) went through seven more printings by 1787. One might also cite *The Entertaining History of Little Goody Goosecap. Containing a Variety of Adventures Calculated to Amuse and Instruct the Lilliputian World* (1788), and *The New Lilliputian Magazine: or, the Young Gentleman and Lady's Gold Library. Being an Attempt to Mend the World . . .* (1775).

That Swift's imitators produced large quantities of sentimental and didactic tracts aimed at young readers should not blind us to the fact that the same qualities that initially endeared the *Travels* to children appealed to older readers as well. While the 'big men and little men' that fill the pages of the first two books of the *Travels* may seem the stuff of nightmares or perhaps fairy tales, they are drawn directly from the dwarves and giants that Swift himself could have seen in the fairs of eighteenth-century London. As Dennis Todd points out (see **pp. 76–9**), there are consistent links between events in the *Travels* and the popular culture of Swift's own day. Swift also drew on well-known stories of giants and pygmies found in such popular chapbooks[4] as *The History of Jack and the Giants, The World Turned Upside Down*, and particularly, *The History of Tom Thumbe* where readers would have recognized similarities between the stories of Tom Thumb and Gulliver in Brobdingnag. For example, Tom is dropped into his mother's pudding while Gulliver is dropped into a bowl of cream. Both are attacked by small animals – birds and insects – larger than themselves, and each finds the gigantic persons of the maids of court physically repellant. Of course as a parodist, Swift delights in upending his reader's expectations for his own satirical purposes. In his retelling of *Gulliver's Travels*, Padraic Colum remarks that it is:

> a fairy tale inverted. In the fairy tale the little beings have beauty and graciousness, the giants are dull-witted, and the beasts are helpful, and humanity is shown as triumphant. In *Gulliver* the little beings are hurtful, the giants have more insight than men, the beasts rule, and humanity is shown, not as triumphant, but as degraded and enslaved.[5]

As M. Sarah Smedman points out, in what is perhaps the best analysis of Swift's success as a children's writer, *Gulliver's Travels* reveals 'qualities deriving from the child always alive in the Swift whose favorite maxim was *vive la bagatelle*'

---

4    Small, inexpensive books sold in the seventeenth century by 'chapmen', or pedlars.
5    *Gulliver's Travels*, retold by Padraic Colum (1919) (New York: Macmillan, 1962), p. 259. This is an expurgated retelling of the *Travels* written for Irish children by a notable member of the Irish literary renaissance.

(long live nonsense or trifles). In effect, children know instinctively, what more serious critics often forget, that above all, Swift is a joker. When he is around, a game is always afoot. Smedman points to one other significant feature linking the *Travels* with the familiar characteristics of writing for children: its style. Whatever else it might be, the *Travels* is an adventure story, 'told with precision and logic in straightforward, unadorned prose, neither inflated nor magniloquent; Swift's logic delights children, whose own thought processes are so direct'.[6] As critics remark in several of the essays included here, Swift's style is closely linked with the circumstantial specificity of travel writers and the immediacy of the emerging novel (see **pp. 79–84**). Many of these details involve excrement, filth and monstrosity, leading modern psychoanalytic critics to speak of Swift's 'excremental vision'. George Orwell reminds us, however, that even Swift's excremental preoccupation can be linked, at least in part, to the imagination of children which is fascinated with precisely those things 'impure' that so angered more squeamish adults:

> A child, when it is past the infantile stage but still looking at the world with fresh eyes, is moved by horror almost as often as wonder—horror of snot and spittle, of the dog's excrement on the pavement, the dying toad full of maggots, the sweaty smell of grown-ups, the hideousness of old men; with their bald heads and bulbous noses. In his endless harping on disease, dirt, and deformity, Swift is not actually inventing anything, he is merely leaving something out.[7]

William Makepeace Thackeray complains most loudly about the filthiness of Swift's imagination, but even his famous remark that Swift enters 'the nursery with the tread and gayety of an ogre' pays oblique tribute to Swift's popularity as a children's book (see **pp. 70–1**).

## Swift and Misanthropy

One might argue that for the past 250 years some version of Thackeray's ogre in the nursery has haunted two of the major branches of Swift criticism: the one being a defence of Swift against charges of misanthropy, the other an attempt to explain the peculiarity and excesses of *Gulliver's Travels* with reference to Swift's own personal pathology. In 1752 the Earl of Orrery's *Remarks on the Life and Writings of Dr. Jonathan Swift* presented a series of charges that would be repeated or refuted by subsequent critics: first, that Swift reveals an intolerable 'misanthropy'; second, that the *Travels* was written when Swift was in declining health and sliding into madness; and third, that the fourth book is so filthy that in

6    M. Sarah Smedman, 'Like Me, Like Me Not: *Gulliver's Travels* as Children's Book', *The Genres of Gulliver's Travels*, ed. Frederick N. Smith (Newark, Del.: University of Delaware Press, 1990), pp. 75, 77. On the notion of play and game in *Gulliver's Travels*, see John Traugott, 'The Yahoo in the Doll's House: *Gulliver's Travels* the Children's Classic', *English Satire and the Satiric Tradition*, ed. Claude Rawson (Oxford: Basil Blackwell, 1984), pp. 128–50.

7    George Orwell, 'Politics vs. Literature: An Examination of Gulliver's Travels' (1950), in *Shooting an Elephant and Other Stories* (London: Secker, 1950), p. 82.

'painting the Yahoos he becomes one himself' (see **p. 64**). Although it attempted to refute many of these charges, Patrick Delany's *Observations upon Lord Orrery's Remarks on the Life and Writings of Dr. Jonathan Swift* (1754) nevertheless shares Orrery's misgivings about the pessimism of Swift's satire (see **p. 64**), and the myth of Swift's misanthropy slowly acquired the status of fact. Such influential figures as Edward Young accused Swift of having 'dipt his pencil' in 'ordure' and having made monstrous 'the human face divine', and in the process having 'blasphemed a nature little lower than that of angels'. With the suggestion that Swift's 'temper' had 'jostled his judgment' (see **pp. 65–6**), Young also hints at an indictment that would become increasingly public with the passage of time: that *Gulliver's Travels* was the product of Swift's actual madness, a myth given unwitting encouragement by Swift's sizeable bequest to establish a hospital for the mentally ill. Swift's reputation did not go entirely undefended. In his own biography of Swift included in his nineteen-volume edition of Swift's *Works* (1784), Thomas Sheridan parodies Young's attack, accusing him of having defamed one of the 'noblest men that ever lived' (see **pp. 67–8**). The damage was done, however, and nineteenth-century readers were left with a caricature, outlined most notoriously by Thackeray, for whom the Swift visible in the fourth voyage was a 'monster gibbering shrieks, and gnashing imprecations against mankind – tearing down all shreds of modesty, past all sense of manliness and shame; filthy in thought, furious, raging, obscene' (see **p. 68**).

## Psychological Approaches to *Gulliver's Travels*

Modern psychological and psychoanalytic critics inevitably begin with some version of the argument that we may explain *Gulliver's Travels* with reference to Swift's own personal neuroses or outright 'madness'. To be sure, such readings are given encouragement by Swift's apparent preoccupation in the *Travels* with images of excrement, filth and human body odour. Aldous Huxley, whose most notable work *Brave New World* echoes Gulliver's Travels in certain respects, argues that: 'Swift's greatness lies in the intensity, the almost insane violence of that "hatred of the bowels" which is the essence of his misanthropy and which underlies the whole of his work.'[8] For J. Middleton Murry, a mid-twentieth-century biographer with a psychoanalytic bent, Swift's 'extremity of loathing of the physical – and primarily the sexual – functions of humanity was self-induced; and arose from his deliberate and prolonged repression of the emotion of love in the name of reason.'[9]

Not surprisingly, psychoanalytic critics treat the *Travels* as evidence in a case study of Swift himself. In what is perhaps the most notable psychoanalytic treatment of *Gulliver's Travels*, Norman O. Brown quotes Phyllis Greenacre to the effect that 'Swift showed marked anal characteristics' including a preoccupation with personal hygiene, intense ambition and a 'stubborn vengefulness in righteous

---

8    Aldous Huxley, *Do What You Will* (London: Chatto & Windus, 1929), p. 32.
9    John Middleton Murry, *Jonathan Swift: A Critical Biography* (London: Jonathan Cape, 1954), p. 351.

causes'. Brown rejects such simplistic readings of Swift's 'excremental vision' which leaves the 'Dean's character without a shred of integrity', and in response to Greenacre's revulsion at Swift's 'marked anal characteristics', he argues that if 'personal immaculateness, ambition and the championship of righteous causes are neurotic traits, who shall 'scape whipping? And certainly no genius will escape if this kind of psychoanalysis is turned loose on literary texts.' Brown recommends a different way of using psychoanalysis to diagnose the 'universal neurosis of mankind'. In this formulation:

> We no longer try to explain away Swift's literary achievements as mere epiphenomena of his individual neurosis. Rather we seek to appreciate his insight into the universal neurosis of mankind. Then psychoanalysis becomes a method not for explaining away but for explicating Swift. We are not disturbed by the fact that Swift had his individual version of the universal human neurosis; we are not even disturbed by the thought that his individual neurosis may have been abnormally acute, or by the thought that his abnormality may be inseparable from his art.[10]

Perhaps no one has made better use of psychoanalytic insights than contemporary feminist critics interested in the cultural implications of such arguments. Carol Barash argues, for example, that such 'classic psychoanalytic theory produces a universal[izing] account of heterosexual norms from a much more unwieldy, historically specific set of sexual narratives'.[11] Responding to Laura Brown's account of Swift's treatment of women (see **pp. 84–9**), Barash argues that Brown suggests it is Gulliver who shrinks from the 'vision of primal physicality' (p. 447) in Book IV, not Swift himself. Barash draws attention to the facts of Swift's childhood which 'suggest ambivalence about both his own mother and things maternal', pointing to all the symbolic mothers in Book II (p. 451). Critics commonly argue that Book IV is defined by its searching anatomy of human nature, but for Barash, 'Gulliver's revulsion with the female body' is what 'structures the fourth voyage' so that in the end even his own marriage disgusts him (p. 457). 'Through psychoanalysis we can account, at once, for Gulliver's hatred of the female body, its smells and fluids and fleshiness, and his childlike pleasure in being engulfed by this same overwhelming and fleshy maternal otherness' (p. 453).

Before it was possible to dispel the myths of Swift's misanthropy and madness, it was necessary to construct a more accurate biography of Jonathan Swift. Now thanks to David Nokes's *Jonathan Swift, A Hypocrite Reversed: A Critical Biography* (1985), Joseph McMinn's *Jonathan Swift: A Literary Life* (1991), and Irvin Ehrenpreis's magisterial *Swift: The Man, His Works, and the Age*, 3 vols (1962–83), one gains a much more nuanced view of a writer who is at once more

---

10  Quoted in Norman O. Brown, 'The Excremental Vision', from *Life Against Death* (Middletown, Conn.: Wesleyan University Press, 1959), rpt. *Swift: A Collection of Critical Essays*, ed. Ernest Tuveson (Englewood Cliff, NJ: Prentice-Hall, 1964), p. 36.

11  Carol Barash, 'Violence and the Maternal: Swift Psychoanalysis, and the 1720s', in *Gulliver's Travels*, ed. Christopher Fox (Boston, Mass.: Bedford Books, 1995), p. 443; see also Margaret Anne Doody, 'Swift and Women', in *The Cambridge Companion to Jonathan Swift*, ed. Christopher Fox (Cambridge: Cambridge University Press, 2003), pp. 91 ff.

complex, more human and intensely more likable than the figure who emerges from the pages of Orrery, Scott, Murry or even Norman O. Brown. For example, the relationship of Swift and 'Stella', his closest friend and companion, seems far more innocent than had been imagined by Murry. Certainly the myth of a secret marriage between them has now been discredited. Although troubled throughout his life by the periodic deafness and giddiness brought on by Ménière's Syndrome, a disorder of the inner ear, Swift was never 'mad' nor reclusive. In fact, Swift enjoyed the company of a large circle of Irish friends with whom he played cards and shared conversation. He followed a course of vigorous exercise and, perhaps most important, he kept up his busy schedule as Dean of St Patrick's Cathedral until 1742, when his deteriorating physical condition required him to withdraw. While Swift was placed under the protection of a committee of guardians late in his life, he did not expire 'a Driv'ler and a Show', as Johnson so memorably asserted.[12] He was merely old and senile, suffering from a series of small strokes and the effects of Ménière's.

## Hard and Soft Schools of Interpretation

While it has been possible for biographers to debunk a number of the more lurid myths surrounding Swift's personal history, his reputation for misanthropy, encouraged by the fourth voyage of the *Travels*, has been harder to shake. Swift had certainly anticipated this reaction when he told Alexander Pope that he was working on a treatise 'proving the falsity of that Definition *animal rationale*' (that is, the familiar notion that humans are rational animals), 'and to show it should be only *rationis capax*' (that is, capable of reason). This is a key definition, for while Swift concedes that it is on this 'great foundation of Misanthropy' that the 'whole Building of my Travells is erected', he makes a point of insisting that such misanthropy is 'not in Timon's manner' (see Letters, pp. 25–6). In other words, he is not like Timon, the misanthrope in Shakespeare's *Timon of Athens*, a disappointed and angry man who flees to the forest where he hurls curses at all who come near him. Instead, Swift suggests that *Gulliver's Travels* offers a hybrid form of misanthropy less desperate and savage than we might otherwise expect. It is perhaps appropriate, then, that such a large proportion of critical energy devoted to *Gulliver's Travels* over the past fifty years has addressed the question of the scope and meaning of Swift's 'misanthropy', as it is reflected in Book IV. Are we meant to see the Houyhnhnms as models of virtue that Gulliver, identified as he is with Yahoo bestiality, cannot hope to emulate? Or does Gulliver, who is neither Yahoo nor Houyhnhnm, represent a middle term, whose rejection of his own humanity in favour of Houyhnhnm rationality finally renders him the comic butt of the tale? (see Sheridan's analysis in Early Critical Reception, pp. 66–7).

---

12 See Samuel Johnson, 'The Vanity of Human Wishes. The Tenth Satire of Juvenal Imitation', in *Samuel Johnson: The Complete Poems*, ed. J. D. Fleeman (Harmondsworth: Penguin, 1971), p. 91, line 318.

James L. Clifford has memorably described this debate as a struggle between the 'soft' and 'hard' schools of interpretation.[13] In this critical schema, the 'soft' school, represented by Kathleen Williams's *Jonathan Swift and the Age of Compromise*[14] argues in general terms that Gulliver stands as a middle term between the Houyhnhnms and the Yahoos, both of which represent undesirable characteristics. Gulliver insists that the Houyhnhnms are 'perfection of nature'. But the adherents to the soft school argue that this endorsement must be understood ironically. Indeed the soft school tends to emphasize all those negative qualities – failure of imagination, a near-deistical elevation of reason, a lack of passionate concern for their own kind, matched by a genocidal hatred of all others – which finally render the Houyhnhnms inappropriate objects of admiration. Swift, the Anglican cleric, could not have meant us to model our behaviour on theirs, and thus, the argument goes, Gulliver's infatuation with the Houyhnhnms must finally render him the butt of Swift's irony. In Book IV we must look elsewhere for moral models, and the soft school finds such a paragon in the figure of Pedro de Mendez, the Portuguese sea-captain who rescues Gulliver and generously returns him to England.

Not surprisingly, the adherents to the 'hard' interpretation pay little attention to this captain as the locus of humane virtue; nor do they accept the argument that Houyhnhnm reason is visibly flawed, or that Gulliver is meant to be the victim of Swift's irony. Rather, the partisans of the hard school tend to agree with George Sherburn's assertion that 'the Houyhnhnms represent Swift's clearly imperfect concept of "perfection of nature" '. And in this portrayal Swift 'did perhaps as well as could be expected'. As for Gulliver, sometimes he speaks for Swift, sometimes only for himself. Certainly he speaks for Swift 'in the passages satirical of political, social and moral corruption in England', but it is 'only through conversations with his critical Houyhnhnm master that Gulliver comes to see in part the baseness of life in what had been his own dear country'. Why then, if the Houyhnhnms were so perfect, did Gulliver's association with them render him 'unfit for life in human society'? Sherburn's answer is simple: 'Swift was driving to a misanthropic conclusion. The Houyhnhnm state was too high; Gulliver could not attain unto unto it.'[15] It is fair to say that given the choice, most readers of Swift, particularly readers in the later decades of the twentieth century, have expressed greater sympathy for the 'soft' interpretation than for the 'hard'. And while the question of the meaning of Gulliver's last voyage no longer inspires the passion it once did, the debate has contributed to our understanding of the *Travels* in a number of significant ways.

## *Gulliver's Travels* and the Novel

From the very beginning, dissatisfaction with an overemphasis on Swift's 'misanthropy' has led critics to turn away from questions of Swift's personality in favour

13 See James L. Clifford, 'Gulliver's Fourth Voyage: "Hard" and "Soft" Schools of Interpretation', *Quick Springs of Sense: Studies in the Eighteenth Century*, ed. Larry Champion (Athens, Ga.: University of Georgia Press, 1974), pp. 33–49.
14 Kathleen Williams, *Jonathan Swift and the Age of Compromise* (Lawrence, Kans.: University of Kansas Press, 1958).
15 George Sherburn, 'Errors Concerning the Houyhnhnms', *Modern Philology*, vol. 56, no. 2 (November 1958), pp. 96–7.

of discussion of the artistry and style of *Gulliver's Travels* itself. James Beattie remarks that Swift's 'fable is well conducted and, for the most part, consistent with itself, and connected with probable circumstances. He personates a sea-faring man; and with wonderful propriety supports the plainness and simplicity of the character. And this gives to the whole narrative an air of truth' (see **p. 69**). This focus on the truth to nature in *Gulliver's Travels*, on its 'verisimilitude', becomes a frequent topic of discussion for later eighteenth-century critics. James Burnett, Lord Monboddo praises the plainness and simplicity of the narrative such that 'those monstrous lies so narrated, have more the air of probability than many a true story unskillfully told' (see **p. 69–70**). Sir Walter Scott builds on this account, noting that Swift's style is actually a parody of the 'manner of old voyagers; their dry and minute style, and the unimportant personal incidents with which their journals are encumbered' (see **pp. 70–1**). Scott is the first to suggest that this 'art of introducing trifling and minute anecdotes, upon which nothing depends, or is made to turn' (**p. 71**) was adapted from Defoe. This fascination with Swift's circumstantial style has also sustained a long-running discussion of the narrative features of the *Travels* which may or may not justify its inclusion in the list of early-eighteenth-century novels.

As J. Paul Hunter remarks:

> *Gulliver's Travels* is not a novel in any meaningful sense of that slippery term ... yet its generic status would be difficult to establish without having the novel in mind. Swift's masterpiece is, in fact, so conceptually dependent upon the novel that it is almost impossible to imagine the existence of the *Travels* outside the context of the developing novelistic tradition.[16]

Certainly, *Gulliver's Travels* invites comparison with that other best-seller, *Robinson Crusoe* (1719), which appeared at approximately the same time as Swift was beginning work on the *Travels*. Like *Robinson Crusoe*, *Gulliver's Travels* includes episodes of dangerous adventure, shipwreck, abandonment, and solitary survival, and yet, as Frederick R. Karl observes, *Robinson Crusoe* is labelled as a novel and *Gulliver's Travels* 'rather warily as a kind of mutation, neither novel nor not novel'.[17] While Swift pretended not to have read *Crusoe*, and claimed even to have forgotten Defoe's name, there is strong evidence that Swift had Crusoe in mind when he described Gulliver's family, background and early career. As Hunter points out, Gulliver's description of how he swam to shore wearing a full suit of clothes, a hat and carrying a large sword, as well as the Lilliputian inventory of Gulliver's pockets (see Key Passages, **pp. 125–6**) is a direct reference to Robinson Crusoe, who strips his clothes off to re-enter his wrecked ship, only to explain pages later how he stuffed biscuits into the pockets of the pants he was presumably not wearing. According to Hunter:

16 J. Paul Hunter, 'Gulliver's Travels and the Novel', ed. Frederick N. Smith, *The Genres of Gulliver's Travels* (Newark, Del.: University of Delaware Press, 1990), p. 56.
17 Frederick R. Karl, *A Reader's Guide to the Eighteenth-Century English Novel* (New York: Farrar, Strauss & Giroux, 1974), p. 279.

The example of the allusive pockets suggests that *Gulliver's Travels* is, among many other impressive things, an accreting generic or class parody not only of travel narratives per se but also of a larger developing class of first-person fictional narratives that make extraordinary claims for the importance of the contemporary.[18]

Early critics were almost unanimous in their praise of Swift's specificity and accuracy of fictional detail (see **pp. 69–71**). Although the realism of *Gulliver's Travels* links it most firmly with the eighteenth-century novel, most readers have not considered its illusion of verisimilitude alone sufficient grounds to classify the work itself as a novel. Part of this difficulty may derive from the absence of a significant plot in *Gulliver's Travels*. The *Travels* certainly has a story; the reader is interested in what happens to Gulliver and what he will do next. Yet, if one accepts E. M. Forster's definition of plot as a 'narrative of events, the emphasis on causality', or R. S. Crane's description of plot as a temporal synthesis of 'action, character and thought', whose organizing principle is 'completed change', then it becomes more difficult to speak of plot in *Gulliver's Travels* (see **pp. 81–4**).[19]

# Gulliver and his Readers

Largely in reaction against the focus on Swift's 'personality' inherent in various biographical and psychoanalytic attempts to account for *Gulliver's Travels*, the New Critics of the mid-twentieth century severed all connections between Swift the man and *Gulliver's Travels* as a free-standing and autonomous work of satiric art. In general terms the New Critics tended to ignore biographical or historical data in the interpretation of literary works in favour of a close analysis of the aesthetic features – image, symbol or metaphor – of the individual work of art. This critical method is perhaps most neatly encapsulated in Ricardo Quintana's 'Situational Satire: A Commentary on the Method of Swift', which seeks to eliminate the confusion between the writer and the written word, stressing instead the 'element of impersonality in literary art'. As in any other work of art, *Gulliver's Travels* creates 'its own, complete universe'. It is an aesthetic 'construct', a 'precisely devised literary composition, a form of rhetoric'.[20] Such critical assertions are more fully developed in works like *Swift's Rhetorical Art: A Study in Structure and Meaning*[21] in which Martin Price defends Swift's literary achievement using such rhetorical criteria as his mastery of the plain style, his exploitation of wit or his use of symbolism. Like all New Critics of the *Travels*, Price places special emphasis on Swift's mastery of the satirical mask or persona. Of course, Swift

18 Hunter, 'Gulliver's Travels and the Novel', p. 69.
19 E. M. Forster, *Aspects of the Novel* (New York: Harcourt, Brace & World, 1955), p. 86; R. S. Crane, 'The Concept of Plot and the Plot of *Tom Jones*', in *Critics and Criticism, Ancient and Modern* (Chicago, Ill.: University of Chicago Press, 1952), pp. 616–47.
20 Ricardo Quintana, 'Situational Satire: A Commentary on the Method of Swift', *University of Toronto Quarterly*, vol. XVII (1948), pp. 130–36. Quoted in *Swift: A Collection of Critical Essays*, ed. Ernest Lee Tuveson (Englewood Cliffs, NJ: Prentice-Hall, 1968), pp. 91, 93.
21 Martin Price, *Swift's Rhetorical Art: A Study in Structure and Meaning* (New Haven, Conn.: Yale University Press, 1953).

clearly encouraged this critical response by adopting a range of fictional identities from the Drapier, the voice we hear in the *Drapier's Letters* (1724), to Gulliver himself.

Perhaps the most extreme reading of Gulliver as a fully 'lifelike and individualized persona' is offered by William Bragg Ewald for whom Gulliver is 'an everyman' who actually 'learns from his experiences'. According to Ewald, Gulliver is a 'real seaman in his genuine fondness for both his family and the sea', an ordinary man whose business failures force him to 'set sail in order to get riches to maintain himself and his family'. Because he is a fictional persona, not a satiric spokesperson, the fact that 'Gulliver, like many men, holds beliefs that are contradictory to one another', is not an issue. Gulliver is 'not only a naïve individual; he is also a patriotic Englishman'. Along with Gulliver's exaggerated ingenuousness and his extreme patriotism goes his powerful admiration for the work of mathematicians, scientists and projectors. 'Swift does not overwork the irony in *Gulliver's Travels*. In many instances, Gulliver is merely an objective reporter; here Swift lets events speak for themselves.'[22]

The whole question of Gulliver's status as a purely fictional construct has inspired considerable debate. In his notable essay 'Personae', Irvin Ehrenpreis questions the attempt to rescue Swift from the biographical criticism of Thackeray and Murry by establishing 'an ideal of impersonal art as the distinguishing property' of writers like Swift. According to Ehrenpreis, critics who stress the centrality or consistency of Swift's 'personae' share certain common assumptions. For example, the presupposition that 'a literary work should be regarded not as an aspect of the author's personality but as a separate thing', means that 'the sentiments expressed' are 'not to be attributed to the author himself' but to a speaker or narrator to whom we may 'assign the attitudes which seem implicit in a literary work'. While the demonstration of a perfect symmetry between character of the speaker and the alleged design of the work may serve to enhance the reputation of the work in question, in the case of *Gulliver*, it simply doesn't work. Swift's characters are not 'fully rounded figures. . . . again and again the veneer of probability is broken.' Swift frequently steps forward to give 'the reader a piece of his mind', as when he denounces the 'English voters of his day for prostituting themselves by accepting bribes'.[23]

The persona is primarily useful as a means of seducing readers into accepting the logical necessity or ideas – like the notion of eating infants – before they realize that they have been victimized. According to Ehrenpreis, Swift's skill as a writer appears in his 'disclosing the wickedness of the doctrines before disclosing the irony of his manner. The longer the reader can be kept in suspense between the two revelations, the sharper is the effect. The greater the degree of fascinated ambivalence that results, the greater is the achievement of the satirist.' In purely narrative terms, each of the four voyages begins the same way, couched in the familiar circumstantial terms of realistic narrative, and the reader assumes that 'the moral character of the speaker is essentially like his own'. The ironic persona must 'retain this sympathy after the reader has contemplated the evil

22  William Bragg Ewald, *The Masks of Jonathan Swift* (Oxford: Basil Blackwell, 1954), pp. 124–49.
23  Irvin Ehrenpreis, 'Personae', in *Literary Meaning and Augustan Values* (Charlottesville, Va.: University Press of Virginia, 1974), p. 50.

or absurdity of the recommendations'. While the reader is 'struggling to disengage his fellow feeling – that is, while he still feels reluctant to admit that he was wrong to give a fair hearing to the author – it must grow obvious that the author himself is not in earnest but is delivering a parody, acting out a caricature of a type of man he loathes or contemns'. As a result, the reader experiences a 'double' effect,

> for he sees himself derided by the very person he has been straining to respect. At the same time, he feels that the author, by taking his initial sympathy for granted, has pinned the loathsome character on him. In fact, it is because of this sympathy that he is being ridiculed. If the maneuver is successful, the reader cannot help exerting himself to reject the character.[24]

Ehrenpreis's argument has given rise to an extended debate over Swift's exploitation of the ironic persona. Perhaps more important, it points to a central concern of later-twentieth-century critics: Swift's ambiguous relationship with his readers. As Clive Probyn remarks: 'One of the most vexing characteristics of Swift's satire is that it seems no part of his strategy to leave clear space between the speaker (or persona) and the "author". Swift moves in and out of dramatic constructions without warning and the effect is destabilizing.'[25] While a number of critics (some listed in the section entitled 'Further Reading') have commented on ambiguous, often tortuous, relationship between Swift, his ironic spokesman, and the 'generous' reader, perhaps no one has exploited the topic to greater or better effect than C. J. Rawson, whose *Gulliver and the Gentle Reader* is excerpted later in this book (see **pp. 93–8**).

Rawson's emphasis on the unstable relationship between Swift and his readers may be seen to partake of a wider modern and postmodern concern with instability and indeterminacy on a number of fronts. In a notable essay applying poststructuralist perspectives to the whole relationship between author, reader and textuality in the *Travels*, Richard H. Rodino points to the epigraph 'Splendide Mendax' (splendidly false) underneath the portrait of Gulliver in the 1735 Faulkner edition as an indication that the text itself is a 'nexus of fiction making'. Gulliver's story also 'conflates the power of language with the language of power. . . . In *Gulliver's Travels*, interpretation, by the human characters at least, is never merely a quest for truth and virtue: it always contains a desire to control the flux of meaning. The potential for fictions and other lies is at once creative and pernicious. Language conceals even as it reveals.' Despite Swift's reputation for clarity and straightforwardness of description, Rodino's description of the relationship between reader and the business of fiction-making in the *Travels* points to just how uncertain Swift's descriptions can be. We can begin with Faulkner's title page which identifies itself as 'Volume III of the Author's Works'. This urges readers to 'infer an author [Swift] who has invented an author [Gulliver] who is inventing a text that urges his own readers to assume a new relationship to him as

---

24  Ehrenpreis, 'Personae', p. 58.
25  Clive Probyn, *Gulliver's Travels* (Harmondsworth: Penguin, 1987), p. 78.

character and through that relationship to construct his desired image of himself, that is, Gulliver as he intends to be understood.'

In other words, throughout the process of reading we are required to remember that we are making sense of the story written by Gulliver who is a character in another larger story written by Swift, neither of which is entirely dependable.

> During any given reading, then, the reader is invited to play at least three roles: docile interpreter of Gulliver's authorial intentions; metacritic of Gulliver's motives and strategies; and metametacritic of Swift, who glimpses the levels and loops of textuality in which the Travels' other readers, authors, and characters are situated. The reader's unstable roles thus also include the parts of author and character.[26]

## Gulliver and the Uncertainties of Language

As this brief redaction of Rodino's argument suggests, poststructuralism has tended to emphasize the fact that works of literature are made objects whose very form and content offer us a texture of words all of which are involved in the production of meaning. The result for Swift is that the texture of language easily undercuts or renders ambiguous the more normative instructions that Gulliver, or Swift, seems to offer. So it is that *Gulliver's Travels* simultaneously advertises the fact that it is perfectly and entirely true, and that its author is a splendid liar. This insight provides the basis for Robert Phiddian's discussion (see **pp. 98–102**) of Swift's ambivalence towards scientific language in what purport to be descriptions of modern experiments in the Academy of Lagado.

Critics have also taken the opportunity to re-examine Swift's use of language as part of a larger political agenda. In her essay on 'The Battle of the Ancients and (Post) Moderns: Rethinking Swift through Contemporary Perspectives', Carole Fabricant reconsiders the complexity of Swift's language through the lens of ideology, conditioned by historical contingency. Although the years before 1715 were spent defending the values of his Tory companions and the orthodox Church of Ireland, and while his writings after his return to Ireland increasingly focus on the defence of his fellow Irishmen, the arc of Swift's career, according to Fabricant, can be described as a 'movement away from the attempt to bolster existing forms of power by strengthening centralized mechanisms of (moral and cultural as well as political) control, and toward an identification with the interests of an emergent though oppressed group for whom such regulatory mechanisms are a hindrance to rather than a promoter of authentic community'.[27] That is to say, Swift moves from defending institutions like the Church of England, identified with established power, to a defence of the Irish who were oppressed

---

26  Richard H. Rodino, ' "Splendide Mendax": Authors, Characters, and Readers in Gulliver's Travels', *PMLA (Publications of the Modern Language Association of America)* vol. 106 (1991), pp. 1056–7.

27  Carole Fabricant, 'The Battle of the Ancients and (Post) Moderns: Rethinking Swift through Contemporary Perspectives', *The Eighteenth Century: Theory and Interpretation*, vol. 32 (fall 1991), p. 259.

**CAPT. LEMUEL GULLIVER**
*Splendide Mendax. Hor.*

*Figure 4* Captain Gulliver, 'Splendide Mendax'.

by many of the same institutions Swift had once championed. Thinking about Swift's 'diverse voices and stances' in relation to the distribution of political power provides a way to think about Swift's changing personae 'in other than traditionally generic or biographical contexts', and offers 'a perspective that avoids the contemporary trap of explaining these identities (away) as purely linguistic constructs' (p. 260). Resisting theories that reduce Swift merely to a 'writing subject' or a 'textual self', Fabricant insists on the relationship between writing and power in the works of Jonathan Swift. It is no accident that twice in his career he had a price put on his head: once for *The Public Spirit of the Whigs*, and then again for one of his *Drapier's Letters*. 'Swift never allows us to forget that he is writing in a situation where the writer (as well as his publisher) can at any moment be thrown in prison, silenced, officially repudiated, and where his texts' can be censured or suppressed 'not so much because of "textual indeterminacy" or "verbal slippage" but because of the wrath or policy of those in power' (p. 261).

Fabricant concedes that Swift's addiction to word play may imply that the signification of his language is unstable, open to multiple interpretations (as Robert Phiddian argues on **pp. 98–102**). Even so, as a political writer Swift also assigns meanings to language and these 'acts are never either innocent or equal since they never occur in a political vacuum'. In an important essay, 'Why the Houyhnhnms Don't Write' (**pp. 102–6**), Terry Castle argues that Gulliver suffers from a form of 'Grammaphobia', a fear of the written text that leads him to prefer the pristine world of 'spoken discourse'. Fabricant modifies this position, arguing that what really matters is not 'the catastrophic fall into the world of letters', but the far more sinister and disastrous fall into a world of censored and confiscated letters, constituting one short step away from complete silence . . .'[28] The argument that Swift's language must be understood in a political context was one that Swift himself understood; his letters are filled with apprehension that his political satire might result in persecution, censorship or even arrest (see Letters, **pp. 25, 27–8**). As J. A. Downie suggests, the whole question of the political specificity of Swift's satire in the *Travels* and his vulnerability to prosecution remains a matter of critical debate (see, **pp. 106–11**).

## Politics, Power and *Gulliver's Travels*

One of the effects of postmodernist and cultural studies has been to redefine *Gulliver's Travels* as a fundamentally Irish text, its satiric messages governed by the same forces that gave rise to the *Drapier's Letters* or *A Modest Proposal*. Fabricant argues that:

> Swift cannot be understood apart from his multi-varied ties to Ireland. There is room for disagreement about the precise nature and meaning of these ties, but there can be no disputing the fundamental connection itself – a kind of umbilical cord which, though sometimes perversely

28 Fabricant, 'The Battle of the Ancients and (Post) Moderns', p. 269.

denied or concealed, was never severed and in fact greatly strengthened during the final quarter-century of his life.[29]

Certainly, Swift felt an ambivalence about his native land that never abated. He could simultaneously describe himself almost proudly as 'a Teague,[30] or an Irishman, or what people please', and as 'an obscure exile in a most obscure and enslaved country'.[31] As Clement Hawes points out, the Irishness of the *Travels* is but part of a larger critique of colonialism, most clearly articulated at the conclusion of the Fourth Voyage where Gulliver talks about the island on which he has been marooned and of which he is, at least for the moment, the new conqueror.[32] For moral critics of the novel, perhaps best represented by Samuel Holt Monk (see **pp. 89–93**), *Gulliver's Travels* is primarily concerned with answering the question of what sort of creatures humans can be said to be. Monk also attempts to determine whether Swift sought to condemn human nature in its entirety or merely to suggest that while we are 'capable of reason', and are therefore a salvageable species, we have fallen short of the mark.

Cultural critics, on the contrary, are interested in the political implications of *Gulliver's Travels*, in particular the relationship between depictions of travel and the mechanics of conquest. Arguing in opposition to those who find no consistent character development in Gulliver, and insisting that the *Travels* is a reaction against the 'bourgeois' or 'realistic' novel, which organizes reality 'around the inner life of a privileged subject or "character" ', Hawes suggests that 'Gulliver is himself now the victimized, radically misanthropic – and, indeed, quite insane – product of repeated colonization.' According to this argument, Gulliver's bizarre behaviour in Book IV should be ascribed not to Swift's own feelings and intentions or his conscious generic choices, 'but rather to Gulliver's narrative enactment of that violent colonial process which it so consistently and lucidly condemns.' Having been colonized himself by the Houyhnhnms, Gulliver comes to identify with the 'otherness' of the Yahoos, with their primitive features – flat noses – etc., and his hatred of his own kind, even his repulsion at their 'smell' are iterations of familiar colonial themes (see Key Passages, **pp. 165–6**). At the same time, and as with other colonized peoples, Gulliver begins to imitate the mannerisms of the colonial masters, who reveal a kind of 'equine chauvinism'. According to this line of argument, the Houyhnhnms are less to be seen as models of reason than as colonial oppressors who maintain the Yahoos in virtual slavery for their own benefit.[33]

Hawes points to the ease with which the Houyhnhnms (in council) can condemn an entire native species to death, or at least fantasize about it (see Key Passages, **pp. 179–8**), a question explored in greater and more troubling depth by Claude Rawson in *God, Gulliver, and Genocide: Barbarism and the European Imagination 1492–1945*. Rawson reiterates the argument outlined earlier, that

29  Carole Fabricant, 'Swift the Irishman', in *The Cambridge Companion to Jonathan Swift*, ed. Christopher Fox (Cambridge: Cambridge University Press, 1993), p. 48.
30  Slang for an Irishman.
31  See *Corr.* IV, p. 229 and *Corr.* IV, p. 468.
32  Clement Hawes, 'Three Times Round the Globe: Gulliver and Colonial Discourse', *Cultural Critique*, vol. 18 (1991), pp. 187–214.
33  Hawes, 'Three Times Round the Globe', pp. 208, 205.

Swift's description of the Yahoos conflates imagery of Hottentots and the primitive Irish (see Contemporary Documents, **pp. 37–8**). More importantly, however, Rawson also suggests connections between the genocidal fantasies entertained by the Houyhnhnms, by Gulliver (and perhaps by Swift himself), and a wider relationship between colonists and the colonized through the ages. Rawson argues that the episode where the female Yahoo leaps on Gulliver while he is bathing (see Key Passages, **p. 176**),

> was expressly planted by Swift to indicate that Gulliver's, and 'our' identity with the Yahoos is an objective fact of the narrative, and not merely a distorted projection of Gulliver's misanthropy. The Yahoos are also 'brutes' in the same sense as the natives of the African bush are to Kurtz or to Marlow in *Heart of Darkness*, eliciting the same troubled suspicion of radical kinship, and the same outbursts of murderous rejection.[34]

As Rawson argues: 'When Kurtz exclaims, in the famous delirious postscript, "Exterminate all the brutes!", he is replaying a grisly commonplace of the litera- ture of empire, ubiquitous in fiction as well as in the narratives or polemics of exploration and conquest, and manifested in the debate in the Houyhnhnm General Assembly as to 'Whether the Yahoos should be exterminated from the face of the Earth (IV, ix p. 96). Rawson points out that there is a troubling ambivalence about such an assertion since it matches Swift's own suggestion regarding the fate reserved for Irish infants in *A Modest Proposal* (1729). In short:

> [The Yahoos are] not simply Irish brutes. They stand more prom- inently not as members of an individual race but as representatives of the human species in its most radical and degraded form. The fact that humanoids are also expressly represented as having the charac- teristics of 'all Savage Nations', and in particular those specifically attributed to the Irish, is a characteristic double-bind. It reflects a deep Swiftian tendency to identify mankind as a whole with its own despised subgroups.[35]

This equation between Yahoos and humans does not necessarily represent Swift's true feelings. Rather, it forms part of a 'large network of small effects of its kind', designed to vex the reader, to 'plant' an impression for the 'reader's discomfort'.[36] As Rawson points out, moreover, Houyhnhnm debates about the extermination of the Yahoos (see Key Passages, **pp. 178–9**) echo the language of Genesis 6:7: 'I will destroy man whom I have created from the face of the earth.' This is not to say that either the Book of Genesis, or *Gulliver's Travels*, is in the business of

---

34  Claude Rawson, *God, Gulliver, and Genocide: Barbarism and the European Imagination 1492– 1945* (Oxford: Oxford University Press, 2001), p. 96.

35  *Rawson, God, Gulliver, and Genocide*, p. 258. In Joseph Conrad's *The Heart of Darkness*, Kurtz writes in the margin of a tract he is writing on native customs, 'Exterminate all the Brutes', an outburst that contradicts the apparent benevolence and high-mindedness of the study he is writing about Africa.

36  Op. cit., p. 260.

suggesting that: 'God, or the Houyhnhnms, are genocidal maniacs, but that mankind, or the Yahoos, deserve punishment.'[37]

It is characteristic of modern discussions of the *Travels* that even the question of Swift and the temptations of genocide inevitably brings us full circle, back to the original question of Swift's misanthropy with which the critical discussion of *Gulliver's Travels* began more than two centuries ago. As we will see, all of these concerns from the role of the narrator, Swift's truth to nature, the ambiguous functions of language, and Swift's attitudes towards mankind in general and women in particular are touched on in the early and more modern critical responses to *Gulliver's Travels* that follow.

37 Op. cit., p. 238.

# Early Critical Reception

From **John Boyle, Fifth Earl of Orrery, Remarks on the Life and Writing of Dr. Jonathan Swift, Dean of St. Patrick's Dublin** (1752) (Dublin: George Faulkner), *quoted in Swift: The Critical Heritage*, ed. Kathleen Williams (New York: Barnes & Noble, 1970), p. 125

In this passage, Swift's acquaintance, Lord Orrery, complains that in Book III the satire on modern politics and modern science is too severe and that the imagery frequently degenerates into outright indecency. This criticism is consistent with the argument made elsewhere in his *Remarks on the Life and Writing of Dr. Jonathan Swift* that *Gulliver's Travels* was a 'real insult upon mankind', (p. 121), and that Swift 'indulged a misanthropy that is intolerable' (p. 117). Lord Orrery initiated a line of criticism that continued into the first half of the twentieth century. Here he connects the 'filth' of many of the episodes in *Gulliver's Travels* with Swift's undeserved reputation for madness, an argument that inspired great critical response.

The sixth chapter [of the Third Book] is full of severity and satyr. Sometimes it is exerted against the legislative power: sometimes against particular politicians: sometimes against women: and sometimes it degenerates into filth. True humour ought to be kept up with decency, and dignity, or it loses every tincture of entertainment. Descriptions that shock our delicacy cannot have the least good effect upon our minds. They offend us, and we fly precipitately from the sight. We cannot stay long enough to examine, wither wit, sense, or morality, may be couched under such odious appearances. I am sorry to say, that these sort of descriptions, which are too often interspersed throughout all SWIFT's works, are seldom written with any other view, or from any other motive, than a wild unbridled indulgence of his own humour and disposition.

## From **Patrick Delany, *Observations upon Lord Orrery's Remarks on the Life and Writings of Dr. Jonathan Swift*** (1754) (Dublin: Robert Main), quoted in *Swift: The Critical Heritage,* ed. Kathleen Williams (New York: Barnes & Noble, 1970), p. 135

> Dr Patrick Delany (1685?–1768) was another friend of Swift's during his later years. Delany was offended by Orrery's attack on Swift, and he attempted to defend Swift's character. Even so, he expresses concern as to whether any satirist, Swift in particular, can ever hope to reform mankind when he places such emphasis on the apparently irredeemable bestiality of human behaviour.

Upon the whole, I am clearly of opinion, that [Swift] would more effectually have endeavoured to amend mankind, by putting the virtues, and the suited practice of one, even imaginary good man, in a fair and amiable light, than by painting the depravities of the whole species in the most odious colours, and attitudes! Who would not wish rather to be the author of one Arcadia, than fifty *Laputa's, Lilliputs*, and *Houyhnhnms*?

I am fully satisfied, that exaggerated satire, never yet did any good, nor ever will. The only satire that can do any good is that which shews mankind to themselves, in their true light; and exposes those follies, vices and corruptions of every kind, in all their absurdities, deformities, and horrors, which flattery, self-love, and passions of any kind, had hitherto hid from their eyes. That magnifying-glass, which enlarges all the deform features into monstrous dimensions, defeats its own purpose: for no man will ever know his own likeness in it: and, consequently, tho' he may be shocked, he will not be amended by it.

## From **Edward Young, *Conjectures on Original Composition in a Letter to the Author of Sir Charles Grandison*** (1759), 2nd edition (London: A. Millar, and R. and J. Dodsley), pp. 61–5

> In this famous rejection of Swift's misanthropy, Edward Young, a self-proclaimed author of kinder, gentler satires, accuses Swift of having libelled human nature and having distorted the 'human face divine'. It was an indictment that would resonate for the next 200 years. The suggestion that Swift's 'temper' had 'jostled his judgment', introduces the notion, influential with later critics, that Swift's apparent hatred of humankind resulted from his own madness.

How have thy Houyhnhnms thrown thy judgment from its seat; and laid thy imagination in the mire? In what ordure has thou dipt thy pencil? What a monster hast thou made of the

> *Human face divine?*
>                    Milton.

This writer has so satirized human nature, as to give a demonstration in himself, that it deserves to be satirized. But, say his wholesale admirers, Few could *so* have written; true, and Fewer *would*. If it required great abilities to commit the fault, greater still would have saved him from it. But whence arise such warm advocates for such a performance? From hence, *viz.* before a character is established, merit makes fame; afterwards fame makes merit. *Swift* is not commended for this piece, but this piece for *Swift*. He has given us some beauties which deserve all our praise; and our comfort is, that his faults will not become common; for none can be guilty of them, but who have wit as well as reputation to spare. His wit had been less wild, if his temper had not jostled his judgment. If his favourite Houyhnhnms could write, and Swift had been one of them, every horse with him would have been an ass, and he would have written a panegyrick on mankind, saddling with much reproach the present heroes of his pen: On the contrary, being born amongst men, and, of consequence, piqued by many, and peevish at more, he has blasphemed a nature little lower than that of angels, and assumed by far higher than they.

From **Thomas Sheridan, *The Life of the Reverend Jonathan Swift***
(1784) in *The Works of the Rev. Jonathan Swift, D. D. Dean of St. Patrick's, Dublin,*
19 vols (rpt. London: 1801), vol. I, pp. 239, 233–4

> Responding to Young's outburst, Sheridan parodies his very language in defence of Swift. Like a number of twentieth-century critics (see **pp. 89–93**), Sheridan argues that the Yahoos are not actually meant to be seen as truly human, and therefore Swift's account of them does not defame human nature.

O doctor Young, how has thy prejudice thrown thy judgment from its seat, and let thy imagination hurry thee beyond all bounds of common sense! In what black composition of spleen and envy hast thou dipped thy pen! What a monstrous character hast thou given of

> *One of the noblest men*
> *That ever lived in the tide of times.*
>             Shakespeare (239)

[. . .] The position I mean to prove is, that the whole apologue of the Houyhnhnms and Yahoos, far from being intended as a debasement of human nature, if rightly understood, is evidently designed to show in what the true dignity and perfection of man's nature consists, and to point out the way by which it may be attained.

In order to this, let us first see with what design the fourth book of the Travels was written. In the first three books he has given various views of the different vices, follies, and absurdities of mankind, not without some mixture of good qualities, of virtue and wisdom, though in a small proportion to the others, as they are to be found in life. In his last book, he meant to exhibit two new portraits; one, of pure unmixed vice; the other, of perfect unadulterated virtue. In order that the native deformity of the one, might excite in us a deeper abhorrence of evil; and the resplendent charms of the other, allure us to what is good. To represent these to us in sensible forms, he clothes the one with the body of a man; the other with that of a horse. Between these two he divides the qualities of the human mind, taking away the rational soul from the Yahoo, and transferring it to the Houyhnhnm. To the Yahoo he leaves all the passions and evil propensities of man's nature, to be exerted without any check or control, as in the case of all other animals. The rational soul in the Houyhnhnm, acts unerringly as by instinct; it intuitively perceives what is right, and necessarily acts up to the dictates of reason. The Yahoo, as here described, is a creature of fancy, the product of the author's brain, which never had any thing similar to it upon earth. It has no resemblance to man, but in the make of its body, and the vicious propensities of its nature. It differs from him wholly in all the characteristical marks which distinguish man from the rest of the animal world. It has not a ray of reason, it has no speech, and it goes, like other quadrupeds, upon all fours. Now as reason, speech, and walking upright on two legs, are the universal properties of the human race, even in the most savage nations, which peculiarly mark their superiority over brutes, how, in the name of Heaven, has it come to pass, that by almost all who have read *Gulliver*, the Yahoos have been considered as beings of the human species, and the odious picture drawn of them, as intended to vilify and debase our nature? But it is evident from the whole account given of this creature of his fancy, that the author intended it should be considered as a mere beast, of a new species; for he has not only deprived it of all the characteristical distinctions of man before recited, but has superadded some material differences even in his bodily organs and powers, sufficient to distinguish it from the human race. [. . .] But it may be asked, to what end has such an odious animal been produced to view? The answer is obvious: The design of the author, in the whole of the apologue, is to place before the eyes of man a picture of the two different parts of his frame, detached from each other, in order that he may the better estimate the true value of each, and see the necessity there is that the one should have an absolute command over the other.

### From **William Makepeace Thackeray, 'Swift'** (1854) in *English Humorists of the Eighteenth Century* (London and New York: Everyman's Library, 1968), pp. 34–5

Perhaps because he was the author of *Vanity Fair* and editor of *The Cornhill*, one of the leading literary journals of the age, William Makepeace Thackeray's essay on Swift, first delivered on a lecture tour of the USA in 1853, had a powerful effect on Victorian attitudes towards Swift. Beginning with Young's suggestion that Swift's wit had somehow 'jostled' his 'judgment', Thackeray offers up one of the most hysterical diatribes ever directed against Swift's character, charging that Swift was not only a misanthrope but also a raving lunatic.

As for the humour and conduct of this famous fable, I suppose there is no person who reads but must admire; as for the moral, I think it horrible, shameful, unmanly, blasphemous; and giant and great as this Dean is, I say we should hoot him. Some of this audience mayn't have read the last part of Gulliver, and to such I would recall the advice of the venerable *Mr. Punch*[1] to persons about to marry, and say "Don't." When Gulliver first lands among the Yahoos, the naked howling wretches clamber up trees and assault him and he describes himself as "almost stifled with the filth which fell about him." The reader of the fourth part of *Gulliver's Travels* is like the hero himself in this instance. It is Yahoo language: a monster gibbering shrieks, and gnashing imprecations against mankind—tearing down all shreds of modesty, past all sense of manliness and shame; filthy in word, filthy in thought, furious, raging, obscene. [. . .]

What had this man done? what secret remorse was rankling at his heart? what fever was boiling in him, that he should see all the world bloodshot? We view the world with our own eyes, each of us; and we make from within us the world we see. A weary heart gets no gladness out of sunshine; a selfish man is skeptical about friendship, as a man with no ear doesn't care for music. A frightful self-consciousness it must have been, which looked on mankind so darkly through those keen eyes of Swift.

## From **James Beattie, 'Essays on Poetry and Music as they affect the Mind'** (1776) in *Essays. On the Nature and Immutability of Truth . . . On Poetry and Music, . . . On Laughter, and Ludicrous Composition. On the Utility of Classical Learning* (Edinburgh: William Creech), p. 379

As part of the moral critique of *Gulliver's Travels*, James Beattie points to Swift's apparent recommendation of the purely rational (and non-Christian) virtue of the Houyhnhnms as further evidence of the corrupt lessons to be taught by *Gulliver*. Beattie is one of the first to raise the question of how a Christian cleric like Swift could produce such an areligious satire.

Again, did Swift believe, that religious ideas are natural to a reasonable being, and necessary to the happiness of a moral one? I hope he did. Yet he has represented his *Houyhnhnms*, as patterns of moral virtue, as the greatest masters of reason, and withal as completely happy, without any religious ideas, or any views beyond the present life. In a word, he would make stupidity consistent with mental excellence, and unnatural appetites with animal perfection. These, however, are small matters, compared with the other absurdities of this abominable tale.—But when a Christian Divine can set himself deliberately to trample upon that nature, which he knows to have been made but a little lower than the angels, and to have been assumed by One far more exalted than they; we need not be surprised if the same perverse habits of thinking which harden his heart, should also debase his judgment.

---

1    Popular puppet who frequently engages in fights with his wife, Judy.

From **James Beattie, 'On Fable and Romance'** (1783) in *Dissertations Moral and Critical* (London: W. Strahan; and T. Cadell; and W. Beattie), pp. 514–15

> Beattie is also one of the first critics to deal seriously with the genre of *Gulliver's Travels* as well as its most characteristic aesthetic features, most notably its apparent truthfulness and its simplicity of style (see Critical History, **pp. 53–5**).

Gulliver's Travels are a sort of allegory; but rather Satirical and Political, than Moral. The work is in every body's hands: and has been criticized by many eminent writers. As far as the satire is levelled at human pride and folly; at the abuses of human learning; at the absurdity of speculative projectors; at those criminal or blundering expedients in policy, which we are apt to overlook, or even to applaud, because custom has made them familiar; so far the author deserves our warmest approbation, and his satire will be allowed to be perfectly just, as well as exquisitely severe. His fable is well conducted and, for the most part, consistent with itself, and connected with probable circumstances. He personates a sea-faring man; and with wonderful propriety supports the plainness and simplicity of the character. And this gives to the whole narrative an air of truth; which forms an entertaining contrast, when we compare it with the wildness of the fiction. The style deserves particular notice. It is not free from inaccuracy: but, as a model of easy and graceful simplicity, it has not been exceeded by any thing in our language; and well deserves to be studied by every person, who wishes to write pure English.—These, I think, are the chief merits of this celebrated work; which has been more read, than any other publication of the present century. Gulliver has something in it to hit every taste. The statesman, the philosopher, and the critick, will admire his keenness of satire, energy of description, and vivacity of language: the vulgar, and even children, who cannot enter into these refinements, will find their account in the story, and be highly amused with it.

From **James Burnett, Lord Monboddo, *Of the Origin and Progress of Language*** (1786) 2nd edition (Edinburgh: T. Cadell and J. Balfour), vol. III, pp. 195–6

> Following Beattie's critical line, Lord Monboddo (1714–99) notes the peculiarity of Swift's style, its combination of 'exquisite ridicule' with the appearance of absolute clarity. Like Beattie, Monboddo is one of the first critics to note the importance of 'verisimilitude', or the semblance of truth, in Swift's style.

The author, in English, that has excelled the most in this style is Dr. Swift, in his Gulliver's Travels; of which the narrative is wonderfully plain and simple, minute likewise, and circumstantial, so much as to be disgusting to a reader without taste or judgment, and the character of an English sailor is finely kept up in it. In short, it has every virtue belonging to this style; and I will venture to say, that those monstrous lies so narrated, have more the air of probability than many a true story unskillfully told. And, accordingly, I have been informed, that they imposed upon many when they were first published. The voyage to Lilliput, in my judgment, is the finest of them all, especially in what relates to the politics of that kingdom, and the state of parties there. The debate in the King's council, concerning Gulliver, is a master-piece; and the original papers it contains, of which he says he was so lucky as to get copies, give it an air of probability that is really wonderful. When we add to all this; the hidden satire which it contains, and the grave ridicule that runs through the whole of it, the most exquisite of all ridicule, I think I do not go too far when I pronounce it the most perfect work of the kind, ancient or modern, that is to be found. For, as to Lucian's true history [see **pp. 29–30**], which is the only antient work of the kind that has come down to us, it has nothing to recommend it, except the imitation of the grave style of the ancient historians, such as Herodotus;[1] but it wants the satire and exquisite ridicule that is to be found in the Dean's work.

From **Sir Walter Scott, 'The Life of Swift'** (1824), in *The Works of Jonathan Swift, D. D. Dean of St. Patrick's, Dublin*, 12 vols, 2nd edition, XI: p. 307, quoted in *Swift: The Critical Heritage*, ed. Kathleen Williams (New York: Barnes and Noble, 1970), pp. 306–07

> The discussion of *Gulliver's Travels* as a work of fiction may be said to have begun with Sir Walter Scott, whose edition of the *Works of Jonathan Swift* includes one of the most balanced early accounts of Swift's career. In the following passage, taken from the *Life of Swift*, Scott compares the realism of Defoe, author of *Robinson Crusoe* (1719) with that of Swift in the *Travels*. Scott also discusses the various imaginary and philosophical voyages from Cyrano de Bergerac's *Comical History of the States and Empires of the Worlds in the Moon and the Sun* (see **p. 31**), to Lucian's *True Story* (see **pp. 29–30**), which served Swift as models.

They are, in comparison, eccentric, wild, and childish fables, neither conveying a useful moral nor an amusing satire. The passages of satirical allusion are few, and thrown at random, among a scattered mass of incoherent fiction. But no word drops from Gulliver's pen in vain. Where his work ceases for a moment to satirize the vices of mankind in general, it becomes a stricture upon the parties, politics, and court of Britain; where it abandons that subject of censure, it presents a lively picture of the vices and follies of the fashionable world, or of the vain pursuits of philosophy, while the parts of the narrative which refer to the traveller's own adventures form a humorous and striking parody of the manner of old voyagers; their dry and minute style, and the unimportant personal incidents with which their journals are encumbered. These are inserted with an address, which,

---

1    Herodotus of Halicarnassus, Greek Historian (fifth century BC), who describes the Greek defeat of Xerxes at the Battle of Salamis (480 BC).

abstracted from the marvelous part of the narrative, would almost induce us to believe we are perusing a real story. This art of introducing trifling and minute anecdotes, upon which nothing depends, or is made to turn, was perhaps imitated by Swift from the romances of De Foe, who carried the air of authenticity to the highest pitch of perfection in his *Robinson Crusoe*, and *Memoirs of a Cavalier*.[1] It is, indeed, a marked difference between real and fictitious narrative, that the latter includes only such incidents as the author conceives will interest the reader, whereas the former is uniformly invested with many petty particulars, which can only be interesting to the narrator himself. Another distinction is, that, in the course of a real story, circumstances occur which lead neither to consequences nor to explanations; whereas the novelist is, generally speaking, cautious to introduce no incident or character which has not some effect in forwarding the plot. For example, Crusoe tells us, in the beginning of his history, that he had a second brother, an adventurer like himself, of whom his family could never learn the fate. Scarcely a man but De Foe himself would have concluded the adventures of Crusoe without again introducing this brother. But he was well aware that a course of human life is as irregular and capricious as the process of natural vegetation; and that a trim parterre[2] does not more accurately point out the operation of art, than a story in which all the incidents are combined with, and depend upon each other with epic regularity, leads us to infer its being the offspring of invention. In these particulars, Gulliver was probably somewhat indebted to Robinson Crusoe.

---

1   *Robinson Crusoe* (1719) and *Memoirs of a Cavalier* (1724) were novels by Daniel Defoe that were celebrated for their truth to nature and particularity of detail. Because it also dealt with shipwreck and the adventures of a solitary Englishman cast adrift on an unknown island, *Robinson Crusoe* was often compared with *Gulliver's Travels* and even cited as a possible influence on Swift (see Critical History, **pp. 53–5**).
2   An ornamental garden planted on a space of flat ground.

# Modern Criticism

From **William Freedman, 'Swift's Struldbruggs, Progress, and the Analogy of History'** (1995) in *Studies in English Literature, 1500–1900*, vol. 35, no. 3 (summer), pp. 458–66

Despite his desire to establish his own fame as a thoroughly modern writer, Swift was a frequent opponent of all things modern, modern science, and modern literary scholarship most particularly. *Gulliver's Travels* forms part of a larger intellectual debate as to whether civilization was progressing and moving forwards or whether human institutions and human behaviour were actually getting worse. A central document in what came to be known as the Ancients/Moderns controversy was Sir William Temple's *Essay upon Ancient and Modern Learning* (1690), a pamphlet dismissing claims that the achievements of modern men and women were superior to those who lived in the world of Homer and Virgil.[1]

At the heart of the debate between Ancients and Moderns was the argument most forcibly asserted by Godfrey Goodman's *Fall of Man* (1616) that all nature was in a state of gradual decay, that modern humans were actually weaker and shorter than their ancestors, and their intellectual capacities diminished as well. As curious as this debate now seems to modern readers, it clearly had resonance for Swift. The King of Brobdingnag, for example, sees Gulliver's minuscule stature as evidence of decline, arguing that 'Nature was degenerated in these latter declining Ages of the World, and could now produce only small abortive Births in Comparison of those ancient Times' (II, vii, p. 171). In the Houyhnhnm general assembly, one of the members suggests that the Yahoos (like their human counterparts) are all descended from an original pair, which 'degenerating by Degrees, became in process of time much more savage than those of their own Species' in the beginning (IV, ix, p. 353). Although the conflict between Ancients and Moderns no longer generates the critical heat it once did, recognizing what was at stake in the controversy is essential to our understanding of

---

1   See Joseph M. Levine, *The Battle of the Books: History and Literature in the Augustan Age* (Ithaca, NY: Cornell University Press, 1991).

Swift's contrariness where the whole notion of human progress is concerned. The following passage from William Freedman's 'Swift's Struldbruggs, Progress, and the Analogy of History', reveals the pattern in Swift's satiric procedure, outlining the specific features of Swift's attack on the idea of progress in the third book of *Gulliver's Travels*.

As I read the four major segments of this voyage, each contributes integrally to the attack on the spreading doctrine of progress that, if accepted, weakened the force of whatever Swift's satire might have achieved in *Gulliver's Travels* and elsewhere. "Perhaps no other century is so completely permeated by the idea of intellectual progress as that of the Enlightenment," observed Ernst Cassirer.[2] And if indeed the human race is progressing toward perfection, as so many argued, what would it matter even if (unlikely prospect) the satirist's jaundiced view of human nature and behavior is correct? All will be remedied by progress in learning and by the incremental heavenward climb of each generation on the back of its predecessor.

It is to sully and discredit this promise, I believe, that Swift, after completing the climactic Voyage to the Country of the Houyhnhnms, returned to his *Travels* and inserted the controversial Third Voyage. There he aims his weapons at the two heads of the monster progress that threatened his argument most ominously: progress through science and the cumulative advance of history. Laputa and Lagado undermine the Moderns' perfervid belief in mathematics and science as sources of progress. The summoning of the dead in Glubbdubdrib is a frontal assault on the notion of historic progress as reflected in the ghostly presences of the Ancient and Modern "heroes" raised from the dead. And the Struldbrugg episode in Luggnagg attacks first the idea of personal progress within a single lifetime, then, through a covert analogy prevalent in contemporary thought and writing, historical progress in its broadest perspective.

Undeniably, the Struldbrugg episode is, at least in part, directed against a wish for worldly immortality that Swift perceived as both irrational and irreligious. When Gulliver first learns of the existence of the Struldbruggs, he cries out in a rapture for the happy nation in which every child has a chance at immortality and for the happy people who benefit from the instruction and example of such ancient virtue. "But, happiest beyond all Comparison," he effuses, "are those excellent *Struldbruggs*, who being born exempt from the universal Calamity of human Nature, have their Minds free and disengaged, without the Weight and Depression of Spirits caused by the continual Apprehension of Death" [*PW*, III, x, p. 208].[3] Similarly, when he is chastened by his interlocutors, confronted with the horrific reality of Struldbruggian infirmity, isolation, and decay, his response again points us toward that wish. "The Reader will easily believe," he remarks, "that from what I had heard and seen, my keen Appetite for Perpetuity of Life was much abated. I grew heartily ashamed of the pleasing Visions I had formed;

2    [Freedman's note.] Ernst Cassirer, *The Philosophy of the Enlightenment* (Princeton, NJ: Princeton University Press, 1951; rpt. Boston, Mass: Beacon Press, 1955), p. 5.
3    Freedman's quotations from the *Travels* refer to *PW*, vol. XI, revised edition 1959.

and thought no Tyrant could invent a Death into which I would not run with Pleasure from such a Life" [*PW*, III, x, p. 214].[4]

Framed on both sides by a lust for immortality that is instantly ignited and as quickly doused, the Struldbrugg episode addresses that wish in order to contaminate or efface it. But the attack on this prideful wish is at the same time part of the wider assault on progress that permeates and organizes book 3. The possibility that Cartesian rationalism and Baconian science[5] would remedy the ills described and depicted in the first two Voyages is explored and dismissed in the descriptions of the flying island and the Academy of Lagado. The belief that mankind naturally improves as it ages is confuted by what we and Gulliver learn in Glubbdubdrib: the glaring superiority of Ancient to Modern statesmen, the wretchedness of Modern history and its "heroes," and "how much the Race of human Kind was degenerate among us, within these Hundred years past" [III, viii, p. 201]. What remains is to eliminate the only remaining refuge—perpetual and substantial improvement within a single lifetime—and, through an analogy that links the individual with his race, to supply the attack on historical progress with its climactic image. As the Lagado episode complements and sharpens the thrust at scientific progress initiated in Laputa, the Struldbrugg incident supplements and vivifies the assault on historical progress brought to the surface in Glubbdubdrib but implicit in the earlier episodes as well.

The attack on personal progress within a single lifetime, on the notion that the individual improves with age and that the errors and vices of youth will be corrected in maturity, requires no gloss. The portrait of the immortals is vividly decisive on this point. It shuts, as each of the episodes in this Voyage does, another door on the hope for melioration or remedy. If we are indeed guilty of the personal vices and follies we have been accused of in the other Voyages, time promises not their diminution or removal, but their proliferation and exacerbation.[6] But the power of Swift's portrayal of individual decline is enhanced by its incorporation of an analogy that extends its reach: the analogy between the individual and the race, a single lifetime and the course of human history.

Articulated first among Modern theorists by Francis Bacon, the idea that the world is analogous to a single man whose lifetime is a metaphor for human history played a significant role in the debate between the Ancients and the Moderns which Swift plunged into in his *Battle of the Books* and which he reenters, intermittently but forcefully, in *Gulliver's Travels*. As it appears in the literature, regardless of the stage of human development at which the writer fixes his own

---

4    See Key Passages, p. 164.
5    René Descartes (1596–1650) adapted the procedures of mathematics to the pursuit of philosophical truth. He argued that we could only deduce the truth from a series of self-evident propositions or axioms. Francis Bacon (1561–1626) emphasized observation and experimental procedure. He argued that the most important truths are derived inductively from sense experience.
6    [Freedman's note.] In a letter to Thomas Sheridan, 15 May 1736, Swift wrote: 'I have often given my Opinion that an honest Man never wished himself to be younger . . . I have seen since the Death of the late Queen (who had few equals before her in every Virtue, since Monarchy began) so great a Contempt of Religion, Morality, Liberty, Learning, and common Sense, among us in this Kingdom: a hundred Degrees beyond what I ever met with in any Writer antient or modern' (*Corr*. IV, pp. 487–8, n. 4). That Swift says an honest man *never* wished himself younger takes his response beyond immediate events to a statement on the relationship between time and decline, individually as well as historically. This passage, it should be noted, was introduced into the letter by Faulkner and is relegated to a footnote by Williams.

era, the analogy almost invariably serves the cause of progressivism in its struggle against the belief in historical degeneration.[7]

Bacon introduces the parallel with the observation that what we term and habitually revere as antiquity was in fact the youth of the world, while our own age is its true and venerable antiquity. We, therefore, are the world's true ancients, the Greeks and Romans mere youths in humbling contrast. "And truly as we look for greater knowledge of human things and a riper judgment in the old man than in the young," argues Bacon, so "much more might fairly be expected [of the modern age] than from the ancient times, in as much as it is a more advanced age of the world, and stored and stocked with infinite experiments and observations."[8] It is precisely this image of both the aging individual and of his own period that Swift stares down in his Medusan[9] portrait of the Struldbruggs.

[. . .] Hastening to conclusions about the likely public benefits of a race of immortals, Gulliver thrills to the belief that the perpetual warning and personal examples of these privileged sages "would probably prevent" that continual Degeneracy of human Nature, so justly complained of in all Ages" [III, x, p. 210]. As living refutations of human degeneration and active agents of its cessation, then, the Struldbruggs enter the dispute between heralds of historical progress and prophets of decline. Gulliver, in this episode, assumes, as he often does, two contradictory stances. An Ancient in his reiteration of the age-old complaint of mankind's continual decline, he is a Modern in his naive belief in perpetual personal melioration and the reversibility of history's downward drift. The failure of the Struldbrugg example, then, marks the victory of Gulliver's Ancient remnants over his Modern inclinations and the triumph, by example and analogy, of the conviction that the only real progress in human history is the progressive degeneration of the race.

That the principle of historical degeneration informs Swift's repugnant image of the Struldbruggs is suggested by a number of features and vices these gracelessly aging creatures share with the abusive Moderns, whose doctrine of progress is emptied by their failure to embody it. The decline suffered within the lifetime of a single immortal, in other words, replicates the decline Swift detected in the

---

7   [Freedman's note.] The analogy between human history and an individual life was probably first introduced by the Roman historian L. Annaeus Florus, who divided Roman history into four periods corresponding to infancy, adolescence, adulthood and old age. The early age of the kings, in this schema, was the infancy of the nation and lasted some four hundred years. This was followed by the nation's 'youth', marked by growth and military expansion over the next century and a half. 'The next period,' Florus continues, 'is the hundred and fifty years down to the time of Augustus Caesar, during which it [Rome] spread peace throughout the world. This was the manhood and, as it were, the robust maturity of the empire. From the time of Caesar Augustus down to our own age there has been a period of not much less than two hundred years during which, owing to the inactivity of the emperors, the Roman people grew old and lost its potency' (Florus, I, Pref: 1:34. 19; 2:13.3). Cited in James William Johnson, 'The Meaning of "Augustan" ', *Journal of the History of Ideas* 19, vol. 4 (October 1958), pp. 507–22, 518. Florus, Johnson points out, was 'used as a basic text during the seventeenth and eighteenth centuries and occup[ied] an important place in the libraries of Swift, Addison, Congreve, and their contemporaries' (pp. 518–19). It may seem odd that the originator of the analogy adapted by the Moderns adhered to a theory of historical degeneration. But Florus confined his analysis to Rome, and by arguing the case of Rome's decline he lent tacit support to the Modern argument for subsequent progress and improvement.

8   [Freedman's note.] *The Works of Francis Bacon*, ed. James Spedding, Robert Leslie Ellis, and Douglas Denon Heath, new ed. 7 vols. (London: Longman and Co, 1875), vol. 4, p. 82.

9   In ancient mythology the Medusa was a maiden whose beautiful locks had been transformed into hissing snakes as a punishment. She was so frightful that those who looked on her turned to stone.

historic slide from Ancient vigor to Modern depletion. The deterioration is both physical and moral. In Glubbdubdrib, after viewing a parade of figures from the ancient and recent past, Gulliver is stricken with the marks of progressive physical degeneration emblematic of the moral turpitude that produced them: "As every Person called up made exactly the same Appearance he had done in the World, it gave me melancholy Reflections to observe how much the Race of human Kind was degenerate among us, within these Hundred Years past. How the Pox under all its Consequences and Denominations had altered every Lineament of an *English* Countenance; shortened the Size of Bodies, unbraced the Nerves, relaxed the Sinews and Muscles, introduced a sallow Complexion, and rendered the Flesh loose and *rancid*" [III, viii, p. 201]. The degenerative consequences of the pox,[10] which stand in both a causal and metaphoric relation to historical decline, are also the defining symptoms of old age. What the pox has done to the recent dead, time alone has brought to the immortals, whose signs of inevitable decay are conducive to the same melancholy reflections on the degeneration of the race.

[...] The Moderns are to the Ancients what recent history is to the more glorious past: living proof of the disheartening doctrine of continuous degeneration. Swift's portrait of the progressive moral and physical deterioration of the immortals—and only history is immortal—is a grotesquely individualized image of that decline. It is historical "progress" humiliatingly reduced to personal senility and decay.

## From **Dennis Todd, 'The Hairy Maid at the Harpsichord: Some Speculations on the Meaning of *Gulliver's Travels*'** (1992), *Texas Studies in Literature and Language,* vol. 34, no. 2 (summer) pp. 244–6

In all four books of *Gulliver's Travels*, Gulliver is examined by the creatures he meets in an effort to discern what sort of creature he himself might be. In Book I he is described as the 'Man Mountain', in Book IV he is defined as a 'gentle Yahoo'. In Book II, the wise men of Brobdingnag examine Gulliver only to determine that he doesn't really fit anywhere in their taxonomy of nature, and they declare him to be *lusus naturae*, a freak of nature (see Key Passages, **pp. 141–2**). Before he becomes the focus of scientific interest, however, Gulliver is displayed as a carnival freak by the farmer who first found him.[1] Monsters of various kinds provided a seemingly limitless source of popular entertainment in eighteenth-century London. While Book I draws heavily on the politics of Swift's day and Book III exploits the seemingly ridiculous experiments of modern science, Book II draws heavily on the popular entertainments of eighteenth-century London, in particular the 'popular diversion of monster-viewing', which, according to Dennis Todd, provides the imaginative centre of *Gulliver's Travels*.

---

10  Syphilis.

---

1  On monsters and science, see Christopher Fox, 'Swift and the Spectacle of Human Science', *Reading Swift: Papers from the Third Munster Symposium on Jonathan Swift*, ed. Hermann J. Real and Helgard Stover-Leidig (Munich: Wilhelm Fink Verlag, 1998), pp. 201–2.

In the opening chapters of Book II, the matter is quite explicit, for Gulliver is shown "as a Sight," and he expresses his resentment at "the Ignominy of being carried about for a Monster" and being "exposed for Money as a publick Spectacle to the meanest of the People" [II, ii, pp. 80–81].[2] The details of his early tour of Brobdingnag (his being trundled from town to town, carried in a box, and exhibited publicly in inns and privately to the wealthy in their homes) are drawn from the actual practices of showing monkeys and dwarfs in eighteenth-century England. And so too are the "diverting Tricks" [II, ii, p. 81] he is forced to perform. He pays his "humble Respects" to the company, drinks "a Thimble filled with Liquor," and then uses a straw "exercised as a Pike" [II, ii, p. 82]. Handbills show that monkeys performed precisely these same tricks: a "Noble Creature, which much resembles a Wild *Hairy Man* . . . pulls off his Hat, and pays his Respects to the Company" and then "drinks a Glass of Ale"; a "Man Teger" takes "a glass of Ale in his hand like Christian, Drinks it, also plays at Quarter Staff."[3]

But monster shows, particularly as practiced at Bartholomew Fair,[4] are omnipresent in *Gulliver's Travels*. For Bartholomew Fair had become a place "for Recreation chiefly; *viz.* To see Drolls, Farces, Rope dancing, Feats of Activity, Wonderful and Monstrous Creatures, wild Beasts made Tame, Giants, Dwarfs &c."[5] Precisely these "Wonderfull and Monstrous Creatures inform much of the structure of *Gulliver's Travels,* made up as it is of little people, big people, intelligent animals, and bestial men, the four most typical monsters exhibited at the Fair.

The giants exhibited in London were not as tall as Gulliver when he was among the Lilliputians (they averaged between seven and eight feet), so no person, let alone an army, could walk with ease between their legs, though one giant who showed himself at Southwark Fair in 1684 remarked in his handbill that "his late Majesty was pleased to walk under his Arm, and he has grown very much since."[6] Giants of another sort—large strongmen—were common too. The feats they performed were fairly uniform. All lifted heavy objects, usually barrels or men; they bent iron bars; and the "*Southwark Sampson,*" William Joyce, "snaps Cables like Twine Thread, and throws Dray Horses upon their backs with . . . ease." Gulliver performs most of these: he can lift horses, men, and the "largest Hogsheads" [I, i, p. 8] effortlessly, and he "twisted three . . . Iron Bars together" [I, v, p. 35] with no difficulty. He had more trouble, however, snapping cables—he had to cut the cables of the Blefuscudian ships—and from the beginning he is a signal failure at

2  Todd's quotations from the *Travels* refer to *PW,* vol. XI (1941).
3  [Todd's note.] Aline Mackenzie Taylor, 'Sights and Monsters and Gulliver's Voyage to Brobding-nag', *Tulane Studies in English* vol. 7 (1957), pp. 29–82.
4  Cloth market in Smithfield, where a two-week carnival was held every August from 1133 to 1855. The fair was famous for puppet shows, acrobats and other spectacles of various kinds.
5  [Todd's note.] Stow, *Survey of the Cities of London* and Westminster (London: 1720), vol. III: p. 285.
6  [Todd's note.] Walking under the arm of a giant was (and still is) a typical way of taking a purchase on his height. See Pepys's comment: '. . . calling the way at Charing-Cross and there saw the great Dutchman that is come over, under whose arm I went with my hat on' (*Diary*, V: pp. 242–3; see also IX: pp. 406–7). [Editor's note.] Every September, Southwark Fair took place south of the River Thames in the Borough of Southwark. Like Bartholomew Fair, it was famous for amusements of various kinds.

the one feat most strongmen performed easily, lifting objects by their hair. Joyce's handbill proclaimed "*HIS STRENGTH PROV'D* before the *KING*," a claim that was made by almost all the giants and strongmen who were exhibited, and so in this way, too, they are like Gulliver, who is asked to perform numerous diversions before the king of Lilliput and is invited by the Court of Blefuscu "to shew them some Proofs of [his] prodigious Strength, of which they had heard so many Wonders" [I, v, p. 38].[7]. . . .

Even more popular than giants were dwarfs. If we are to trust their handbills, they too were regularly exhibited before royalty. And they appeared to be valued not only because of their size. First, a premium was put on a dwarf who was well-proportioned. The dwarf who attracted an audience (judging from handbills and the reactions of spectators) was one who was "straight, well proportioned and well-made in every way," one who, as John Wormberg boasted of himself in his handbill, "is so very well proportioned to his bigness that all that sees him, admires him." Second, dwarfs had to display some intelligence and an ability to interact socially—thus the "Woman Dwarf but Three Foot and one Inch high, who discourses excellently well"; the dwarf "not above eighteen inches long," who "hath all her sense of Admiration, and Discourses, Reads very well"; and the "Little Scotchman," who "discourses of the Scriptures, and of many Eminent Histories, very wisely." These are the very qualities in Gulliver that so fascinate the Brobdingnagians. The farmer advertises Gulliver as "exactly shaped in every Part like a human Creature" and as having "the finest Limbs in the World" [II, ii, p. 80]. Gulliver's show itself—conversing with Glumdalclitch and the spectators and delivering "Speeches [he] had been taught" [II, ii, p. 82]—displays his intelligence and his skill at "discourse," just like the shows of the dwarfs at Bartholomew Fair. And the Brobdingnagian king's desire to get "a Woman of [Gulliver's] own Size" so that he might "propagate the Breed" [II, iii, p. 123] was anticipated by the sensation of the winter of 1711–12. The "Black Prince," a three-foot dwarf from the West Indies, and his pregnant wife, "the *Fairy Queen* . . . the least woman that ever was with child in Europe," were shown daily at Charing Cross. Her condition was avidly reported in the press, as were the details of her delivery in March of 1712.[8]

7  [Todd's note.] Examples are legion. Paris remarks that the giant he saw in 1716 'was seen by George I, the Queen, the prince of Wales, the rest of the Royal Family and the Court, at Windsor'. The 'tall *Britain*' claimed that he had 'Travelled abroad, and has been shown before all the Foreign Kings and Princes in Christendom, and is not lately come into *England*, and had the Honour to have been shown before Her Present *Majesty of Great Britten* and her Royal Consort the *Prince*.' 'The Living Colossus . . . has had the honour to show himself to most princes in Europe, particularly to his late majesty the King of France, who presented him with a noble scymiter, and a silver mace.' A German giant was advertised as having 'had the Honour to be presented with a piece of Armour proportionable to his Bigness, by the King of the *Romans*.' (One recalls that the emperor of Blefuscu presented Gulliver with 'fifty Purses of two hundred *Sprugs* a piece, together wit his Picture at full length'.)

8  [Todd's note.] Swift certain knew of the 'Little Family' (which included the 'little Horse'), probably firsthand, and certainly through Arbuthnot, for the Black Prince plays a prominent role in the 'Double-Mistress' episode of *Memoirs of Martinus Scriblerus*; see Taylor, 'Sights and Monsters', pp. 63–9. The cruelty of the King's desire ('I think I should rather have died,' says Gulliver, 'than undergone the Disgrace of leaving a Posterity to be kept in Cages like tame Canary Birds; and perhaps in time sold about the Kingdom to Persons of Quality for Curiosities', p. 123) was nicely captured in a letter purportedly written by 'S. T.', the owner of the 'Little Family': 'I am forced to comply with her Demand while she is in her present Condition, being very willing to have more of

Along with giants and dwarfs, the third popular attraction at the Fair were creatures which blurred the distinction between men and beasts. Apes and monkeys were taught to mimic human actions, and other animals were trained so that they appeared to have the skills or intelligence of men: an elephant that could raise a flag and shoot a gun, a troop of eight dancing dogs, dressed in the newest French fashions, who appeared at Southwark Fair in the early eighteenth century and later performed before Queen Anne, the single dog Evelyn saw "that seemd to do many rational actions."[9] And an almost unbroken succession of Clever Mares. None of these was as virtuous as the Houyhnhnms nor, I suspect, as intelligent, but all of them were smart enough to count, to ferret out hidden objects, to tell time, and to perform "many things to admiration,"[10] some of which, if we are to trust the handbills, were "past human Faith to believe unless seen done."

## From **Clarence Tracy, 'The Unity of *Gulliver's Travels*'** (1962)
*Queen's Quarterly*, vol. 68, no. 4, pp. 598–601

> Because of its similarities to Defoe's *Robinson Crusoe*, *Gulliver's Travels* has often been treated as if it were a novel, with a familiar narrative structure and a traditional fictional hero who changes over time. In the following excerpt, Clarence Tracy questions all of these assumptions, asking whether Gulliver can be said to develop at all over the course of the narrative. While it is true that Gulliver fails to recover his 'youthful zest, and he is sad and bewildered!' at the end of Book IV, 'fundamentally he has been little altered by his experience and is still the same old booby. Almost the last thing we hear from him is the uproariously naïve remark that his book had not made any noticeable change in human nature even after six months.' Tracy also asks us to reconsider whether the four-book structure of *Gulliver's Travels* offers us a traditional plot or some other form of organizational pattern.

[C]onsidering all the time that we spend in his company, we get remarkably little feeling for Lemuel Gulliver as an individual. I was about to say that he is little more than a name, but I remembered in time that not even once in all of the four voyages is he called by his own name. He is a presence constantly felt, a yardstick by means of which we take the measure of things in strange lands, at times our personal representative and spokesman there, and at other times the butt of our ungrateful laughter. But he is not a character we get inside of. It is hard even to think of him as one man. The big, awkward, embarrassed, self-effacing Gulliver of the first voyage seems a different man from the strutting braggart of voyage two, and although the difference is explained by his altered environment,

---

the same Breed. I do not know what she may produce me, but provided it be a *Show*, I shall be well satisfied' (*Spectator*, 271 [10 January 1712]; in *The Spectator*, ed. Donald F. Bond, 5 vols (Oxford: Clarendon Press, 1965), vol. II: pp. 557–8).

9  [Todd's note.] *The Diary of John Evelyn*, ed. E. S. de Beer, 6 vols (Oxford: Clarendon Press, 1955), vol. III: p. 359.

10  [Todd's note.] Pepys, *Diary*, IX: p. 297; see also IX: p. 301.

the change under these circumstances is hardly 'a realistic, believable course of character development'. Moreover, our first impression of him (if we start our reading with the beginning of the first voyage) is that he is intelligent and has had a good education in medicine and mathematics. Later we are struck by his facility with languages and by his knowledge of European history, literature, and philosophy—enough to enable him to brief the ghost of Aristotle on Scotus and Ramus.[1] But if we get our first impression instead from the introductory letter written by him to his Cousin Sympson, we will be apt to think of him rather as a simple sailor, like William Dampier, whose 'very loose and incorrect account' of his travels ought to have been revised before publication by 'some young gentleman of either university'. This is the other pole of his character. When we see him from this angle, he appears stupid, incapable of knowing when he makes a fool of himself, and an easy prey for any sort of imposition—in short, the *gull* that his name implies. Between these poles his character oscillates. He runs through the whole human spectrum from dolt to near genius, from addle-pated projector[2] to man of common sense, from realist to idealist. He is not so much a man as 'all mankind's epitome'.[3] He is the personification of the discordant humours of that being Pope described as 'the glory, jest, and riddle of the world'.[4]

The usual concept of plot is equally irrelevant. 'The plot of any novel or drama,' writes Ronald Crane, 'is the particular temporal synthesis effected by the writer of the elements of action, character, and thought.' The synthesizing principle, he goes on to say, is a 'completed change' in either the situation, the moral character, or the thought and feelings of the protagonist.[5] Obviously a sense of the passing of time is basic. Accordingly some critics find, or imagine that they find, a completed change in the character of Lemuel Gulliver. Arthur Case, for example, wrote that Gulliver changed in the course of the work from a naïve optimist to a naive pessimist. Case could not fit voyage three into this temporal synthesis, but John Sutherland, coming to his rescue, writes that it was needed 'to fill yawning gaps in the organization of the satire', and that Gulliver had to go through the dead-center of 'superficial disillusionment and sophistication' described in that

---

1    Aristotle (384–22 BC), Greek philosopher and student of Plato. His *Poetics* was the most influential authority in eighteenth-century literary criticism, but his various scientific theories were rejected by modern science; Duns Scotus (1268–1308), one of the most important and most subtle philosopher/theologians of the high Middle Ages; Peter Ramus (1515–1572), rhetorician and educational theorist.

2    Projector: someone who invents foolish and impractical schemes; addle-pated: someone whose brains have literally been stirred or confused.

3    John Dryden, *Absalom and Achitophel*, in *John Dryden: Selected Works*, ed. William Frost, second edition (New York: Rinehart & Winston, 1971), p. 36, line 545. Dryden is describing Zimri (the Duke of Buckingham) who, like Gulliver, is 'everything by starts, and nothing long / But in the course of one revolving moon, / Was chymist, fiddler, statesman and buffoon' (lines 548–50).

4    Tracy is quoting from Alexander Pope's *Essay on Man*, canto I, line 18, a poem which, like *Gulliver's Travels*, seeks to determine where human beings fit in the universal scheme of things. Brady repeats an argument popular with Swift critics (particularly those of the 'soft' school) that Gulliver somehow represents the mediate position of all mankind somewhere between the angels and beasts (see Critical History, **p. 79**). For a quick version of this argument, see Clive Probyn, *Jonathan Swift: Gulliver's Travels* (Harmondsworth: Penguin, 1989), pp. 35–6.

5    R. S. Crane, 'The Concept of Plot and the Plot of Tom Jones', in *Critics and Criticism, Ancient and Modern* (Chicago, Ill.: University of Chicago Press, 1952), pp. 616–47.

voyage in order to make his development convincing.[6] Other critics have worked
that development out in even greater detail, endeavouring to show by a minute
psychological analysis how step by step through four voyages and over fifteen
years Gulliver altered from 'an optimistic and benevolent' man into 'an asinine
but pitiable misanthrope'.[7] [. . .]

Instead of a temporal synthesis, the structural principle of *Gulliver's Travels* is a
series of contrasts, echoes, and anticipations—intersecting links that hold the
work together as firmly as the pack threads held Gulliver to the soil of Lilliput.
These contrasts are unlike the chronological ones that we make in reading a novel
[. . .] In *Gulliver's Travels* the contrasts are antithetical rather than chronological:
we compare Lilliputian with Balnibarbian, Yahoo with Houhynhnm, Gulliver
big with Gulliver little, or Gulliver stupid with Gulliver acting like a man of
common sense. We can make these contrasts either backwards or forwards. Time
is of so little importance that it would not be disastrous to read the voyages out of
sequence. Swift's order is undoubtedly the best, but not because he had a precisely
datable schedule of events in mind, as Sterne had behind the apparent chaos of
*Tristram Shandy*,[8] but because, like a good concert program, it was planned to
provide variety and to build up towards a finale. There is a gradually deepening
seriousness in the tone of the frame-story, and also a steadily increasing extravagance of fantasy in the voyages themselves, from the doll's house realism of
Lilliput to the unworldliness of Houyhnhnmland. But these developments have
nothing to do with time; indeed the world of *Gulliver's Travels* is timeless. The
Lilliputian inspectors who made an inventory of Gulliver's pockets could not
comprehend the use to which he put his watch. Swift's imagination compelled
him to give dates for the voyages, along with latitudes, longitudes, and sailing
directions, but these must have been inspired rather by an impulse to parody the
travel books than by a desire to give any sense of real time. In the same way the
charts give no sense of real place. For Gulliver's world hangs suspended in space
like the flying island of voyage three, or like the mobile constructed of pendants
hanging on a wire.

## From **Frank Brady, 'Vexations and Diversions: Three Problems in *Gulliver's Travels*'** (1978), *Modern Philology*, vol. 75, pp. 350–1.

Beginning with Monboddo and Scott (see Early Critical Reception, **pp. 69–71**),
critics have praised the specificity of detail in *Gulliver's Travels* that produces
the appearance of truth and accuracy. More recent critics have noted the
care with which Swift has calculated the relative size of objects in Lilliput and
Brobdingnag. In the following excerpt, Frank Brady questions the accuracy of

6   See A. E. Case, *Four Essays on 'Gulliver's Travels'* (Princeton, NJ: Princeton University Press,
    1945), and John Sutherland, 'A Reconsideration of Gulliver's Third Voyage', *Studies in Philology*,
    vol. 54 (1957), pp. 45–52.
7   Someone who has adopted a foolish and ridiculous hatred of humankind.
8   The narrative of Laurence Sterne's *Tristram Shandy* (1760–7) is deliberately disjointed. Chapters
    are routinely inserted out of sequence, and although the novel claims to be the history of Tristram
    Shandy, the boy doesn't even get christened until the fourth volume of a nine-volume work.

all the specific details in the *Travels*, suggesting that Swift's apparent truth to nature, about which critics have been so enthusiastic, may also be part of some elaborate joke at the reader's expense.

It is easy to find jokes (errors ? misstatements ?) in *Gulliver*; what is difficult in some instances is to determine whether they are (1) accidental, (2) incidental (local, restricted), or (3) significant. In any case, my premise is that Gulliver never makes a joke; all of them are Swift's. Swift said as much to his egregious translator, the Abbé des Fontaines: "Vous serez sans doute surpris de scavoir qui'ils [English admirers of *Gulliver*] regardent ce chirugien de vaisseau comme un Auteur grave, qui ne sort jamais de son serieux, qui n'emprunte aucun fard, qui ne se pique point d'avoir de l'esprit, et qui se contente de communiquer au public, dans une Narration simple et naive, les avantures qui luy sone arrivées, et les choses qu'il a vû ou entendu dire pendant ses voyages" (July 1727).[1] Beyond this premise, the problem lies partly in the relation of wit to the conscious. When Gulliver translates what one critic has pleasantly called the "Hanoverian"[2] of Luggnagg,[3] "*Fluft drin Yalerick Dwuldum prastrad mirplush,*" as "*My Tongue is in the Mouth of my Friend*" [III, ix, p. 205],[4] the joke seems accidental (always a shaky presumption, however, to make in the case of Swift). But when "a Sink" is deciphered as "a C—t" [III, v, p. 191], the original filler "court" may be insufficient, since another common English word fits equally well, and Swift could easily be suggesting the equivalence of all three terms.[5]

The most difficult joke of this kind to place is the first joke to occur in *Gulliver*, that on "Master *Bates*" [I, i, p. 20]. There it is, apparently gratuitous but inescapable,[6] in the midst of the humdrum detail that establishes Gulliver's background and character. Most critics have hurried past with averted eyes, but Dr. Phyllis Greenacre pounced with psychoanalytic vigor: *Gulliver* represents the "acting out of Lemuel's masturbatory fantasies."[7] Here, as often in criticism of *Gulliver*, levels of reality get confused. But the best explanation I can give of this joke is that Swift is warning the reader that this story is as unreal as most masturbatory fantasies, or simply, "Be sure to read with care, and you'll find some very odd

---

1   *Corr.* III, p. 226. 'You will undoubtedly be surprised to know that they [English admirers of *Gulliver*] regard this ship's surgeon as a grave author who is never anything but serious, who does not borrow a disguise, who never engages in wit and who takes every chance to communicate to the public in a simple and naive narration the adventures that happened to him and the things which he saw or heard about during his voyages.'

2   It was a standing joke that George I, who had been the Elector of Hanover before becoming King of England, couldn't speak English.

3   [Brady's note.] J. S. Lawry, 'Dr. Lemuel Gulliver and "The Thing Which Was Not" ', *Journal of English and Germanic Philology*, vol. 67 (1968), p. 226.

4   Brady's quotations refer to the *PW*, vol. XI (1959).

5   [Brady's note.] ' "Court" is written out in the editions of 1726 and 1727; Swift may have noted the flexibility of the dash later.' The same joke was made at the expense of David Hamilton, man-midwife to Queen Anne, who when knighted was satirized as a 'c—t knight'.

6   [Brady's note.] The manipulation of Bates's name is unique in *Gulliver*. The *Oxford English Dictionary* first cites 'masturbation' as of 1766, but it occurs in Florio's translation of Montaigne (1603) (London, 1910) 2: 303.

7   [Brady's note.] Phyllis Greenacre, *Swift and Carroll* (New York: International Universities Press, 1955), p. 115.

things here." Certainly the reader must be expected to notice, almost immediately after this pun, that Gulliver washes up on Lilliput on Guy Fawkes Day [I, i, pp. 20–1], the day on which Tristram Shandy is born.[8]

But most readers are quickly taken in by small marvels. Critic after critic has praised that "extraordinary illusion of verisimilitude,"[9] that shower of circumstantial detail in which Gulliver arrives in Lilliput. The illusion is indeed extraordinary. [. . .] Still, it was annoying to discover that so many Lilliputian details were haywire. Some might pass with a generous reader: Gulliver picks up six Lilliputians in his right hand [I, ii, p. 31]; his hair is "long and thick" [I, i, p. 21] enough for the children to play hide-and-seek in [I, iii, p. 38]; the Lilliputians march twenty-four abreast through his legs as he stands "like a *Colossus*" [I, iii, p. 42]; his handkerchief stretches to an exercise field for a Lilliputian troop of twenty-four horse [I, iii, pp. 40–1]. When fantasy acts as the literal level of a work, the only sure test of unreliability is internal contradiction: "As the common Size of the Native is somewhat under six Inches, so there is an exact Proportion in all other Animals, as well as Plants and Trees: For Instance, the tallest Horses and Oxen are between four and five Inches in Height, the Sheep an Inch and a half, more or less; their Geese about the Bigness of a Sparrow" [I, vi, p. 37]. These are very small sheep and very large geese.

While Gulliver may exaggerate or just be "a little too circumstantial" ("Publisher to the Reader," p. 9) in these details, others admit of no debate. The largest warships in the Lilliputian world are nine feet long [I, i, p. 26], but Gulliver "with great Ease" draws "fifty of the [Blefuscudian] Enemy's largest Men of War" after him [I, v, p. 52], an accomplishment sharply contrasted with Gulliver's struggle to beach the "real Boat" he later comes upon [I, viii, pp. 75–6]. Readers have long smiled at his gallant denial of an intrigue with the treasurer's wife, and talked of his loss of perspective. But when in the same passage Gulliver defies the treasurer and his informers, Clustril and Drumlo ("I will name them, and let them make their best of it"—I, vi, p. 65), to prove that anyone except Reldresal ever visited him incognito, then three paragraphs later describes an incognito visit in detail, surely the reader is meant to spot the contradiction—and to conclude that Gulliver is no more to be trusted than the speakers in *A Tale of a Tub*, *An Argument Against Abolishing Christianity*, or *A Modest Proposal*.[10] At the end of the work his allusion to Sinon [IV, xii, p. 292][11] warns the reader that Gulliver is a liar, but he has been an "unreliable narrator" from the beginning and handsomely

8  Guy Fawkes Day, 5 November. A day commemorating the failure of the Gunpowder Plot to blow up Parliament. Tristram Shandy's birth, in Laurence Sterne's *Tristram Shandy* (1760–7) is accompanied by a host of comic misadventures.
9  [Brady's note.] R. C. Elliott's phrase in *The Power of Satire* (Princeton, NJ: Princeton University Press, 1960), p. 197.
10  The speaker in *A Tale of a Tub* (1704) is a writer whose recommendations of all things modern is meant to be rejected by the reader; the speaker in *An Argument Against Abolishing Christianity* (1708) claims to be a Christian who argues that it would be wrong to abolish nominal Christianity, while 'real' Christianity may be impossible to preserve. Swift's most outrageous spokesman is the public-spirited pamphleteer in *A Modest Proposal* (1729), who argues that the best way to reduce Irish poverty and to cut down on the number of Irish Catholics is to eat Catholic babies when they are one year old.
11  One of the greatest liars in history. In Virgil's *Aeneid*, Sinon is the man responsible for convincing the Trojans that the great horse was actually an offering to the gods and therefore safe to bring inside the walls of Troy (see Key Passages, pp. 181–2).

deserves the legend, *splendide mendax*, with which his picture is adorned in Faulkner's edition of 1735. Indeed, Gulliver's repeated assertion that he tells nothing but the truth is suspicious in itself.[12]

From **Laura Brown, 'Reading Race and Gender: Jonathan Swift'** (19??) *Eighteenth-Century Studies* vol. 23, no. 4 (summer 1990), pp. 433–6

In the letter from Gulliver to his cousin Sympson that begins *Gulliver's Travels*, Swift admits that: 'I see myself accused of . . . abusing the Female Sex' (see Key Passages, **pp. 120–2**), and accusations of misogyny have continued straight through the twentieth century. Swift's private life was marked by his ambiguous relationships with women. Margaret Doody suggests that his difficulty with mothers – his own and those of the other women in his life – is reflected in two 'bad mothers' in *Gulliver's Travels*: the Empress of Lilliput, who complains about his dousing the palace fire with his own urine; and the Queen of Brobdingnag, who is large and controlling.[1] The exception is his little nurse Glumdalclitch in Book II, who seems to be a 'meditation, wholly or partly conscious, upon the Nurse of Whitehaven' who is said to have taken Swift back to England with her when he was but an infant. Certainly Swift felt a lifelong suspicion of marriage, and yet he also maintained deep attachments to a series of younger women: Esther Johnson (Stella), Esther Vanhomrigh (Vanessa), and Jane Waring (Varina) to whom Swift was briefly engaged.[2] Swift was also surrounded by a bevy of adoring females. The Earl of Orrery complains of the 'command which SWIFT had over all his females; and you would have smiled to have found his house a constant seraglio of very virtuous women, who attended him from morning to night, with an obedience, an awe, and an assiduity, that are seldom paid to the richest, or the most powerful, lovers.'[3] Among these women were such writers as Mary Davys, Mary Barber and Letitia Pilkington, who left us this encomium on the Dean: 'As the Irish are the eternal Ridicule of the English for their Ignorance, I am proud *Hibernia* had the Happiness of producing this brilliant Wit, to redeem the Credit of the Country; and to convince the World, a Man may draw his first Breath there, and yet be learned, wise, generous, religious, witty, social and polite.'[4] For a writer noted for his poetic misogyny, this is high praise. Doody remarks that while there are a 'number of digs at women's physicality and sexuality in his work, there are fewer than we would expect

---

12  [Brady's note.] For the sake of completeness, I note other suspicious details: the size of Gulliver's handkerchief (I, ii, p. 34), the number of fowl he could hold on the end of his knife (I, vi, p. 64), his three-minute urination (I, ii, p. 56), and the size and capacity of Mildendo – only 500 feet square but capable of holding 500,000 Lilliputians (I, iv, 46–7).

---

1  Margaret Anne Doody, 'Swift and Women', in *The Cambridge Companion to Jonathan Swift*, ed. Christopher Fox (Cambridge: Cambridge University Press, 2003), p. 91.
2  'Stella', 'Vanessa', and 'Varina' were the nicknames that Swift gave to these three women.
3  Orrery, quoted in Doody, 'Swift and Women', p. 106.
4  Letitia Pilkington, *Memoirs* (vol. 1, p. 67), quoted in Margaret Doody, 'Swift Among the Women', *Critical Essays on Jonathan Swift*, ed. Frank Palmieri (New York: G. K. Hall, 1993), p. 15.

from a major satirist'. Indeed, as Felicity A. Nussbaum has argued, the traditional notion of misogyny, meaning 'hatred for women', implies a 'personally motivated vendetta against the female sex', a vendetta not easily demonstrated given Swift's personal history. Nussbaum suggests instead that we 'redefine *misogyny* as a cluster of discourses circulating within the culture and directed against women everywhere'.[5] In the following passage, Laura Brown undertakes a political critique of Swift's misogyny in *Gulliver's Travels*. Citing such poems as 'The Lady's Dressing Room' and 'The Progress of Beauty', Brown argues that Swift links female beauty, female adornments and dress with the corruptions of mercantile capitalism. 'It is only one quick step from the equation of women and commodities to an attack on the hypocritical female as the embodiment of cultural corruption, the visceral epitome of the alienating effects of commodification and the disorienting social consequences of capitalist accumulation.'

If we bring this reading of the misogynist poetry[6] to bear upon *Gulliver's Travels*, we can move from the ideological status of women in Swift's writing and the connection of the representation of women with capitalist expansion to the historical problem of colonialism as it shapes the most important satire of the eighteenth century, and we can begin to see the mutual interaction of race and gender in Swift's major satire. Predictably, Gulliver's account of female luxury in Book IV reproduces the economic trope of the Irish tracts[7] and of Mandeville's more fully-faceted account of capitalism:

> 'I assured him, that this whole globe of earth must be at least three times gone round, before one of our better female yahoos could get her breakfast, or a cup to put it in'. [I, vi, p. 203][8]

But Book II supplies the famous images of the gigantic female body which put Gulliver in precisely the place of Strephon in "The Lady's Dressing Room" when he picks up the magnifying mirror:

---

5   Felicity A. Nussbaum, 'Gulliver's Malice: Gender and the Satiric Stance', *Gulliver's Travels*, ed. Christopher Fox (Boston, Mass.: Bedford Books, 1995), p. 321.
6   In a number of poems, Swift suggests that women must somehow assemble themselves from the bits and pieces of make-up and fashion, with emphasis on the sheer nastiness of the whole process. In 'The Lady's Dressing Room' (1730), Strephon steals into the Celia's dressing room only to discover soiled underwear, dirty combs, filthy make-up jars, scrapings from her teeth and gums, towels begrimed with sweat and ear-wax and, finally, Celia's overflowing chamber pot. His response 'Oh! Celia, Celia, Celia Shits!' reveals the depth of his naïvety and his revulsion. Similarly, in 'A Beautiful Nymph Going to Bed' (1731), Swift describes Corinna, a prostitute who literally disassembles herself when she comes home, removing her wig, glass eye, false eyebrows, dentures, false breasts, corset and make-up.
7   In *The Drapier's Letters* and *A Modest Proposal*, Swift argues that part of the Irish economic problem is due to the expensiveness, pride and vanity of the Irish women. In *The Fable of the Bees* (1724), Bernard Mandeville associates the pursuit of female luxury with the stimulation of a capitalist economy (see Key Passages, **p. 172**).
8   Brown's quotations from the *Travels* refer to *Gulliver's Travels and Other Writings*, ed. Louis A. Landa (Boston, Mass.: Houghton Mifflin, 1960).

The Virtues we must not let pass,
Of *Celia*'s magnifying Glass.
When frighted *Strephon* cast his Eye on't
It shew'd the Visage of a Gyant.
A Glass that can to Sight disclose,
The smallest Worm in *Celia*'s Nose,
And faithfully direct her Nail
To squeeze it out from Head to Tail. [lines 59–66]

Brobdingnagian gigantism is intimately linked to misogyny. Indeed, the scenes that emphasize the scale of size in Book II are all centered around the female figure. The hideous, gigantic corporeality of the Brobdingnagian women is represented first in the anti-madonna scene that Gulliver witnesses almost upon his arrival in Brobdingnag – the woman nursing her child:

The nurse to quiet her babe made use of a rattle ... but all in vain, so that she was forced to apply the last remedy by giving it suck. I must confess no object ever disgusted me so much as the sight of her monstrous breast, which I cannot tell what to compare with, so as to give the curious reader an idea of its bulk, shape and colour. It stood prominent six foot, and could not be less than sixteen in circumference. The nipple was about half the bigness of my head, and the hue both of that and the dug so varified with spots, pimples and freckles, that nothing could appear more nauseous. ... This made me reflect upon the fair skins of our English ladies, who appear so beautiful to us, only because they are of our own size, and their defects not to be seen but through a magnifying glass. [II, i, p. 74]

The nauseous scent against which Strephon ought to stop his nose almost overwhelms Gulliver in the apartments of the maids of honour:

They would often strip me naked from top to toe, and lay me at full length in their bosoms; wherewith I was much disgusted; because, to say the truth, a very offensive smell came from their skins. [II, v, p. 95]

And disease, like that which wastes Celia in "The Progress of Beauty," gives Gulliver his most horrific fantasy of female corruption in Brobdingnag:

One day the governess ordered our coachman to stop at several shops, where the beggars, watching their opportunity, crowded to the sides of the coach, and gave me the most horrible spectacles that ever an European eye beheld. There was a woman with a cancer in her breast, swelled to a monstrous size, full of holes, in two or three of which I could have easily crept, and covered my whole body. [II, iv, p. 90]

Though Gulliver thinks to stop his nose with rue[9] only at the end of Book IV, the

---

9   Strong smelling herb, popular as an insect repellant and as a disguise for unpleasant odours.

nauseous scent, the disease and corruption, and the hideous corporeality that we have seen elsewhere in Swift's texts to be so powerfully and specifically associated with the female figure pervade the second book of his *Travels*. But if we look to the fourth book, we can see all these qualities again embodied in the Yahoos: their offensive smell, their naked corporeality, their connection with disease, and their uncontrolled sexuality are, as we have seen, the essential attributes of the female figure. From this perspective, the whole context of Book IV takes on a new significance. The Yahoos are the prototypical women of Swift's works.

But Gulliver's relationship with the Yahoos themselves suggests another dimension to the role of the woman in the *Travels*. Gulliver begins at a seemingly unbridgeable distance from the Yahoos, which are represented as some species of monkey, perhaps, having little in common with the human. But the main import of Book IV is the increasing proximity and eventual identification between the Yahoo and the human, despite Gulliver's own resistance and disgust. This process of association with the creatures that seem at first utterly and hideously other suggests a dynamic of aversion and identification that we will find to be central to the ideological significance of the satire. In Book II, likewise, Gulliver's disgust with the maids of honor is balanced by a titillating voyeurism that singles out the "handsomest" and suggests that he is sexually implicated in the scene: figuratively, in the sense that he is evidently desirous himself, but also – and more grotesquely – physically, in that once we entertain the fantasy of a sexual connection between Gulliver and the maids of honor, we are implicitly invited to imagine the actual physical incorporation of the tiny male figure into the sexual body of the woman:

> The handsomest among these maids of honor, a pleasant frolicsome girl of sixteen, would sometimes set me astride upon one of her nipples, with many other tricks, wherein the reader will excuse me for not being over particular. [II, v, p. 96]

The story of the cancerous breast, in this context, supplies a parallel image of explicit incorporation, in which Gulliver responds to the sight of female corruption with the extraordinary and unexpected fantasy of creeping inside and covering his whole body in the "nauseous unwholesome living carcase" of the diseased woman.

In fact, Gulliver actually does take the place of the female figure at more than one prominent point in the *Travels*. In the relativist comparison between Gulliver's own form as a giant in Lilliput and his encounter with the giants of Brobdingnag, he repeatedly occupies the position of a woman. The overpowering scent of the Brobdingnagian maids of honor puts Gulliver in mind of the occasion in Lilliput when:

> an intimate friend of mine . . . took the freedom, in a warm day, when I had used a good deal of exercise, to complain of a strong smell about me . . . I suppose his faculty of smelling was as nice with regard to me, as mine was to that of this people. [II, v, p. 95]

And similarly, in the anti-madonna scene, after describing the "spots, pimples and freckles" of the nursing woman's skin, Gulliver provides a Lilliputian account of his own skin for comparison:

> an intimate friend of mine . . . said that my face appeared much fairer and smoother when he looked on me from the ground, than it did upon a nearer view when I took him up in my hand, and brought him close, which he confessed was at first a very shocking sight. He said he could discover great holes in my skin . . . and my complexion made up of several colours altogether disagreeable . . . On the other side discoursing of the ladies in that emperor's court, he used to tell me, one had freckles, another too wide a mouth, a third too large a nose, nothing of which I was able to distinguish. [II, i, pp. 74–5]

These comparisons too establish a routine and consistent interchangeability between Gulliver and the female figures of his narrative.

Similarly, in Book II Gulliver is dressed by his little nurse, Glumdalclitch, in a manner that would have evoked a common contemporary female image. As Neil McKendrick has shown, the fashion doll was the major implement of the rise and popularization of female fashion in the eighteenth century. Originally imported singly from Paris and displayed in the London shops wearing the latest Parisian dress, these life-sized dolls were subsequently miniaturized and made widely available in rural as well as urban parts of England. Supplied with sample suits of the latest fashion, they were dressed both by clothing merchants and by children and adult women, and served as a major means of teaching the new and unfamiliar concept of rapidly changing styles of dress, and of spreading the notion of a market-conditioned obsolescence.[10] In Brobdingnag, Gulliver plays precisely this role; for Glumdalclitch and the contemporary reader he takes the place of this miniature commodified female figure.

To say that Gulliver occupies the place of the woman at recurrent moments in the *Travels* is not to say that Gulliver is the same as a woman, but to suggest a systematic pattern of implication, which moves from the various forms of interchangeability that we have seen in Gulliver's connection with the fashion doll and the Yahoos to a full incorporation like that offered by Gulliver's relation to the cancerous breast and the maids of honor, and which begins to problematize Swift's attack on women and to complicate our understanding of his relation with the female other. Gulliver's implicit identification with the female figure—a figure which we have seen to be systematically underlying the ideology of mercantile capitalism—suggests that his *Travels* must be read in the context of that major historical conjuncture. Those panegyrics on women that I cited earlier to exemplify the mercantile capitalist context of Swift's misogyny unconsciously function, as we saw, to displace responsibility for the historical consequences of capitalism upon womankind, to make her a locus for the male anxieties of

---

10  [Brown's note.] Neil McKendrick, 'The Commercialization of Fashion', in McKendrick, John Brewer, and J. H. Plumb, *The Birth of of Consumer Society: The Commercialization of Eighteenth-Century England* (Bloomington, Ind.: Indiana University Press, 1982), pp. 43–9.

empire.[11] Swift's Irish tracts certainly participate in this common assumption of displaced responsibility, though with a different valuation. But the implicit dynamic of aversion and identification that we have begun to discern in *Gulliver's Travels* suggests that in this major text that effort of displacement partly fails, that the shifting status of the male observer (which we have been taught by formalist criticism of Swift to describe as the "persona controversy") makes the designation of a separable other, upon whom the anxieties and responsibilities of mercantile capitalism and imperialism can be displaced, symptomatically impossible.

## From **Samuel Holt Monk, 'The Pride of Lemuel Gulliver'** (1955), *Sewanee Review*, vol. 63, no. 1 (winter), pp. 65–71

As selections in the 'Early Critical Reception' section of this book suggest, the question of Swift's misanthropy provided a subject of debate well into the twentieth century (see **pp. 64–8**). The following is an excerpt from one of the most frequently cited 'soft' readings of Book IV (see Critical History, **pp. 52–3**). Like a number of critics at the middle of the twentieth century, Monk concludes that the conclusion of the *Travels* is not tragic, not hopelessly misanthropic, as so many had argued, but rather, it is finally comic. It is not Swift who mistakes human beings for Yahoos, but Gulliver himself.

The legend of Swift as a savage, mad, embittered misanthrope largely rests upon this wrong-headed, sensational reading of the last voyage. In my opinion the work is that of a Christian-humanist[1] and a moralist who no more blasphemes against the dignity of human nature than St. Paul and some of the angrier prophets of the Old Testament.[2] Swift has been misunderstood for several reasons.

1. The sheer intensity and violent rhetoric of the voyage are overwhelming and may well numb the critical sense of certain readers.

2. Gulliver in the frenzy of his mad misanthropy has been too facilely identified with Swift. Gulliver speaks for Gulliver and not for his creator in the final pages of the book, and careful reading should reveal the plain fact that he becomes the victim of Swift's irony as he grows to hate the human race. The final pages of the book are grimly comic.

3. The primary symbols of the voyage have been totally misunderstood. The Houyhnhnms have been regarded as Swift's ideal for man, and the Yahoos have

---

11 Specifically, Brown has in mind Alexander Pope's *The Rape of the Lock* (1714), a poem in which Belinda's beauty is enhanced by a list of cosmetics, perfumes and jewellery – all of which are the products of trade and commerce.

---

1 According to Paul Fussell, Christian humanism 'suggests a sort of wise and broad piety, a rich, civilized amalgam of Christian devotion and pagan wisdom – or even worldly wisdom'. *The Rhetorical World of Augustan Humanism* (Oxford: Clarendon Press, 1965), p. 3.

2 According to many Protestant theologians, St Paul emphasizes the struggle against the sin in each person's own nature and his/her inability to fulfil God's law without God's grace. Old Testament prophets are equally preoccupied with human sin and depravity constantly warning, in the words of Isaiah 13:11, that God 'will punish the world for their evil, and the wicked for their iniquity'.

been identified as his representation of what men are. Neither of these opinions, I believe, is correct.

Let us begin with the Houyhnhnms and the Yahoos. In the first two voyages Gulliver is shown uncomfortably situated on the isthmus[3] of a middle state between the very large and the very small. In this voyage he also stands on an isthmus, but now it is between the purely rational and the purely sensual— between Houyhnhnm and Yahoo. Neither of these symbols can stand for man, since Gulliver himself is the symbol of humanity. Unfortunately for poor Gulliver, he shares somehow in the nature of both extremes. Swift simply isolates the two elements that combine in the duality of man, the middle link, in order to allow Gulliver to contemplate each in its essence.

Does Swift recommend that Gulliver (who, remember, is we) should strive to become a Houyhnhnm? We discover that in every sense Houyhnhnmland is a rationalistic Utopia. The Houyhnhnms are the embodiment of pure reason. They know neither love nor grief nor lust nor ambition. They cannot lie; indeed they have no word for lying and are hard put to it to understand the meaning of *opinion*. Their society is an aristocracy, resting upon the slave labor of the Yahoos and the work of an especially-bred servant class. With icy, stoical calm they face the processes of life—marriage, childbirth, accident, death. Their society is a planned society that has achieved the mild anarchy that many Utopian dreamers have aspired to. They practice eugenics, and since they know no lust, they control the size of their population; children are educated by the state; their agrarian economy is supervised by a democratic council; government is entirely conducted by periodic assemblies. The Houyhnhnms feel natural human affection for each other, but they love everyone equally. It is all very admirable, but it is remote from the possibilities of human life.

Does Swift intend us to accept this as his ideal way of life? He who loved and hated and fought and bled internally through *saeva indignatio*?[4] I think not. The Houyhnhnms are obviously Cartesians and are obviously stoics.[5] "Neither is *Reason* among them a Point problematical as with us," reports Gulliver, "where Men can argue with Plausibility on both Sides of a Question; but strikes you with immediate Conviction;...." This is the Houyhnhnm version of Descartes' rational intuition of clear and distinct ideas.[6] Now Swift was anti-Cartesian from his first published satire, for the simple reason that he held that Descartes was self-deluded and that man's reason was incapable of the feats that Descartes

---

3  Narrow land bridge between two larger land areas – the isthmus of Panama, for example. Here Monk alludes to Pope's argument in *Essay on Man*, that humans constitute a middle term between animal and angels between pure spirit and pure animal passion. 'Plac'd on this isthmus of a middle state / A being darkly wise, and rudely great. . . . He hangs between; in doubt to act, or rest, / In doubt to deem himself a God, or Beast' (vol. II, lines 3–8).

4  'Savage indignation.' Swift's epitaph in St Patrick's Cathedral, Dublin reads: 'Here lies the Body of Jonathan Swift, Doctor of Divinity, Dean of this Cathedral Church, Where savage indignation can no longer Rend his heart.'

5  In rough terms, Cartesians may be described as those who, following the teachings of René Descartes, make all decisions beginning with a set of self-evident or a-priori maxims. The Stoics were a philosophical movement of the Hellenistic period who held that strong emotions like fear, envy or even sexual passion could be overcome through the exercise of discipline of the will. The Houyhnhnms, for example, display no affection for their colts.

6  Descartes argued that 'clear and distinct ideas' might be obtained not from sense impressions, but through the pure act of intuition.

attributed to it. The Houyhnhnms are stoics, and Swift recorded his view of stoicism in *Thoughts on Various Subjects*: "The Stoical Scheme of supplying our Wants, by lopping off our Desires, is like cutting off our Feet when we want Shoes." It is Gulliver, not Swift, who is dazzled by the Houyhnhnms and who aspires to rise above the human condition and to become pure intelligence as these horses and the angels are.

The most powerful single symbol in all Swift is the Yahoos. They do not represent Swift's view of man, but rather of the bestial element in man—the unenlightened, unregenerate, irrational element in human nature—the id or the libido, if you will.[7] Hence the Houyhnhnms classify Gulliver with them; hence the female Yahoo wishes to couple with him; hence despite his instinctive recoiling from them, Gulliver has to admit with shame and horror that he is more like them than he is like the Houyhnhnms. This I think is clear. Because of his neglect or misuse of human reason, European man has sunk nearer to the Yahoo pole of his nature than he has risen toward the Houyhnhnm pole. The seeds of human society and of human depravity, as they exist in Europe, are clearly discerned in the society and conduct of the Yahoos. Gulliver looks into the obscene abyss of human nature unlighted by the frail light of reason and of morality, and the sight drives him mad.

Repelled by what he sees, he, not Swift, identifies the Yahoos with man; and he, not Swift, turns misanthrope. Since he will not be a Yahoo, he seeks to become, as nearly as possible, a Houyhnhnm. But he can do so only by denying his place in and responsibility to the human condition, by aspiring above the middle link, which is man, to the next higher link, that of the purely rational. The wise Houyhnhnm, to whom he gives his terrifying account of European man and society, concludes that "the corruption of reason" is worse than brutality itself, and that man is more dangerous than the Yahoo. This is profoundly true. But its effect on Gulliver is to awaken loathing of all that is human.

Lear, gazing on the naked, shivering Edgar, disguised as a Tom o' Bedlam, cries: "Thou art the thing itself; unaccommodated man is no more but such a poor, bare, forked animal as thou art."[8] And in that intense moment, he goes mad. Something of the same thing befalls Gulliver. He thinks he has seen the thing itself. Though the Houyhnhnms never acknowledge that he is more than an unusually gifted Yahoo, he aspires to their rationality, stoicism, and simple wisdom; and persuaded that he has attained them, he feeds his growing misanthropy on pride, which alienates him not only from his remote kinsmen, the Yahoos, but eventually from his brothers, the human race. Looking back with nostalgia on his lost happiness in Houyhnhnmland, he recalls:

> I enjoyed perfect Health of Body, and Tranquility of Mind; I did not feel the Treachery or Inconstancy of a Friend, nor the Injuries of a secret or open Enemy. I had no Occasion of bribing, flattering, or pimping, to

---

7  According to Freudian theory, the Id is the irrational or emotional part of the mind, the source of the libido associated with the sexual instinct.

8  In Shakespeare's *King Lear*, Act III, scene iv, Lear, who has been thrown out into the storm by his own daughters, encounters Edgar who is pretending to be a madman to escape detection by his brother who seeks to kill him. When Lear gazes on 'Poor Tom', as Edgar calls himself, he realizes that his own grandeur and pomp are a sham and that each human being is nothing more than a 'poor, bare, forked animal' like the one shivering in front of him.

procure the Favour of any great Man, or of his Minion. I wanted no Fence against Fraud or Oppression: Here was neither physician to destroy my Body, nor Lawyer to ruin my Fortune: No Informer to Watch my words and Actions, or forge Accusations against me for Hire: Here were no Gibers, Censurers, Backbiters, Pickpockets, Highwaymen, Housebreakers, Attorneys, Bawds, Buffoons, Gamesters, Politicians, Wits, Spleneticks, tedious Talkers, Controvertists, Ravishers, Murderers, Robbers, Virtuoso's; no Leaders or Followers of Party and Faction; no Encouragers to Vice, by Seducement or Examples: no Dungeon, Axes, Gibbets, Whippingposts, or Pillories; No cheating Shopkeepers or Mechanicks; No Pride, Vanity or Affection: No Fops, Bullies, Drunkards, strolling Whores, or Poxes: No ranting, lewd, expensive Wives: No stupid, proud Pedants: No importunate, over-bearing, quarrelsome, noisy, roaring, empty, conceited, swearing Companions: No Scoundrels raised from the Dust upon the Merit of their Vices; or Nobility thrown into it on account of their Virtues: No Lords, Fiddlers, Judges or Dancing-masters.

From the moment that the banished Gulliver despairingly sets sail from Houyhnhnmland, his pride, his misanthropy, his madness are apparent. Deluded by his worship of pure reason, he commits the error of the Houyhnhnms in equating human beings with the Yahoos. Captured by a Portuguese crew and forced to return from sullen solitude to humanity, he trembles between fear and hatred. The captain of the ship, Don Pedro de Mendez, like Gulliver himself, shares the nature of the Houyhnhnm and the Yahoo; and like the Gulliver of the first voyage he is tolerant, sympathetic, kindly, patient, and charitable; but Gulliver can no longer recognize these traits in a human being. With the myopic vision of the Houyhnhnms, he perceives only the Yahoo and is repelled by Don Pedro's clothes, food, and odor. Gradually, however, he is nursed to back to partial health, and is forced to admit in the very accent of his admired horses, that his benefactor has a "very good *human* Understanding." But the Gulliver who writes this book is still under the control of his *idée fixe*, and when we last see him he prefers the smell and conversation of his two horses to the company of his wife and children. This is misanthropy in Timon's manner, not Swift's.[9] In the brilliant and intricately ironic coda with which the book ends, Swift directs his savage, comic gaze straight at Gulliver and his insane pretensions.

My Reconcilement to the Yahoo-kind in general might not be so difficult, if they would be content with those Vices and Follies only which Nature hath entitled them to. I am not in the least provoked at the Sight of a Lawyer, a Pickpocket, a Colonel, a Fool, a Lord, a Gamester, a Politician, a Whoremunger, a Physician, an Evidence, a Suborner, an Attorney, a Traytor, or the like: This is all according to the due Course of Things: But when I behold a Lump of Deformity, and Diseases in both of

---

9    Swift argued that his own satire was 'not in Timon's manner' (see Contemporary Documents, **pp.** 25–6). Timon, the central character in Shakespeare's *Timon of Athens*, loathes mankind and exiles himself to the forest where he hurls curses at all who come to visit him and at the world in general.

Body and Mind, smitten with *Pride*, it immediately breaks all the Measures of my Patience; neither shall I ever be able to comprehend how such an Animal and such a Vice could tally together.

The grim joke is that Gulliver himself is the supreme instance of a creature smitten with pride. His education has somehow failed. He has voyaged into several remote nations of the world, but the journeys were not long, because of course he has never moved outside the bounds of human nature. The countries he visited, like the Kingdom of Heaven, are all within us. The ultimate danger of these travels was precisely the one that destroyed Gulliver's humanity—the danger that in his explorations he would discover something that he was not strong enough to face. This befell him, and he took refuge in a sick and morbid pride that alienated him from His species and taught him the gratitude of the Pharisee— "Lord, I thank Thee that I am not as other men."[10]

Swift himself, in his personal conduct, displayed an arrogant pride. But he was never guilty of the angelic dehumanizing pride of Gulliver, who writes in a letter to his Cousin Sympson:

I must freely confess, that since my last Return, some corruptions of my *Yahoo* nature have revived in me by Conversing with a few of your Species, and particularly those of my own Family, by an unavoidable Necessity; else I should never have attempted so absurd a Project as that of reforming the *Yahoo* Race in this Kingdom; but, I have now done with all such visionary Schemes for ever.

Jonathan Swift was stronger and healthier than Lemuel Gulliver. He hated the stupidity and the sinfulness and the folly of mankind. He could not accept the optimistic view of human nature that the philosophers of the Enlightenment proposed. And so he could exclaim to his contemporaries: "O wicked and perverse generation!" But, until he entered upon the darkness of his last years, he did not abandon his fellow man as hopeless or cease to announce, however indirectly, the dignity and worth of human kind.

### From **C. J. Rawson, *Gulliver and the Gentle Reader: Studies in Swift and Our Time*** (London: Routledge, Kegan & Paul, 1973), pp. 6–10

Readers of *Gulliver's Travels* have often suspected that Swift's hostility was directed at them as well as the objects of satire in the text itself.[1] As C. J. Rawson argues in the following except, nowhere is Swift's ambiguous attitude towards

---

10  These are the words of the Pharisee in Luke 18:11, a devout adherent of the Jewish law who was proud that he was better than the mere publican who was praying beside him, but whose prayer, Jesus points out, is more acceptable to God because it is sincere and humble.

---

1  See Richard H. Rodino, ' "Splendide Mendax": Authors, Characters, and Readers in *Gulliver's Travels*' (*Publications of the Modern Language Association of America*), vol. 106 (1991), pp. 1054–70.

his readers more clearly marked than in Gulliver's direct and continuous engagement of the 'gentle reader', the 'candid reader', and above all, the 'curious reader', whose desire for strange adventures is assumed to equal Gulliver's own. At times, Gulliver invokes the reader's curiosity as the pretext for narrative digression. Of his long description of the Laputans and their flappers, Gulliver observes: 'It was necessary to give the Reader this Information, without which he would be at the same Loss with me, to understand the Proceedings of these People' [III, ii, p. 199]. Such information is almost never 'necessary', revealing one aspect of Swift's ambiguous attitude towards the inconsequential detail which was the raw material of the novel, where digressions and authorial asides would be standard features. More frequently, however, these digressions serve to create the illusion of familiarity between Gulliver and the reader. All satires are in some sense rhetorical, and as H. W. Sams has argued: 'One of the prerequisites of successful rhetoric is the creation of cooperative relationship between speaker and audience.' As readers, we recognize a distinction between Gulliver and Swift, and join with Swift in his various satirical attacks. Swift's scorn encourages readers to feel personally superior to the objects of his satire. This is what Sams describes as satire of the 'third person', but there is another kind of satire of 'the second person', in which the reader comes to suspect that, thanks to a complex interrelationship 'between Swift, Gulliver, and the reader', he himself has become the object of Swift's satire.[2] So it is that our identification with Gulliver leaves us doubly vulnerable to the suspicion that when he rejects all the Yahoos for qualities that are identifiably human, he rejects his readers as well. In the following excerpt, Rawson builds upon Sams' 'satire of the second person', to explore an 'aggressiveness towards the reader' which is 'pervasive in his major satires'.

This aggressiveness towards the reader is what chiefly distinguishes Swift from the later writers to whom he can be compared, and who imitate him or are prefigured in his work. It takes many forms, and is not confined to contexts of parody. In the *Tale*, however, parody cannot help being closely involved, and Swift's determined and naked hostility to the targets of his parody has several immediate consequences which differentiate his effects from those of similar passages in Sterne or Mailer. The primacy of the parodic element diverts formal attention (as distinct from our informal sense of Swift's teasing and often explosive presence) away from Swift to his satiric victims. The parody prevents by this means that unSwiftian note of self-cherishing which sometimes creeps into Sterne's, or Mailer's,[3] use of 'self-conscious' mannerisms and other 'modern' postures, and correspondingly discourages easy complicities in the reader, without freeing the reader from an

---

2   Henry W. Sams, 'Swift's Satire of the Second Person', *ELH* (*English Literary History*), vol. 26 (1959), in *Twentieth-Century Interpretations of Gulliver's Travels*, ed. Frank Brady (Englewood Cliffs, NJ: Prentice-Hall, 1968), p. 36.

3   In Laurence Sterne's *Tristram Shandy* (1760–7), the author's address to the reader is often confusing. Norman Mailer, author of 'factions' like *The Armies of the Night* (1968), frequently makes himself a central character in his own fictions.

awkward sense of relationship. But whether parody is present or not, the aggression I speak of is usually quite inescapable in Swift's satire. What is involved is not necessarily a 'rhetoric' or thought-out strategy, so much as an atmosphere or perhaps an instinctive tone. This is not to mistake Swift for his masks, but to say that behind the screen of indirections, ironies, and putative authors a central Swiftian personality is always actively present, and makes itself felt.

Consider a scatological[4] passage in *Gulliver*. I do not wish to add here to the available theories about the scatology and body-disgust as such. Psychoanalysts have examined it; C. S. Lewis says, sturdily, that it is 'much better understood by schoolboys than by psychoanalysts'; another critic says the 'simplest answer is that as a conscientious priest [Swift] wished to discourage fornication';[5] others say that Swift was just advocating cleanliness, mocking the over-particularity of travel-writers, or doing no more any way than other writers in this or that literary tradition. But most people agree that there is a lot of it, and it has been a sore point from the start. Swift knew it, and knew that people knew, and early in book I he has a characteristic way of letting us know he knows we know [I, ii, p. 29].[6] Gulliver had not relieved himself for two days, and tells us how in his urgency he now did so inside his Lilliputian house. But he assures us that on future occasions he always did 'that Business in open Air', and that the 'offensive Matter' was disposed of 'every Morning before Company came' by two Lilliputian servants. Gulliver thinks the 'candid Reader' needs an explanation, so he tells us why he tells us this:

> I would not have dwelt so long upon a Circumstance, that perhaps at first Sight may appear not very momentous; if I had not thought it necessary to justify my Character in Point of Cleanliness to the World; which I am told, some of my Maligners have been pleased, upon this and other Occasions, to call in Question.

It is Gulliver and not Swift who is speaking, but it is Swift and not Gulliver who (in any sense that is active at this moment) has had maligners. Gulliver does have enemies in Lilliput, notably after urinating on the palace-fire, but the reader does not know this yet, and it is difficult not to sense behind Gulliver's self-apology a small egocentric defiance from the real author. This would be true whether one knew him to be Swift or not: but it comes naturally from the Swift whose writings, and especially *A Tale of a Tub*, had been accused of 'Filthiness', 'Lewdness', 'Immodesty', and of using 'the Language of the Stews'[7] (Swift called it being 'battered with Dirt-Pellets' from 'envenom'd . . . Mouths'.)[8] Swift's trick consists

4    Having to do with excrement or filth.
5    [Rawson's note.] C. S. Lewis, 'Addison', in *Essays on the Eighteenth-Century, Presented to David Nichol Smith* (Oxford: Oxford University Press, 1945), p. 1; Irvin Ehrenpreis, *The Personality of Jonathan Swift* (London, 1958), p. 39.
6    Rawson's quotations from the *Travels* refer to *PW*, vol. XI (1959).
7    Stews: brothels or whorehouses.
8    [Rawson's note.] William King, *Some Remarks on the Tale of a Tub* (1704), cited by Ricardo Quintana, *The Mind and Art of Jonathan Swift* (Oxford: Oxford University Press, 1936), p. 75; William Wotton, *A Defense of the Reflections upon Ancient and Modern Learning . . . With Observations upon the Tale of a Tub* (1705), in *A Tale of a Tub*, ed. A. C. Guthkelch and D. Nicol Smith, 2nd edn (Oxford: Clarendon Press, 1958), pp. 322, 323, 326; *PW*, vol. I, p. 5.

of doing what he implies people accuse him of, and saying that this proves he isn't like that really: the openly implausible denial becomes a cheeky flaunting of the thing denied, a tortuously barefaced challenge. This self-conscious sniping at the reader's poise occurs more than once: a variant instance of mock-friendly rubbing-in, for the 'gentle Reader's' benefit, occurs at the end of II.i, where the particularity of travel-writers is part of the joke.

A related non-scatological passage, which Thackeray praised as 'the best stroke of humour, if there be, a best in that abounding book',[9] is Gulliver's final farewell to his Houyhnhnm master, whose hoof he offers to kiss, as in the papal ceremony.[10] (Gulliver seems to have leanings that way: he also wanted to kiss the Queen of Brobdingnag's foot, but she just held out her little finger—II, iii, p. 101.) 'But as I was going to prostrate myself to kiss his Hoof, he did me the Honour to raise it gently to my Mouth. I am not ignorant how much I have been censured for mentioning this last Particular' [IV, x, p. 282]. Since the passage occurs in the first edition, Gulliver or Swift could hardly have been censured for mentioning this before. 'Detractors' would be presumed by the reader to object that human dignity was being outraged, and Swift was of course right that many people would feel this about his book in general. But this is not Gulliver's meaning at all, and the typical Swiftian betrayal that follows gains its real force less from mere surprise than from its cool poker-faced fanning of a reader's hostility which Swift obviously anticipated and actually seemed on the point of trying to allay: 'Detractors are pleased to think it improbable, that so illustrious a Person should descend to give so great a Mark of Distinction to a Creature so inferior as I. Neither have I forgot, how apt some Travellers are to boast of extraordinary Favours they have received. But . . .' Thackeray's praise ('audacity', 'astounding gravity', 'truth topsy-turvy, entirely logical and absurd') comes just before the famous 'filthy in word, filthy in thought, furious, raging, obscene' passage:[11] it is perhaps appropriate that such coarse over-reaction should be the counterpart to a cheerful complacency in the face of the subtler energies of Swift's style.

The mention of travellers in the hoof-kissing passage brings us back to parody, but emphasizes again how readily Swiftian parody serves attacking purposes which are themselves non-parodic. Edward Stone's view that this reference is proof that Swift is merely joking at the expense of boastful travellers misses most of the flavour of the passage.[12] (One might as easily say that the main or only point of the passage is to guy a papal rite. I do not, of course, deny these secondary jokes, or their piquancy.) But parody is important, almost as much in its way as in the *Tale*. Gulliver is an author, who announces forthcoming publications about Lilliput [I, iv, pp. 47–8; I, vi, p. 57] and Houyhnhnmland [IV, ix, p. 275]—which is a common enough device—and whose putative authorship of the work we are actually reading, as well as being the source of many of its most central

9 [Rawson's note.] William Makepeace Thackeray, *The English Humorists of the Eighteenth Century* (London and New York: Everyman's Library, 1949), p. 32. [see Early Critical Reception, pp. 70–1.]
10 [Rawson's note.] For other satirical treatments of the papal ceremony, see *Tale*, Chapter IV (*PW* I, p. 71), and Rabelais I.ii; I.xxxiii; II.xxx.
11 [Rawson's note.] *English Humorists*, pp. 34–5.
12 [Rawson's note.] Edward Stone, 'Swift and the Horses: Misanthropy or Comedy?' *Modern Language Quarterly*, vol. X (1949), p. 374 n.

ironies, enables Swift to flaunt his own self-concealment in some amusing and disconcerting ways.[13] A portrait of Gulliver was prefixed to the early editions, and in 1735 this acquired the teasing caption 'Splendide Mendax'.[14] The elaborate claims to veracity in 'The Publisher to the Reader' and in the text itself gain an additional piquancy from this. The 1735 edition also prints for the first time Gulliver's letter to Sympson, which, as prefatory epistles go, is a notably unbalanced document, providing advance notice of Gulliver's later anti-social state and by the same token giving a disturbing or at least confusing dimension to the sober opening pages of the narrative. [...]

We are hardly expected to take *Gulliver's Travels* as a straight (even if possibly mendacious) travel story. But the sea captain who claimed to be 'very well acquainted with Gulliver, but that the printer had Mistaken, that he lived in Wapping & not in Rotherhith', the old gentleman who searched for Lilliput on the map, the Irish Bishop who said the 'Book was full of improbable lies, and for his part, he hardly believed a word of it'[15] [...] do tell a kind of truth about the work. Swift's whole ironic programme depends on our not being taken in by the travel-book element, but it does require us to be infected with a residual uncertainty about it; and these instances of an over-successful hoax fulfil, extremely a potential in the work to which all readers must uneasily respond. This is not to accept the simpler accounts of Swiftian betrayal, which suggest that the plain traveller's, or modest proposer's, factuality lulls the reader into a false credulity, and then springs a trap. With Swift, we are always on our guard from the beginning (I believe this is true of sensitive *first* readings as well as later ones), and what surprises us is not the fact of betrayal but its particular form in each case. But if we are on our guard, we do not know what we are guarding against. The travel-book factuality, to which we return at least at the beginning and end of each book (even the end of book IV, in its strange way, sustains and elaborates the pretence), is so insistent, and at its purest so lacking in obvious pointers to a parodic intention, that we really do not know *exactly* how to take it. What saves the ordinary reader from being totally taken in is, obviously, the surrounding context. (The very opening of the narrative, from the 1735 edition onwards, is coloured by the letter to Sympson: but even before 1735 one would have needed to be exceptionally, obtuse to think, by the end of the first chapter, that one was still reading a travel-book.) But not being taken in, and knowing the plain style to be parodic, do not save us from being unsure of what is being mocked: travelbooks, fictions posing as travel-books, philosophic tales (like *Gulliver* itself) posing as fictions posing as travel-books.[16] Bewilderment is increased by the uncertainty of how much weight to give, moment by moment, to the fact of parody as such and to whatever the style may be mocking, since the parody as we

13  [Rawson's note.] Real concealment seemed a necessity with such a subversive book, though Pope told Swift on 16 November 1726 that people were not worried by 'particular reflections', so that he 'needed not to have been so secret upon this head' (*Corr*, III, p. 181). In any case, simple anonymity or pseudonymity would have served the practical purposes. Swift's authorship soon became fairly well known anyway.

14  [Rawson's note.] Horace, *Odes*, III. xi. 35.

15  See Contemporary Documents, p. 29.

16  [Rawson's note.] See Ricardo Quintana, *Swift: An Introduction* (Oxford: Oxford Paperbacks, 1962), pp. 53ff., 159ff.

have seen is continuously impregnated with satiric purposes which transcend or exist outside it, but which may still feed on it in subtle ways. And we cannot be sure that some of the plainness is not meant to be taken straight, not certainly as factual truth, but (in spite of everything) momentarily as realistic fictional trimmings: at least, the style helps to establish the 'character' of the narrator, though this 'character' in turn has more life as the basis of various ironies than as a vivid fictional personality. No accurate account can exhaust the matter, or escape an element of giddy circularity. The proper focus for Swift's precise sober narrative links is paradoxically a blurred focus because we do not know what to make of all the precision. The accumulation of unresolved doubt that we carry into our reading of more central parts of *Gulliver's Travels* creates, then, not a credulity ripe for betrayal, but a more continuous defensive uneasiness. This undermining of our nervous poise makes us peculiarly vulnerable, in more than the obvious sense, to the more central satiric onslaughts.

## From **Robert Phiddian, 'A Hopeless Project: Gulliver Inside the Language of Science in Book III'** (1998), *Eighteenth-Century Life*, vol. 22, n.s., 1 (February), pp. 51–3

Book III of *Gulliver's Travels* has always been regarded as an ugly duckling. Dr Arbuthnot told Swift (5 November 1726) that 'the Part of the projectors is least brilliant' (see **p. 27**) and according to Gay (17 November 1726), other critics 'think the flying island is the least entertaining' (see **p. 28**). With regard to Swift's satire on science, certain modern critics have been even less kind. Says John Middleton Murry: 'About science, abstract or applied, Swift knew nothing.'[1] Satires on modern scientists, or 'virtuosi' as they were called, were common in the late seventeenth century, and Swift adopts hints from such contemporary satires as Thomas Shadwell's play *The Virtuoso* (1676), Samuel Butler's *Hudibras* (1680), and the parodies of the *Philosophical Transactions* contained in William King's *Transactioneer* (1700) and *Useful Transactions in Philosophy* (1709). Marjorie Hope Nicolson and Nora M. Mohler were the first modern scholars to demonstrate the extent to which Swift drew his inspirations for the satire on science from the *Philosophical Transactions of the Royal Society* (see Sources, **pp. 34–5**, and Key Passages, **pp. 159–61**).[2] These conclusions have been modified by Douglas Lane Patey, who argues that Swift's satire in Book III is directed at new definitions of knowledge that overturned the traditional distinctions between the older 'arts of certainty', like mathematics and the 'arts of prudence'. According to Patey, Swift complains that the Laputans would 'extend demonstrative methods' of mathematics 'through all education and knowledge', applying them inappropriately to the various 'arts' of politics, agriculture, language and architecture in ways that are both inappropriate and

1    John Middleton Murry, *Jonathan Swift: A Critical Biography* (London: Jonathan Cape, 1954), p. 332.
2    Marjorie Nicolson and Nora M. Mohler, 'The Scientific Background of Swift's "Voyage to Laputa" ', in *Fair Liberty Was All His Cry*, ed. A. Norman Jeffares (London: Macmillan, 1967), pp. 226–69.

self-defeating. The Laputans fail in all practical arts from tailoring to home construction. As Patey suggests, when we say that Swift satirized modern science, we must be careful what we are describing, since 'science' as we have come to know it did not yet exist as anything other than a branch of natural philosophy.³ However, in the passage I have excerpted, Robert Phiddian points out the extent to which Gulliver, as a 'scientific traveler', becomes both the conduit and the subject matter of Swift's satire on the new enthusiasm for empirical observation. Like parodies of other literary forms in the *Travels*, 'the writing lives off the discursive energies it subverts, and exploits while it rejects' (see Contextual Overview, **pp. 12–13**).

The setting for the language of *Gulliver's Travels*, the genre it apparently belongs to if read unironically, is the travel book. The sort of travel book that Gulliver thinks he is writing is certainly no belletristic exercise in subjectivity, but rather a practical man's practical description of exotic places, people, and things. Gulliver is generally an empirical tourist, and is especially so in Book III, where he disappears to an extraordinary extent into the language of science. Obviously, as Patey points out so clearly, it is important to have a historical sense of what science means in this context;⁴ for it is the popular form of the language of natural philosophy that Gulliver writes, a style that represses the appearance of subjectivity in a narrator and focuses on describing visible or material phenomena. For example, when the flying island approaches for the first time, Gulliver records,

> I turned back, and perceived a vast Opake Body between me and the Sun, moving forwards towards the Island: It seemed to be about two Miles high, and hid the Sun six or seven Minutes, but I did not observe the Air to be much colder, or the Sky more darkned, than if I had stood under the Shade of a Mountain. As it approached nearer over the Place where I was, it appeared to be a firm Substance, the Bottom flat, smooth, and shining very bright from the Reflexion of the Sea below. I stood upon a Height about two Hundred Yards from the Shoar, and saw this vast Body descending almost to a Parallel with me, at less than an *English* Mile Distance. I took out my Pocket-Perspective,⁵ and could plainly discover Numbers of People moving up and down the Sides of it, which appeared to be sloping, but what those People were doing, I was not able to distinguish. [pp. 156–7]⁶

This is not the famous "philosophical Account" [. . .] where Gulliver describes the motion of the island in a manner that parodies the style of the Royal Society;

---

3    Douglas Lane Patey, 'Swift's Satire on "Science" and the Structure of Gulliver's Travels', *ELH*, vol. 58, no. 4 (winter, 1991), pp. 809–39.
4    Douglas Lane Patey, 'Swift's Satire on "Science" and the Structure of *Gulliver's Travels*', *ELH* (*English Literary Heritage*), vol. 58, no. 4 (winter, 1991) pp. 809–39.
5    Small telescope; spyglass.
6    Phiddian's quotations from the *Travels* refer to *PW*, vol. XI (1959).

that is too obvious for my present purposes. This example illustrates more subtly the pervasiveness of the empirical eye. Gulliver is more a cipher in Book III than in the other books, and becomes something very like a reader's "Pocket-Perspective." He describes what he sees and does this in material terms marked by the linguistic assumptions of Bacon, Sprat, Boyle, and the rest of the "new" scientists.[7] His is the testimony of the objective eye, circumstantially describing things.[8]

Though clearly parody, this is more than simple ridicule: Swift does not allow the text to accede to its own rhetoric's conventions of sincerity. Gulliver is clearly a vehicle for ridicule when he leaves for the Academy of Lagado expectantly because he had been "a sort of Projector[9] in . . . younger Days" (p. 178); and it is as a not-much-reformed projector that Gulliver delivers the majority of his observations. Projectors allege that

> [O]ne Man shall do the Work of Ten: a Palace may be built in a Week, of Materials so durable as to last for ever without repairing. All the Fruits of the Earth shall come to Maturity at whatever Season we think fit to chuse, and increase an Hundred Fold more than they do at present: with innumerable other happy Proposals.
>
> (p. 177)

But there is a problem:

> The only Inconvenience is, that none of these Projects are yet brought to Perfection: and in the mean time, the whole Country lies miserably waste, the Houses in Ruins, and the People without Food or Cloaths. By all which, instead of being discouraged, they are Fifty Times more violently bent upon prosecuting their Schemes.
>
> (p. 177)

However, the animosity toward materialist schemes is not always as easily decipherable as this. The projecting spirit is the voyage's main *vehicle* as well as its main target. There are many patently ludicrous things, such as the Lagadan language machine whereby "the most ignorant Person at a reasonable Charge, and with a little bodily Labour, may write Books in Philosophy, Poetry, Politicks, Law, Mathematicks and Theology, without the least Assistance from Genius or Study" (pp. 182–4)—an advertisement for the wonders of the Internet?—and the philosophers who converse only with things they can carry on their backs. However, to work at all, Book III relies on the reader's provisional assent to empirical

---

7    Francis Bacon, father of the experimental method, Thomas Sprat, author of the *History of the Royal Society* (1667), and Robert Boyle, himself a scientist and author of numerous books, all subscribed to a belief that scientific description should be free of all rhetorical figures – metaphors, similes, hyperboles, etc. (see Contemporary Documents, **pp. 34–5**).

8    [Phiddian's note.] On the nature and social significance of testimony in science, specifically of this period, see Steven Shapin, *A Social History of Truth: Civility and Science in Seventeenth-Century England* (Chicago, Ill.: University of Chicago Press, 1994).

9    Person who concocts extraordinary schemes, sometimes for public benefit. The speaker in Swift's *A Modest Proposal* (1729), is a 'projector' whose plan to eat the Catholic children of Ireland is designed to solve the problem of Catholic poverty and overpopulation.

language, to materialist conventions of mimesis.[10] Gulliver sees ghosts in Glubb-dubdrib and immortals in Luggnagg: he describes the conventions and physical appearances of various courts. He acts routinely as if he were a reliable empirical observer, a traveler who writes with a circumstantial flatness and transparency that encourages a reader to trust the account. This transaction of interpretive trust is undermined but not obliterated by the fact that he is the simulacrum of an empiric, rather than the real thing. By providing the skeleton of a rhetorical structure, empirical mimesis provides at least the surface coherence that carries the reader on and conveys the first layer of meaning.

Even ghosts are described materially, circumstantially, and without any apparent sense of the fantastic or the bizarre:

> I proposed that *Homer* and *Aristotle*[11] might appear at the Head of all their Commentators; but these were so numerous, that some Hundreds were forced to attend in the Court and outward Rooms of the Palace. I knew and could distinguish those two Heroes at first Sight, not only from the Croud, but from each other. *Homer* was the taller and comelier Person of the two, walked very erect for one of his Age, and his Eyes were the most quick and piercing I ever beheld. *Aristotle* stooped much, and made use of a Staff. His Visage was meager, his Hair lank and thin, and his Voice hollow. I soon discovered, that both of them were perfect Strangers to the rest of the Company, and had never seen or heard of them before.
>
> (p. 197)

Aristotle is ultimately responsible for the theory of language that equates words with things, but he is not treated straightforwardly as a fool. Like Sprat and Gulliver, he treats transparent lucidity as the goal of all rhetoric, but he also shares this position with Swift in his unironic statements on the matter.[12] On his appearance in Glubbdubdrib, he cuts a slighter figure than Homer, but his right to be the metonymic representative of ancient philosophy does not seem to be questioned. The hollowness of his voice conveys ambivalence, but not outright repudiation.

The presentation of Homer and Aristotle, and the ridicule of their disciples which follows, depend on the superficial coherence of empirical observation and narratorial objectivity. Though it is ludicrous to propose that Swift simply approves of the materialist language Gulliver spouts, a lot of its energy still comes through; and the nature of Swift's animosity is not easily decipherable, at least from within the text. Simply to reverse the polarities, and assume that Gulliver is systematically "saying the thing which is not" [. . .] will only take you so far. The bad natural philosophy that Patey (and most readers) see as the target of this

---

10  Fictional mimesis (that is, the imitation of nature) depends on a faith that what the writer describes actually exists as he/she describes it.

11  Homer's *Iliad* and Aristotle's *Poetics* were literary works that had attracted the attention of dozens of seventeenth- and eighteenth-century literary critics, many of whom simply 'made up' the information they purveyed as fact, and many of whom simply copied the criticism (and errors) of other contemporary critics.

12  [Phiddian's note.] Anne Cline Kelly, *Swift and the English Language* (Philadelphia, Pa.: University of Pennsylvania Press, 1988) surveys Swift's expressed views on language thoroughly.

parody is also its medium. The writing lives off the discursive energies it subverts, and exploits while it rejects.

## From **Terry J. Castle, 'Why the Houyhnhnms Don't Write: Swift, Satire and the Fear of the Text'** (1980), *Essays in Literature*, vol. 7 (spring), pp. 39–42

One of the themes connecting almost all Scriblerian satires is an interest in the modern abuses of language (see Critical History, **pp. 58–60**). In his *Proposal for Correcting, Improving, and Ascertaining the English Tongue* (1712) Swift produced what is perhaps his most definitive and, paradoxically, his most uncertain statement regarding the correction of the English language. On the one hand, Swift sought to rid the language of all the additions and 'Alterations' (*PW*, vol. IV, p. 15) that had crept into common usage largely as a result of the increased rate of publication. Swift also wished to eliminate certain fashionable abbreviations and newly coined phrases. While he was not entirely hostile to the addition of new words to English lexicon – Swift was particularly fond of new scientific vocabulary – he sought to prevent obsolete expressions from being dropped from the language.[1] One of Swift's goals (and one he shared with Alexander Pope) was to halt the evolution or, as he would say, the deterioration of language so that works of literature would remain intelligible over a long period of years. This concern for the stabilization of language is reflected in Book III of the *Travels* where the Struldbruggs express their fear that they will live so long that their language will no longer be understood by their descendants (see Key Passages, **p. 163–4**). Paradoxically, however, Swift recommends that this project for 'Correcting, Improving, and Ascertaining the English Tongue' should be entrusted to an academy, the sort of organization for which Swift elsewhere expresses unalloyed contempt.

There is irony as well in a stated determination to somehow 'fix' the language, since there is no one more devoted to punning wordplay and verbal equivocation than Jonathan Swift, as we see in Gulliver's extended pun on 'Master Bates' in Book I (see Key Passages, **pp. 122–3**). Carole Fabricant suggests that Swift's lifelong indulgence in puns, riddles and invented languages must be understood as a function of his Irish culture where 'words could have dual (or more) meanings and often functioned on several different levels at once, creating the possibilities for both linguistic plenitude and semantic confusion'.[2] In his *Proposal for Correcting . . . the English Tongue* (1712), Swift had suggested that closer attention to word etymology would help to slow the rate of language change. In practice, however, Swift seems as fascinated with mock-etymologies as he is with puns as we see in Gulliver's explication of the meaning of *Laputa* in Book III. Gulliver is quite vain about his 'wonderful facility' with

---

1   See Anne Cline Kelly, *Swift and the English Language* (Philadelphia, Pa.: University of Pennsylvania Press, 1988), pp. 89–103.
2   Carole Fabricant, 'Swift the Irishman', *The Cambridge Companion to Jonathan Swift*, ed. Christopher Fox (Cambridge: Cambridge University Press, 2003), p. 64.

languages, and throughout the *Travels* he treats his readers to a series of translations, some of them straightforward, as in his assertion that the words *Trameck-san* and *Slamecksan* equate to low heels and high heels in English, and some of them misleading, like Gulliver's explanation that *Grildrig*, Glumdalclitch's pet name for him, means 'what the *Latins* call *Nanunculus*, the *Italians Homunceletino*' (II, ii, p. 95), words, which, as Deborah Wyrick points out, don't exist.[3]

Not all critics have adopted Wyrick's scepticism regarding Swift's intentions, and some, like Ian Higgins, have gone so far as to suggest that the 'plain-style simplicity and propriety' that we find in Houyhnhnm conversation represents a 'Swiftian ideal' that is 'offered as a contrast to a European corruption. Their language, which is oral not written, and so presumed to have escaped the corruption of textuality, is wryly implied at one point to be an appropriate model for a universal language.' Indeed, 'utopian Houyhnhnm culture in Book IV seems immemorial. Their poetry is Homeric in character. The speech of these horses "approaches nearest to the *High Dutch* or *German*" ' (IV, iii, p. 234), one of the languages Swift listed in the *Proposal* as admitting little change.[4] In the following excerpt, Terry J. Castle offers a contrasting account of Swift's intent where Houyhnhnm language is concerned. Castle argues that in *Gulliver's Travels* Swift's development of the very theme of 'Grammaphobia' isolates for his readers 'the radical indeterminacy of the very texts we allow to influence our lives'. As a result, she argues, Swift may be indulging in a critique of the very notion of writing itself. As was suggested in the Contexts section (see **pp. 8–9**), the very structure of *Gulliver's Travels*, the fact that it simultaneously imitates and satirizes a great number of literary texts, makes it easy for Swift to satirize the very idea of writing itself.

The themes Swift associates with writing—its fallen aspect, its hermeneutic indeterminacy,[5] and physical and moral degeneracy—all reappear, finally, within the fictional context of *Gulliver's Travels*. One might even be tempted to claim that satire of the written word is an underlying principle of organization in that work. No matter how other perspectives shift from book to book (most notoriously our view of the narrator himself), a critique of the written word seems to remain a constant. It works as a symbolic reference point against which other elements of the satire may be aligned.

Texts exert a different pressure on each of the societies Gulliver visits, inviting the hypothesis that this pressure is a Swiftian index to the nature of each place. In Book I, for instance, when Swift satirizes the pettiness and pomposity of the Lilliputians he shows us that their society is pre-eminently text oriented. The

3   See Deborah Baker Wyrick, *Jonathan Swift and the Vested Word* (Chapel Hill, NC: University of North Carolina Press, 1988), p. 80–5.
4   Ian Higgins, 'Language and Style', *The Cambridge Companion to Jonathan Swift*, ed. Christopher Fox (Cambridge: Cambridge University Press, 1993), pp. 149, 154. One may wonder just how exemplary these languages are meant to seem, since German was the language of the Hanoverians, High Dutch a variation frequently ridiculed by the Scriblerians.
5   Linguistic indeterminacy: linguistic ambiguity inherent in texts themselves that makes it impossible for the reader to determine exactly what the writer means.

Lilliputians are compulsive writers: they organize their lives around significant texts-published "Edicts" (such as the one which initiates the Big- and Little-Endian controversy), the "Proclamations" and "Orders of State" of their prince, treaties (which do not hold), and "Articles" of behavior like those presented to Gulliver on his arrival. The Lilliputians tend to formalize all their experience—silly as it is—as text. Yet this process of textualizing is, as elsewhere in Swift, a suspect one. Witness the distortion that creeps in as the Lilliputians set out to describe, in scientific discourse, the contents of Gulliver's pocket. Likewise, Gulliver's plight in Book I worsens precisely as texts intervene. The palace fire—the event that initiates Gulliver's fall from favor—starts because of the "careless-ness of a Maid of Honour, who fell asleep while she was reading a Romance" [I, v, p. 44].[6] The Englishman's fate is sealed by the "Articles of Impeachment" ordered against him by corrupt Lilliputians. The text, the satirist suggests, disrupts both the physical and social order of things; it is the primary cause of Lilliputian error and the primary tool of their injustice. The Lilliputians are condemned by the intimacy they share with it.

The Brobdingnagians, in proportion to their greater magnanimity as a people, denigrate and restrict the influence of the text. Gulliver notes that they have printing, "But their Libraries are not very large." Similarly, "they avoid nothing more than multiplying unnecessary Words" [II, vii, p. 110], and institute—arbitrarily but as best they can—against the process of interpretation itself: "No Law of their Country must exceed in Words the Number of Letters in their Alphabet; which consists only of two and twenty. But indeed, few of them extend even to that Length. They are expressed in the most plain and simple Terms, wherein those people are not Mercurial enough to discover above one Interpret-ation. And, to write a Comment upon any Law, is a capital Crime" [II, vii, p. 110]. Gulliver comments that as a result Brobdingnagian learning is very "confined," but the joke is on him. We predicate Swift's satire on his narrator on a pre-existing satire of the text. Thus, when Gulliver's own pettiness is exposed in this book by the Brobdingnagian king, we find the king analogizing England and its inhabitants to a corrupted text: "I observe among you some Lines of an Institu-tion, which in its Original might have been tolerable; but these half-erased, and the rest wholly blurred and blotted by Corruption" [II, vi, p. 106]. The immediate focus of Swiftian satire shifts, of course, between Books I and II, but its underlying assumption remains the same: the "little odious Vermin," whether Lilliputian or Gulliver himself, has pen in hand.

Again, in Book III, the satire of the text underlies Swift's satire on the Academy of Projectors. Laputan writing is perhaps the most nightmarish in *Gulliver's Travels*. Among the various ridiculous inventions that Gulliver finds in Laputa, for example, is that implement "for improving speculative Knowledge by prac-tical and mechanical Operations" [III, v, p. 148]—the text-breeding machine. With this device "the most ignorant Person may write Books in Philosophy, Poetry, Politics, Law, Mathematicks and Theology, without the least Assistance from Genius or Study" [III, v, p. 148]. The invention generates arbitrary assort-ments of letters by mechanical rearrangement of bits of wood and paper, on which

---

6    Castle's quotations from Gulliver's Travels are taken from *PW*, vol. XI (1941).

are written "all the Words of their Language in their several Moods, Tenses, and Declensions, but without any Order." As in *A Tale of a Tub*, writing is figured as a non-intellectual process; it is automatic, mindless replication. "The Pupils at Command took each of them hold of an Iron Handle, whereof there were Forty fixed round the Edges of the Frame; and giving them a sudden Turn, the whole Disposition of the Words was entirely changed. He then commanded Six and Thirty of the Lads to read the several Lines softly as they appeared upon the Frame; and where they found three or four Words together that might make Part of a Sentence, they dictated to the four remaining Boys who were Scribes" [III, v, p. 148]. Already the texts created thus are many; "several Volumes" exist of "broken Sentences," and the inventor of the machine intends more. With the prospect of five hundred such devices in operation, the number of "Rich Materials" still to be produced is incalculable [III, v, p. 150]. Swift here discovers, then, an appropriate physical model for meaningless, inhuman and infinitely reproducing writing. The text factory is the central locus for grammaphobia in Book III, but one might note, too, the satirist's exposure again of the "Anagrammatick Method" [III, vi, p. 156] in the section on political projectors, and his dismissal of "Commentary" [III, viii, pp. 150–60] and interpretation in the episode in which Gulliver calls back the Ancient writers from the dead. At all points in the Laputan scenes, even more so perhaps than in Lilliput, the reader encounters a world replete with writing, a world controlled by a technology of the text. In both societies, however, writing itself becomes the mark of an intrinsic intellectual and moral degeneracy.

And here we come back, of course, to the horses. As Gulliver has already told us, "their Knowledge is all traditional" [IV, ix, p. 220]. Unlike any other society in *Gulliver's Travels*, the Houyhnhnms have not taken the catastrophic fall into a world of letters. Their complete ignorance of books suggests an improvement even upon the relatively text-free Brobdingnagians.

The situation, however, is not without paradox. The pattern of grammaphobia in *Gulliver's Travels* conditions the appalling problem that confronts the reader in Book IV. Houyhnhnm society is indeed pure to the extent that it is free from textuality. It is a naturalized society. The Houyhnhnms are bound by a community of the voice; they are bound by a language of pure sound, the neigh. This is the sense in which Houyhnhnm society qualifies (as some critics would like to see it[7]) as a Swiftian version of the Platonic utopia.[8] The secondary mode of signification[9] is absent, along with its attendant corruption. No demonic texts here, getting in the way of the spoken discourse.

Swift queers the pleasant resolution of the grammaphobic situation—the escape to a Platonic Utopia—however, by one simple and ludicrous transformation. The residents in Utopia are not human. By virtue of the essential difference between Houyhnhnm and human, the naturalized society is not, and can never

---

7    [Castle's note.] See, in particular, John F. Reichert, 'Plato, Swift, and the Houyhnhnms', *Philological Quarterly*, vol. 47 (1968), pp. 179–92.

8    According to Reichert, 'Plato, Swift, and the Houyhnhnms', pp. 181–3, both Book IV of *Gulliver's Travels* and the ideal society described by Plato include an emphasis on intuitive conviction that excludes conflicting opinion, the adoption of eugenic principles of reproduction, and the strenuous and identical education of both sexes.

9    That is, writing.

be, our own. Gulliver tries to imitate the gait and speech of the horses, but, most significantly, he is never able to stop writing. Already fallen, he cannot emulate the Houyhnhnms in this crucial respect. (Indeed, Swift hints everywhere of Gulliver's inescapable resemblance to the Yahoos—who, with their enthusiastic and decorative shit-smearing seem, anthropologically speaking, on the way to the discovery of a script.) Thus the satirist's examination of textuality takes its most damning turn. The Houyhnhnms model that situation suggested at all points in Swift from *A Tale of a Tub* on as a good—no writing at all. But they are not we. For humankind, Swift suggests, the text is inevitable. It is already here. The evil text and human presence constitute an inseparable unit in the world.

This extension of the grammaphobic argument places the reader in an impossible position. Swift leaves us in Book IV with confirmation of a logical tautology[10]—because we are human, we are open to dehumanization. Indeed, we already possess the necessary tool. He infects us everywhere with the malignancy of the text, and then says there is nothing we can do about it. Attempted return to the innocence of the Houyhnhnm is doomed to be an incomplete gesture. Meanwhile, the Yahoos drop excrement upon us from the trees. They inscribe our very bodies with a text.

From **J. A. Downie, *Jonathan Swift, Political Writer*** (1984) (London: Routledge & Kegan Paul), pp. 275–8

Even before *Gulliver's Travels* was published, Swift expressed the fear that persons in power would find it politically objectionable. Although his fear of official reprisals was exaggerated, Whig pamphleteers certainly objected that Swift's satire, particularly in Book I, formed part of the larger campaign against Walpole's government launched by Swift's friends in the Opposition (see Contemporary Documents, **pp. 39–40**). Even moderate Whig journalists like Abel Boyer argued that 'the Allusions and Allegories . . . are for the most part so strong, so glaring, and so obvious' that no further explanation was necessary.[1] The presumed transparency of the allusions and allegories did not prevent a number of anonymous hacks from preparing Keys to the *Travels*, just the same, variously identifying Flimnap with Robert Walpole, the Prime Minister, and Reldresal with Lord Townsend, the Treasurer. For twentieth-century critics, Arthur E. Case's influential argument that 'Gulliver's career in Lilliput represents the joint political fortunes of Oxford and Bolingbroke during the latter half of Queen Anne's reign'[2] gave rise to a veritable cottage industry devoted to demonstrating particular parallels between Gulliver's adventures and the political actions of contemporary politicians. Irvin Ehrenpreis argues, for example,

---

10   Statement in which the premise and conclusion are identical – e.g. 'All circles are round.'

1   Quoted in Phyllis Guskin, ' "A very remarkable Book": Abel Boyer's View of Gulliver's Travels', *Studies in Philology*, vol. 72 (1975), p. 439.

2   Arthur E. Case, *Four Essays on Gulliver's Travels* (Princeton, NJ: Princeton University Press, 1945), p. 70.

that the treason charges brought against Gulliver for his failure to destroy Blefuscu is an allegorical rendering of the charges filed against Bolingbroke by a vengeful Whig ministry.[3] Characteristic of more recent responses to the politics of the *Travels* has been the argument advanced by Phillip Harth and F. P. Lock that while Book I contains numerous allusions to particular figures and events, Swift invites the reader to 'generalize to all courts from this exemplary tale of the ingratitude of princes, and the jealousy of ministers'.[4] A notable exception to this trend among more recent critics is the argument of Ian Higgins, that the allegory and political innuendo sprinkled throughout *Gulliver's Travels* bears a close resemblance to the political rhetoric of the Jacobite opposition to the Hanoverian government of England. According to Higgins: 'Gulliver's Travels can be shown not only to share the disaffected political discourse of Jacobite publications but also to entertain recognized Jacobite alternative options' including 'ideas of resistance and tyrannicide'.[5] Why Jonathan Swift, a devoted clergyman of the Church of England, should have secretly longed for the return of the Roman Catholic Stuarts is not a question that Higgins answers. If we turn to a critic like J. A. Downie we find that this is not even a question worth asking, since, as Downie argues in a number of publications, far from being a Jacobite, Swift was almost certainly a lifelong Whig, however loosely we construe that term. The following passage, excerpted from Downie's *Jonathan Swift: Political Writer* provides a clear and measured version of the debate over Swift's politics and the significance of political analogy in the *Travels*.

Only the most obvious parallels between Lilliput and England can be noted here, but the comparison is not merely one of size. There are two 'struggling Parties' in Lilliput, known as '*Tramecksan*, and *Slamecksan*, from the high and low Heels on their Shoes, by which they distinguish themselves' (p. 48).[6] The analogy with the Tory and Whig parties, which were also known as the High Church and Low Church parties, is sufficiently obvious to require no elaboration. Although the High-Heels are more numerous, the Low-Heels have all the power, just as in the England of 1726, in which, despite a natural Tory majority in the kingdom, the government was entirely in the hands of the Whigs. George I was an enemy of the Tories, but his son, the Prince of Wales, less obviously so. The Emperor of Lilliput's heels were 'lower at least by a *Drurr* than any of his Court', but 'the Heir to the Crown' was thought to 'have some Tendency towards the

3    See Irvin Ehrenpreis, 'The Origins of Gulliver's Travels', *Publications of the Modern Language Association of America* (1957), pp. 880–99; see also Maurice J. Quinlan, 'Treason in Lilliput and England', *Texas Studies in Literature and Language*, vol. 11 (1970), p. 1323.
4    Phillip Harth, 'The Problem of Political Allegory in *Gulliver's Travels*', *Modern Philology*, vol. 73 (1976), p. 45. See also F. P. Lock, *The Politics of Gulliver's Travels* (Oxford: Clarendon Press, 1980) and Sir Charles Firth, 'The Political Significance of Gulliver's Travels', *Proceedings of the British Academy*, vol. 9 (1919–20), pp. 237–59.
5    Ian Higgins, *Swift's Politics: A Study in Disaffection* (Cambridge: Cambridge University Press, 1994), p. 171.
6    Downie's quotations from *Travels* refer to *PW*, vol. XI (1959).

High-Heels' (p. 48). In this way England and Lilliput can be seen to have certain significant similarities.

By representing familiar things in an unusual light, Swift's satiric mirror invites us to examine our own prejudices. The conflict between Catholic and Protestant is reduced to a debate over whether one should break one's egg on the bigger or the smaller end. 'Many hundred large Volumes have been published upon this Controversy', Gulliver informs us, 'It is computed, that eleven Thousand Persons have, at several Times, suffered Death, rather than submit to break their Eggs at the smaller End.' These 'civil Commotions' including 'six Rebellions raised on that Account,' are constantly fomented by the Monarchs of *Blefuscu*; and when they were quelled, the Exiles always fled for Refuge to that Empire' (p. 49). In this way, Swift deliberately invites us to compare the situation in Lilliput and that in England. France becomes analogous to Blefuscu, the supporters of the Old Pretender[7] to the Big-Endian exiles, and so on. The contemporary application is there to be made, as well as the universal significance to be derived from recognising the pettiness of the disputes from which confrontations develop.

The recent controversy over the topicality of the political allusions in *Gulliver's Travels* stems from the question of whether or not Blefuscu *represents* France, or whether or not the quaintly named Lilliputian characters are meant to suggest contemporary political figures.[8] The rope-dancers, for instance, provide a ready metaphor for those who wish to gain and keep political office. The passage retains a universal significance. Dancing on figurative ropes can be seen to be the customary practice of aspiring ministers. But when Gulliver states that '*Flimnap*, the Treasurer, is allowed to cut a Caper on the strait Rope, at least an Inch higher than any other Lord in the whole Empire' (p. 38), Flimnap is openly compared to Walpole, the Prime Minister, who is also Lord Treasurer of England. It would be pointless to say that Flimnap *is* Walpole, for the characterisation is never developed, although the identification is readily made. It is even more futile to speculate upon whether or not Skyresh Bolgolam is the Earl of Nottingham or the Duke of Marlborough,[9] because Swift's allusions are seldom sufficiently specific.[10]

'A Voyage to Lilliput' nonetheless comments on the state of the nation under the Walpole ministry. This is readily apparent when that other Lilliputian 'Diversion' of leaping over or creeping under a stick is taken in to account. In 1725 George I revived the Order of the Bath.[11] Swift satirised the event in verse:

7   James III (1688–1766), son of the deposed James II. On his father's death (1701), he was recognized as King of England by France and Spain.

8   [Downie's note.] I have dealt with this problem at length in 'Political Characterization in Gulliver's Travels', *Yearbook of English Studies*, vol. 7 (1977), pp. 108–21. More recently, F. P. Lock, in *The Politics of Gulliver's Travels*, has rejected the idea that Swift was referring to particular events and politicians through 'specific allegories and allusion' (p. 89). But I see no reason to alter my own, earlier views on the topicality of *Gulliver's Travels*, although, as I have explained, Swift's method is one of allusion and analogy, rather than of allegory.

9   Daniel Finch (1647–1730), Second Earl of Nottingham. Secretary of State under Queen Anne, President of the Council under George I. John Churchill, Duke of Marlborough (1650–1722). Leader of the armies in the War of the Spanish Succession (1702–1713).

10  [Downie's note.] Downie, 'Political Characterization', pp. 112–14; Lock, pp. 115–16.

11  An order of knighthood, late medieval in origin. It name derives from ritual washings emblematic of the purifications of baptism. The order was revived in 1725 by George I as a regular military order to serve the purposes of Robert Walpole, his prime minister, who needed a new source of political rewards.

> Quoth King Robin, our Ribbands I see are too few
>   Of S$^t$ Andrew's the Green, and S$^t$ George's the Blue
> I must have another of Colour more gay
>   That will make all my Subjects with pride to obey.

Thus 'he who will leap over a Stick for the King / Is qualified best for a Dog in a String.'[12] This 'Ceremony' is described in detail in 'A Voyage to Lilliput':

> The Emperor holds a Stick in his Hands, both Ends parallel to the Horizon, while the Candidates advancing one by one, sometimes leap over the Stick, sometimes creep under it backwards and forwards several times, according as the Stick is advanced or depressed. Sometimes the Emperor holds one End of the Stick, and his first Minister the other; sometimes the Minister has it entirely to himself. Whoever performs his Part with most Agility, and holds out the longest in *leaping* and *creeping*, is rewarded with the Blue-coloured Silk; the Red is given to the next, and the Green to the third . . . (p. 39)

Through comparing the English nobility's pursuit of empty honours with the undignified antics of the Lilliputians, Swift satirises Walpole's creation of 'jobs for the boys,' and exposes the tactics of the Robinocracy[13] to buy off potential opposition – a policy which is connived at by George I himself.

Swift employs different satiric techniques when dealing with the laws, customs and education of the Lilliputians. 'There are some Laws and Customs in this Empire very peculiar,' Gulliver remarks, 'and if they were not so directly contrary to those of my own dear Country, I should be tempted to say a little in their Justification' (p. 58). The strange practices he proceeds to enumerate are all eminently sensible, and they coincide with what we know to have been Swift's own views on certain subjects. These, too, have contemporary applications as well as universal significance. For instance, in the wake of the Atterbury trial,[14] the Lilliputian law relating to informers is of interest:

> All Crimes against the State, are punished here with the utmost Severity; but if the Person accused make his Innocence plainly to appear upon his Tryal, the Accuser is immediately put to an ignominious Death; and out of his Goods or Lands, the innocent Person is quadruply recompensed. [. . .] (p. 58)

12 [Downie's note.] *Poems of Jonathan Swift*, ed. Harold Williams, 3 volumes, 2nd edition (Oxford: Oxford University Press, 1958), vol. II, p. 389. In the first edition of *Gulliver's Travels*, the colours of the silks were given as purple, yellow and white, and although Ford included the correct colours in his list of necessary emendations in his 'interleaved' copy of the first edition [Forster Collection, Accession no. 8551, held in the Victoria and Albert Museum, London, UK], these were retained in the so-called 'Second Edition Corrected' (See *PW*, vol. XI, p. 303).
13 Name given to describe Robert 'Robin' Walpole and his various ministers, who used rewards, titles, positions and even bribes to guarantee that parliamentary votes went their way.
14 Francis Atterbury (1663–1732), Bishop of Rochester and friend of Swift, was accused of plotting a Jacobite restoration of James III and was exiled (1722).

So is the view that fraud is 'a greater Crime than Theft,' especially with regard to the recent South Sea Bubble.[15]

In these instances, Swift is exposing the shortcomings of British society by comparing it with a Lilliputian ideal which, it must be said, the Lilliputians also patently fail to live up to. They are his habitual objects of concern. In Lilliput, for example, 'Males of Noble or Eminent Birth ... are bred up in the Principles of Honour, Justice, Courage, Modesty, Clemency, Religion, and Love of their Country' (p. 61), whereas his constant complaint about post-Restoration England is that the lines of once-virtuous families have degenerated sadly, to the inestimable loss of the nation. It is the decay of this natural aristocracy which has allowed upstarts like Walpole to dominate affairs. This is the theme developed in 'A Voyage to Brobdingnag' in Gulliver's conversations with the King, for they constitute the heart of the matter of this book.

'NOTHING but an extreme Love of Truth could have hindered me from concealing this Part of my Story,' Gulliver admits. 'It was in vain to discover my Resentments, which were always turned into Ridicule: And I was forced to rest with Patience, while my noble and most beloved Country was so injuriously treated.' And yet he 'gave to every Point a more favourable turn by many Degrees than the strictness of Truth would allow' (p. 133). The sagacious reader once again perceives that Gulliver protests too much. To try to retrieve the situation and win the King of Brobdingnag's admiration for the achievements of his own society, Gulliver offers to give him the secret of making gunpowder, but he is amazed at his reaction. 'The King was struck with Horror at the Description I had given of those terrible Engines, and the Proposal I had made', he recalls. 'A strange *Effect of narrow Principles* and *short Views~*!' He finds it incomprehensible

> that a Prince possessed of every Quality which procures Veneration, Love and Esteem; of strong Parts, great Wisdom and profound Learning; endued with admirable Talents for Government, and almost adored by his Subjects; should from a *nice unnecessary Scruple*, whereof in *Europe* we can have no Conception, let slip an Opportunity put into his Hands, that would have made him absolute Master of the Lives, the Liberties, and the Fortunes of his People. (pp. 134–5)

The *leitmotif* of Swift's political writings sounds once more, as *Gulliver's Travels* brings into focus the question of the royal prerogative and the rights and privileges of the people. The King of Brobdingnag is 'almost adored' by his subjects precisely because he is a paternalistic Prince who respects the liberty and property of his dependants. The contrast with George I is marked. Gulliver's question-and-answer sessions with the benevolent King are a serious indictment of the state of the nation under Walpole. Gulliver's descriptions of the House of Lords – 'the Ornament and Bulwark of the Kingdom; worthy Followers of their most renowned Ancestors, whose Honour had been the Reward of their Virtue;

15 A financial crisis that hit England in 1720. Stock of the South Sea Company, which was devised to trade with Latin America, became vastly overvalued, and in the market crash that followed, one blamed on corrupt administration, share values plummeted, bankrupting many Englishmen.

from which their Posterity were never once known to degenerate' – the House of Commons – 'all principal Gentlemen, *freely* picked and culled out by the People themselves, for their great Abilities, and Love of their Country' – the laws, religion, customs and history of England 'for about an hundred Years past,' provoke searching queries:

> He asked, what Methods were used to cultivate the Minds and Bodies of our young Nobility; and in what kind of Business they commonly spent the first and teachable Part of their Lives. What Course was taken to supply that Assembly, when any noble Family became extinct. What Qualifications were necessary in those who are to be created new Lords: Whether the Humour of the Prince, a Sum of Money to a Court-Lady, or a Prime Minister; or a Design of strengthening a Party opposite to the publick Interest, ever happened to be Motives in those Advancements. . . .
>
> He then desired to know, what Arts were practised in electing those whom I called Commoners. Whether, a Stranger with a strong Purse might not influence the vulgar Voters to chuse him before their own Landlord, or the most considerable Gentleman in the Neighbourhood. How it came to pass, that People were so violently bent upon getting into this Assembly, which I allowed to be a great Trouble and Expence, often to the Ruin of their Families, without any Salary or Pension: Because this appeared such an exalted Strain of Virtue and publick Spirit, that his Majesty seemed to doubt it might possibly not be always sincere. . . . (pp. 129–30)

The King of Brobdingnag's queries express Swift's own views on English government and society. By presenting them in this manner, he avoids any possible confusion that might have resulted from using Gulliver as his mouthpiece. It is not Gulliver, but the King of Brobdingnag, who suggests that MPs might consider 'sacrificing the publick Good to the Designs of a weak and vicious Prince, in Conjunction with a corrupted Ministry' (p. 130). The naïve Gulliver is exerting his puny eloquence in *defence* of the system of Walpole, blind to the pertinence of his royal adversary's observations. Brobdingnag is a sort of England in pristine condition. Instead of permitting the ancient constitution to fall into a state of disrepair, the King of Brobdingnag actively promotes the fulfillment of the paternalistic duties advocated so strenuously by Swift. It is for that reason that, in conclusion, the 'least corrupted' society is held to be that of the Brobdingnagians, 'whose wise Maxims in Morality and Government, it would be our Happiness to observe' (p. 292). Given man's fallen condition, it would be the most he could hope for – and Swift did, fervently.

# 3

# Key Passages

# Introduction

There will, perhaps, never be complete agreement as to the most significant passages in *Gulliver's Travels*. One of the consequences of Swift's success at 'vexing' his readers is that each critic has necessarily chosen to focus on passages that seem most closely attuned to the argument he or she is making. As the interests of critics have changed so, too, have notions of what readers of *Gulliver's Travels* should notice first or attend to most carefully. Readers of the selections offered here will undoubtedly notice that my own choices reflect certain critical preferences. That is unavoidable. In a rather limited space, I have, however, tried to select passages from a long book that reflect the main thematic currents of Swift criticism over the years. I have been particularly concerned to select passages that exemplify and support the interpretations outlined in the 'Interpretations' section of this book, and I have supplied headnotes and footnotes designed to call attention to the continuing dialogue between Swift's text, the historical background, and the critical commentary included here. Although this section of the book does not attempt any systematic abridgement of Swift's *Travels*, the student who reads the headnotes together with the selections offered here should obtain a relatively clear sense of the main outlines of the plot and thematic development of the book.

There has long been a debate as to which text of *Gulliver's Travels* ought to be considered authoritative. The *Travels* was first published in London by Benjamin Motte (1726) after Swift had returned to Ireland and could take no direct part in the printing and proofreading. Negotiations with the printer were handled either through letters written by 'Richard Sympson' (a pseudonym for Swift himself) or by Charles Ford (see Letters, **p. 26**). 'Sympson's' apprehension that some passages might be thought a 'little Satyrical' and his advice to Motte that he must 'Judge for yourself' whether they would give offence, may have led Motte to understand that he was free to 'edit the manuscript much as he pleased' (*PW*, XI, p. xxv). On receipt of the published volume, Swift certainly complained about unauthorized changes – complaints that have inspired a long debate about the authenticity of the Motte edition as well as a scholarly crusade to reconstruct a truly definitive text, using the various changes and textual variants found in a number of other editions as well as corrections pencilled into the margins of individual copies of the Motte edition thought to be Swift's own annotations. When *Gulliver's Travels* was republished as Volume III of the collected *Works* in the Dublin edition of George Faulkner (1735), Swift disclaimed any participation in this edition as well, but he did allow Faulkner to claim that his revisions had been made with the help of an 'intimate friend of the Author's' (*Corr.* V, p. 263), whatever that might mean. Swift's failure (or refusal) to acknowledge any authoritative version of the *Travels* has meant a long debate among scholars as to which text – Motte (1726) or Faulkner (1735) – ought to be considered standard. While this scholarly discussion continues, there has developed at least a rough consensus that the Faulkner edition is the most dependable. Since it is not my intention to solve these debates here but to provide students with a readable text, the following excerpts have been taken from the original Faulkner edition of 1735 with minor corrections for clarity or usage. For those students wishing to follow this debate at closer range, I have included the bibliographical sources in the section entitled 'Further Reading'.

# Summary of Key Passages

## Part I: A Voyage to Lilliput

Gulliver is shipwrecked on the island of Lilliput, which is inhabited by a race of tiny people who look and act very much like the English, but who are only 6 inches tall. The Lilliputians tie Gulliver to the ground with ropes, and when he awakes and attempts to rise, they shoot him with tiny arrows. Gulliver does not respond in kind, however, and the Emperor is so impressed with his gentleness that Gulliver is eventually released on condition that he does not injure the people nor accidentally destroy their cities. Gulliver entertains the members of the Court, lets them walk on his hand, and stands with his legs spread so the King's armies can march underneath them. Much of Gulliver's time is spent in discussing the political institutions of Lilliput, which seem a great deal like those of Swift's England. Gulliver is told about the 'high heels' and the 'low heels', the two political parties in Lilliput, which resemble the English Whigs and Tories. And he learns about the religious divisions between those who break their eggs at the big end and those who break them at the little end – an allegorical representation for the split between Roman Catholics and Protestants in England. Lilliput has been at war with Blefuscu, just as the Protestant English had long fought with the Roman Catholic French. Gulliver saves Lilliput from a Blefuscudian invasion by dragging their ships to Lilliput, but he refuses to destroy Blefuscu completely – a decision that creates enemies at the court. Gulliver deepens their resentment when he puts out a fire in the palace by urinating on it. Soon his enemies accuse him of treason and threaten him with death. On learning this news, Gulliver escapes to Blefuscu, where he finds a suitable boat, refits it and returns to England.

## Part II: A Voyage to Brobdingnag

Blown off course in a storm, the ship's landing party goes ashore to refill the water casks, and is frightened by the giants on the island. The landing party abandons Gulliver, who is picked up by a giant farmer who first takes Gulliver home and then transports him to the city to display Gulliver as a circus freak. The farmer sells Gulliver to the Queen of Brobdingnag, who considers him to be a charming little animal. But because he is so small, Gulliver is harassed by the Queen's dwarf, pummelled by apples shaken from a tree, attacked by rats and even kidnapped by a monkey who carries him up to a rooftop and threatens to drop him. Above all, he is humiliated when the young maids at court undress him like a doll and treat him as if he were a sex toy. Once he has learned the language, Gulliver talks at length with the King and Queen about the culture and history of England, about English politics, law, religion and warfare, and he is surprised when the King rejects all human beings as 'little odious vermin'. Throughout his stay in Brobdingnag, Gulliver is overwhelmed by the sheer horror of things when seen at close range, like the sight of flies leaving their excrement on his food, or babies suckling a monstrous breast 6 feet across. Gulliver is suddenly rescued when the box he lives in is carried off by an eagle, dropped into the sea and rescued by a passing ship.

## Part III: A Voyage to Laputa, Balnibarbi, Luggnagg, Glubbdubdrib and Japan

In Book III, Gulliver goes back to sea as a ship's surgeon. This time he is captured by pirates and abandoned on a small island. Gulliver is rescued by an island flying overhead that lets down a chair and pulls him up to safety. The inhabitants of the flying island of Laputa are an odd race of creatures who are preoccupied with music and mathematics, crazed astronomers who worry about the possibility that they may be hit by a comet or that the sun might go out. The Laputans are so abstracted and self-absorbed that they notice nothing until a special servant, called a 'flapper', jogs their attention by hitting them in the eyes or ears with a bag full of peas. The flying island of Laputa moves across the sky powered by an enormous magnet. If the King so chooses, the island can hover over the mainland below, blotting out the sun and rain, and causing drought.

Gulliver is given permission to visit the mainland where he meets Lord Munodi, the most reasonable man in the country, whose beautiful and well-ordered estate has been built on principles handed down from ancient authorities. Everywhere else, Gulliver sees poverty, architectural confusion and agricultural devastation, thanks to the theories of scientific speculators whose hare-brained theories have destroyed the kingdom. These speculators, or projectors as they are called, are headquartered in the Academy of Lagado, and are engaged in a series of mad experiments including the attempt to transform excrement into food, to produce coloured spider webs, to breed naked sheep and to make gunpowder from ice. Other projectors propose to limit confusion by reducing the number of words, or by replacing words altogether with the objects they stand for.

In Glubbdubdrib, the next place Gulliver visits, he meets sorcerers who can raise the dead, and who call up various heroes and writers from the past who explain to Gulliver how many lies subsequent historians and critics have told about them. In Luggnagg, Gulliver hears about creatures called Struldbruggs, men and women who live forever. At first, Gulliver is excited at the prospect of eternal life, but when he discovers that these creatures are old, decrepit and despised by all who know them, he loses his enthusiasm for long life.

## Part IV: Voyage to the Country of the Houyhnhnms

Gulliver sets sail one last time as the captain of a merchant vessel. His crew fall ill and the men Gulliver chooses to replace them turn out to be pirates who strand Gulliver on an island populated by two classes of animals: the Yahoos, who are nasty, ape-like creatures whose favourite recreation is climbing into trees and shitting on those below; and the Houyhnhnms, wise horses who speak in a whinnying sort of dialect and who save Gulliver from the assaults of the Yahoos. The Houyhnhnms tell Gulliver that the word 'Houyhnhnm' means 'perfection of nature', and they live according to the rule of reason. They have no written language, they do not argue and they never lie. They have a simple moral code, based on reason and benevolence, and their only word for evil is 'Yahoo'. As in Brobdingnag, Gulliver's hosts are puzzled by his speech, his clothing and his physical features. After examining him closely, they conclude he must be a more intelligent kind of Yahoo. At first, Gulliver insists on his differences from the Yahoos, but when a female Yahoo tries to mate with him, Gulliver begins to suspect that he might actually be a Yahoo after all. As in Brobdingnag, Gulliver's lengthy descriptions of the culture of Europe with its wars, lawsuits and religious controversies convince the Houyhnhnms that while the Yahoos are loathsome, human Yahoos are worse because their reason gives them the capacity to commit atrocities that the regular Yahoos could never imagine. In the meantime, Gulliver comes to worship the Houyhnhnms; he begins to imitate their speech, whinnying when he talks and trotting when he walks. His desire to stay with the Houyhnhnms is frustrated when the Houyhnhnm assembly decides that he is much too danger- ous to stay on the island with the Yahoos, since he might corrupt them, and he is told he must leave. Heartbroken, Gulliver prepares a boat and sets sail. Gulliver is finally picked up by a Portuguese ship, which eventually returns him to England. But because Gulliver has convinced himself that he is a Houyhnhnm, he treats the Portuguese as if they are Yahoos. He hates their smell, refuses to eat their food and will not talk to them. They assume that Gulliver is deranged and care for him as best they can. When Gulliver sees his home, he cannot stand the sight of his own family: he faints at the embrace of his wife and can only find comfort in the company of horses, whose smell and conversation he prefers. *Gulliver's Travels* ends as it began, with Gulliver's insistence that he tells the absolute truth and he expresses his disappointment that the lessons he has offered have not instantly persuaded his fellow Yahoos that they ought to behave more like Houyhnhnms.

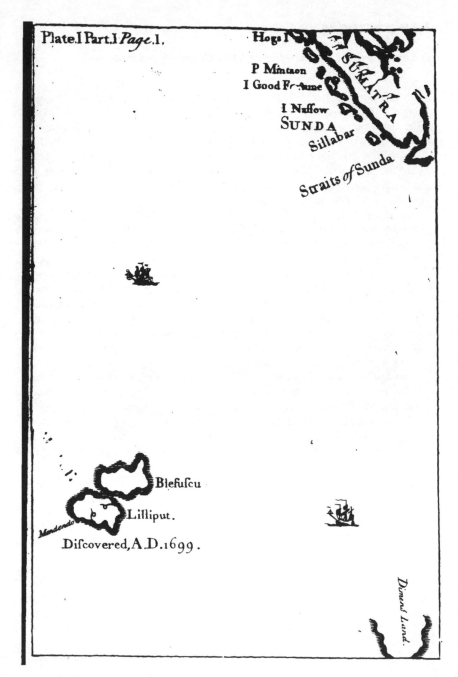

*Figure 5* Map of Lilliput.

# Key passages

## A Letter from Capt. Gulliver to his Cousin Sympson

To the 1735 edition of *Gulliver's Travels* Swift added a prefatory letter, presumably written by Gulliver himself (dated 2 April 1727) and sent to his 'Cousin' Richard Sympson, said to be the publisher of the *Travels*. This is a continuation of the ruse that Swift had pursued in his letters to Benjamin Motte, the first publisher of the *Travels* (see Contemporary Documents, **p. 26**). But nine years after the initial publication of the book, Swift exploits this fictional resurrection of Gulliver himself to correct many of the misconceptions or misreadings that the first edition presumably had created. Swift takes this opportunity to disclaim the deletions and additions that Motte had made in the text, to deny charges that the *Travels* contains political 'innuendo', or that it was meant to offend the 'Female Sex' (see Modern Criticism, **pp. 84–9, 106–11**). Swift also reminds his readers of the parodic significance of Gulliver and the importance of mock-verisimilitude and its parody of 'Sea-Language' (see Contemporary Documents, **pp. 32–3**). Additionally, Swift makes it clear that more than a decade after his return from Houyhnhnmland, Gulliver still swells with pride as he excoriates the British Yahoos for not abandoning their vices once they had been so clearly inventoried in the pages of Gulliver's wonderful book. And he calls attention to his own ambiguous status as narrator, condemning those critics who suggest that the *Travels* might be a 'Fiction' out of his 'own Brain', reminding his readers that because of his internship with the Houyhnhnms, who do not know how to lie, he has successfully rid himself of the habit of prevarication and deception; therefore his tale of vicious pygmies, gentle giants, flying islands and talking horses must be believed. Just as his *Apology* for *A Tale of a Tub* (1710) provides instruction on how to read Swift's satire, so this introductory 'Letter' signposts many of the major themes that will recur in the course of the *Travels*.

I Hope you will be ready to own publickly, whenever you shall be called to it, that by your great and frequent Urgency you prevailed on me to publish a very loose and uncorrect Account of my Travels; with Direction to hire some young Gentleman of either University to put them in Order, and correct the Style, as my Cousin *Dampier* did by my Advice, in his Book called, *A Voyage round the World*. But I do not remember I gave you Power to consent, that any thing should be omitted, and much less that any thing should be inserted. [. . .] When I formerly hinted to you something of this in a Letter, you were pleased to answer, that you were afraid of giving Offence; that People in Power were very watchful over the Press; and apt not only to interpret, but to punish every thing which looked like an *Inuendo* (as I think you called it.)[1] But pray, how could that which

---

1    Swift had reason to be nervous. The whole question of hidden or encoded meanings became increasingly worrisome to English courts during Walpole's ministry. The trial of *The Craftsman* (1729), a journal whose satires attacked Walpole with a series of thinly veiled historical fables,

I spoke so many Years ago, and at above five Thousand Leagues distance, in another Reign, be applied to any of the *Yahoos*, who now are said to govern the Herd; especially, at a time when I little thought on or feared the Unhappiness of living under them. (*Letter*, iii)

[. . .] Behold, after above six Months Warning, I cannot learn that my Book hath produced one single Effect according to mine Intentions: I desired you would let me know by a Letter, when Party and Faction were extinguished; Judges learned and upright; Pleaders honest and modest, with some Tincture of common Sense; and *Smithfield*[2] blazing with Pyramids of Law-Books; the young Nobility's Education entirely changed; the Physicians banished; the Female *Yahoos* abounding in Virtue, Honour, Truth and good Sense: Courts and Levees of great Ministers thoroughly weeded and swept; Wit, Merit and Learning rewarded; all Disgracers of the Press in Prose and Verse, condemned to eat nothing but their own Cotten, and quench their Thirst with their own Ink. These, and a Thousand other Reformations, I firmly counted upon by your Encouragement; as indeed they were plainly deducible from the Precepts delivered in my Book. And, it must be owned, that seven Months were a sufficient Time to correct every Vice and Folly to which *Yahoos* are subject; if their Natures had been capable of the least Disposition to Virtue or Wisdom: Yet so far have you been from answering mine Expectation in any of your Letters; that on the contrary, you are loading our Carrier every Week with Libels, and Keys, and Reflections, and Memoirs, and Second Parts; wherein I see myself accused of reflecting upon great States-Folk; of degrading human Nature, (for so they have still the Confidence to stile it) and of abusing the Female Sex. I find likewise, that the Writers of those Bundles are not agreed among themselves; for some of them will not allow me to be Author of mine own Travels; and others make me Author of Books to which I am wholly a Stranger. . . . (*Letter*, iii–iv)[3]

I HEAR some of our Sea-*Yahoos* find Fault with my Sea-Language, as not proper in many Parts, nor now in Use. I cannot help it. In my first Voyages, while I was young, I was instructed by the oldest Mariners, and learned to speak as they did. But I have since found that the Sea-*Yahoos* are apt, like the Land ones, to become new fangled in their Words; which the latter change every Year; insomuch, as I remember upon each Return to mine own Country, their old Dialect was so altered, that I could hardly understand the new. And I observe, when any *Yahoo* comes from *London* out of Curiosity to visit me at mine own House, we neither of us are able to deliver our Conceptions in a Manner intelligible to the other.[4]

---

turned on whether libellous or seditious 'innuendos' could be detected there. See my 'Irony as Subversion: Thomas Woolston and the Crime of Wit', in *The Margins of Orthodoxy: Heterodox Writing and Cultural Response, 1660–1750*, ed. Roger D. Lund (Cambridge: Cambridge University Press, 1995), pp. 178–81.

2   Smithfield was an area just outside the city walls of London which had been the primary site for the burning of heretics in the sixteenth century.

3   This refers to all those writers who used Gulliver as their own pseudonym (see Critical History, pp. 46–7) and others who offer keys to the secret meanings of the *Travels* (see Contemporary Documents, pp. 32–3).

4   Here Swift repeats the argument first made in his *Proposal for Correcting . . . the English Tongue* (1712) that English was changing so quickly that earlier works of literature would soon become unintelligible to later readers. This is the same problem that Gulliver encounters with the Struldbruggs in Book III (see Modern Criticism, pp. 102–6).

If the Censure of *Yahoos* could any way affect me, I should have great Reason to complain, that some of them are so bold as to think my Book of Travels a meer Fiction out of mine own Brain; and have gone so far as to drop Hints, that the *Houyhnhnms* and *Yahoos* have no more Existence than the Inhabitants of *Utopia*.⁵ [. . .] (*Letter*, v)

Do these miserable Animals presume to think that I am so far degenerated as to defend my Veracity; *Yahoo* as I am, it is well known through all *Houyhnhnmland*, that by the Instructions and Example of my illustrious Master, I was able in the Compass of two Years (although I confess with the utmost Difficulty) to remove that infernal Habit of Lying, Shuffling, Deceiving, and Equivocating, so deeply rooted in the very Souls of all my Species; especially the *Europeans*. (*Letter*, vi)

# Part I: A Voyage to Lilliput

## Chapter I

*The Author giveth some Account of himself and Family; his first Inducements to travel. He is shipwrecked, and swims for his Life; gets safe on shoar in the Country of* Lilliput; *is made a Prisoner, and carried up the Country.*

In what is perhaps a parody of Daniel Defoe's *Robinson Crusoe* (1719), *Gulliver's Travels* begins with a brief account of Gulliver's family background (on Swift and Defoe, see Critical History, **p. 54**, and Early Critical Reception, **pp. 69–71**). But as is often the case in the *Travels*, this seemingly straightforward account contains within it a number of verbal ambiguities designed to entrap the reader or to undermine his/her faith in the accuracy of the details presented (see Modern Criticism, **pp. 78–81**). In this example, Swift exploits the apparent straightforwardness of the biographical account to insinuate an extended and entirely gratuitous pun on masturbation (see Modern Criticism, **pp. 93–8**).

My Father had a small Estate in *Nottinghamshire*; I was the Third of five Sons. He sent me to *Emanuel-College* in *Cambridge*, at Fourteen Years old, where I resided three Years, and applied my self close to my Studies: But the Charge of maintaining me (although I had a very scanty Allowance) being too great for a narrow Fortune; I was bound Apprentice to Mr. *James Bates*, an eminent Surgeon in *London*, with whom I continued four Years; and my Father now and then sending me small Sums of Money, I laid them out in learning Navigation, and other Parts of the Mathematicks, useful to those who intend to travel, as I always believed it would be some time or other my Fortune to do. When I left Mr. *Bates*, I went down to my Father; where, by the Assistance of him and my Uncle *John*, and some other Relations, I got Forty Pounds, and a Promise of Thirty Pounds a Year

---

5  Swift slyly alludes to his own adaptation of More's *Utopia* in the *Travels* (see Contextual Overview, **p. 7**).

to maintain me at *Leyden*: There I studied Physick[1] two Years and seven Months, knowing it would be useful in long Voyages.

Soon after my Return from *Leyden*, I was recommended by my good Master Mr. *Bates*, to be Surgeon to the Swallow, Captain *Abraham Pannell* Commander; with whom I continued three Years and a half, making a Voyage or two into the *Levant*, and some other Parts. When I came back, I resolved to settle in *London*, to which Mr. *Bates*, my Master, encouraged me; and by him I was recommended to several Patients. I took Part of a small House in the *Old Jury*; and being advised to alter my Condition, I married Mrs. *Mary Burton*, second Daughter to Mr. *Edmond Burton*, Hosier, in *Newgate-street*, with whom I received four Hundred Pounds for a Portion.

But, my good Master *Bates* dying in two Years after, and I having few Friends, my Business began to fail; for my Conscience would not suffer me to imitate the bad Practice of too many among my Brethren. Having therefore consulted with my Wife, and some of my Acquaintance, I determined to go again to Sea. (I, i, pp. 1–3)

Gulliver sets sail from Bristol onboard the *Antelope*, headed for the South Seas. Off the coast of Van Dieman's Land (Tasmania), the *Antelope* is sunk in a storm and Gulliver is washed up on the shore of an unknown island. Exhausted, he falls asleep; when he awakes he discovers that he has been tied down by a race of miniature people who look and act remarkably like the natives of England.

I attempted to rise, but was not able to stir: For as I happened to lie on my Back, I found my Arms and Legs were strongly fastened on each Side to the Ground; and my Hair, which was long and thick, tied down in the same Manner. I likewise felt several slender Ligatures across my Body, from my Armpits to my Thighs. I could only look upwards; the Sun began to grow hot, and the Light offended mine Eyes. I heard a confused Noise about me, but in the Posture I lay, could see nothing except the Sky. In a little time I felt something alive moving on my left Leg, which advancing gently forward over my Breast, came almost up to my Chin; when bending mine Eyes downwards as much as I could, I perceived it to be a human Creature not six Inches high, with a Bow and Arrow in his Hands, and a Quiver at his Back. In the mean time, I felt at least Forty more of the same Kind (as I conjectured) following the first. I was in the utmost Astonishment, and roared so loud, that they all ran back in a Fright; and some of them, as I was afterwards told, were hurt with the Falls they got by leaping from my Sides upon the Ground. However, they soon returned; and one of them, who ventured so far as to get a full Sight of my Face, lifting up his Hands and Eyes by way of Admiration, cryed out in a shrill, but distant Voice, *Hekinah Degul*: The others repeated the same Words several times, but I then knew not what they meant. I lay all this while, as the Reader may believe,[2] in great Uneasiness: At length, struggling to get loose, I had

---

1    The study of medicine.
2    This is the first of Gulliver's many direct addresses to his reader (see Modern Criticism, **pp. 55–8**, 93–8).

the Fortune to break the Strings, and wrench out the Pegs that fastened my left Arm to the Ground; for, by lifting it up to my Face, I discovered the Methods they had taken to bind me; and, at the same time, with a violent Pull, which gave me excessive Pain, I a little loosened the Strings that tied down my Hair on the left Side; so that I was just able to turn my Head about two Inches. But the Creatures ran off a second time, before I could seize them; whereupon there was a great Shout in a very shrill Accent; and after it ceased, I heard one of them cry aloud, *Tolgo Phonac*;[3] when in an Instant I felt above an Hundred Arrows discharged on my left Hand, which pricked me like so many Needles; and besides, they shot another Flight into the Air, as we do Bombs in *Europe*, whereof many, I suppose, fell on my Body, (though I felt them not) and some on my Face, which I immediately covered with my left Hand. (I, i, pp. 5–6)

> Gulliver is famished and communicates his hunger with hand gestures. The sheer quantity of Gulliver's appetite and the description of Lilliputian foodstuffs provides a point of comparison with the voyages to Brobdingnag and to Houyhnhnmland, where Swift pays particular attention to the things Gulliver finds to eat (see Key Passages, **pp. 138–9**). Gulliver's consumption is particularly important in this first voyage, because his appetite literally threatens to eat the Lilliputians out of house and home, strongly influencing their decision to get rid of Gulliver any way they can.

The *Hurgo* (for so they call a great Lord, as I afterwards learnt) understood me very well: He descended from the Stage, and commanded that several Ladders should be applied to my Sides, on which above an hundred of the Inhabitants mounted, and walked towards my Mouth, laden with Baskets full of Meat. [. . .] I observed there was the Flesh of several Animals, but could not distinguish them by the Taste. There were Shoulders, Legs, and Loins shaped like those of Mutton, and very well dressed, but smaller than the Wings of a Lark. I eat them by two or three at a Mouthful; and took three Loaves at a time, about the bigness of Musket Bullets. They supplied me as fast as they could, shewing a thousand Marks of Wonder and Astonishment at my Bulk and Appetite. I then made another Sign that I wanted Drink. They found by my eating that small Quantity would not suffice me; and being a most ingenious People, they slung up with great Dexterity one of their largest Hogsheads; then rolled it towards my Hand, and beat out the Top; I drank it off at a Draught, which I might well do, for it hardly held half a Pint, and tasted like a small Wine of *Burgundy*, but much more delicious. They brought me a second Hogshead, which I drank in the same Manner, and made Signs for more, but they had none to give me. (I, i, pp. 8–9)

## Chapter II

*The Emperor of* Lilliput, *attended by several of the Nobility, comes to see the Author in his Confinement. The Emperor's Person and Habit described. Learned*

---

3  Neither this phrase, nor *Hekinah Degul*, cited earlier, can be translated, but may be seen as evidence of Swift's love of language games and mystification.

*Men appointed to teach the Author the Language. He gains Favour by his mild Disposition. His Pockets are searched, and his Sword and Pistols taken from him.*

> The Lilliputians put a sleeping potion in Gulliver's drink and, while he is asleep, they build a huge carriage, drawn by horses only 4½ inches high and haul him to the capital city where they imprison him in an abandoned temple. When he awakes, Gulliver feels the need to defecate and, having no other options, relieves himself in the temple itself. It is this preoccupation with his own faeces that has led critics to accuse Swift of having an 'excremental vision' (see Critical History, **pp. 50–7** and Modern Criticism, **pp. 93–8**).

I had been for some Hours extremely pressed by the Necessities of Nature; which was no Wonder, it being almost two Days since I had last disburthened myself. I was under great Difficulties between Urgency and Shame. The best Expedient I could think on, was to creep into my House, which I accordingly did; and shutting the Gate after me, I went as far the Length of my Chain would suffer; and discharged my Body of that uneasy Load. But this was the only Time I was ever guilty of so uncleanly an Action; for which I cannot but hope the candid Reader will give some Allowance, after he hath maturely and impartially considered my Case; and the Distress I was in. From this Time my constant Practice was, as soon as I rose, to perform that Business in open Air, at the full Extent of my Chain; and due Care was taken every Morning before Company came, that the offensive Matter should be carried off in Wheel-barrows, by two Servants appointed for that Purpose. I would not have dwelt so long upon a Circumstance, that perhaps at first Sight may appear not very momentous; if I had not thought it necessary to justify my Character in Point of Cleanliness to the World; which I am told, some of my Maligners have been pleased, upon this and other Occasions, to call in Question. (I, ii, pp. 16–17)

> Gulliver begs to be released. But before he can be freed, he must be searched, and in what seems like a parody of Defoe's *Robinson Crusoe*, Gulliver translates and transcribes the Lilliputian inventory of what they find in his pockets. Such details suggest that Swift had read *Robinson Crusoe* and that he was reflecting in some fashion on the new popularity of first-person narratives as well as the travel account (see Critical History, **pp. 54–5**).

IMPRIMIS, in the right Coat-Pocket of the *Great Man Mountain* (for so I interpret the Words *Quinbus Flestrin*) after the strictest Search, we found only one great Piece of coarse Cloth, large enough to be a Foot-Cloth for your Majesty's chief Room of State. In the left Pocket, we saw a huge Silver Chest, with a Cover of the same Metal, which we, the Searchers, were not able to lift. We desired it should be opened; and one of us stepping into it, found himself up to the mid Leg in a sort of Dust, some part whereof flying up to our Faces, set us both a sneezing for several Times together. In his right Waistcoat-Pocket, we found a prodigious

Bundle of white thin Substances, folded one over another, about the Bigness of three Men, tied with a strong Cable, and marked with Black Figures; which we humbly conceive to be Writings; every Letter almost half as large as the Palm of our Hands. In the left there was a sort of Engine, from the Back of which were extended twenty long Poles, resembling the Pallisado's[4] before your Majesty's Court; wherewith we conjecture the *Man Mountain* combs his Head [. . .] In the large Pocket on the right Side of his Middle Cover, (so I translate the Word *RanfuLo*, by which they meant my Breeches) we saw a hollow Pillar of Iron, about the Length of a Man, fastened to a strong Piece of Timber, larger than the Pillar; and upon one side of the Pillar were huge Pieces of Iron sticking out, cut into strange Figures; which we know not what to make of. In the left Pocket, another Engine of the same kind. In the smaller Pocket on the right Side, were several round flat Pieces of white and red Metal, of different Bulk: Some of the white, which seemed to be Silver, were so large and heavy, that my Comrade and I could hardly lift them. In the left Pocket were two black Pillars irregularly shaped: we could not, without Difficulty, reach the Top of them as we stood at the Bottom of his Pocket: One of them was covered, and seemed all of a Piece; but at the upper End of the other, there appeared a white round Substance, about twice the bigness of our Heads. Within each of these was inclosed a prodigious Plate of Steel; which, by our Orders, we obliged him to shew us, because we apprehended they might be dangerous Engines. He took them out of their Cases, and told us, that in his own Country his Practice was to shave his Beard with one of these, and to cut his Meat with the other. There were two Pockets which we could not enter: These he called his Fobs; they were two large Slits cut into the Top of his Middle Cover, but squeezed close by the Pressure of his Belly.[5] Out of the right Fob hung a great Silver Chain, with a wonderful kind of Engine at the Bottom.[6] We Directed him to draw out whatever was at the End of that Chain; which appeared to be a Globe, half Silver, and half of some transparent Metal: For on the transparent Side we saw certain strange Figures circularly drawn, and thought we could touch them, until we found our Fingers stopped with that lucid Substance. He put this Engine to our Ears, which made an incessant Noise like that of a Water-Mill. And we conjecture it is either some unknown Animal, or the God that he worships: But we are more inclined to the latter Opinion, because he assured us (if we understood him right, for he expressed himself imperfectly) that he seldom did any Thing without consulting it. He called it his Oracle, and said it pointed out the Time for every Action of his Life.[7] (I, ii, pp. 24–6)

---

4   Fences. Each of the tines on Gulliver's comb is like a fencepost.
5   Special pockets in the vest designed to hold a pocket watch.
6   The common objects that the Lilliputians discover in Gulliver's pockets include a handkerchief, a snuff box filled with tobacco, a small book, a comb, a pistol, coins, a razor, a watch chain and a pocket watch.
7   In Book II, the scholars of Brobdingnag conclude that Gulliver himself must be a piece of clockwork (see Key Passages, p. 141). Here Swift refers to the contemporary fascination with automata of various kinds and the argument from design, popular with Christians and Deists alike that the intricacy of a watch implied a conscious designer.

## Chapter III

*The Author diverts the Emperor and his Nobility of both Sexes, in a very uncommon Manner. The Diversions of the Court of* Lilliput *described. The Author hath his Liberty granted him upon certain Conditions.*

While Gulliver is waiting for his freedom, the Emperor entertains him with descriptions of curious Lilliputian customs, many of which offer allegorical equivalents in miniature to English institutions and practices with which Swift is familiar. For example, Gulliver describes the practice of rope-dancing by performers 'upon a slender white Thread, extended about two Foot, and twelve Inches from the Ground'. What seems to be a quaint description of a popular pastime at fairs and carnivals is also a metaphor for the pursuit of political preferment from Walpole's government. The description of Flimnap's rope-dancing is generally regarded as a swipe at Robert Walpole, Head of the Government from 1715 to 1717 and again from 1721 to 1742. Walpole's political cleverness led him to a long and successful parliamentary career, but it also inspired the contempt of many, like Swift, who felt that his political dexterity disguised a much deeper corruption. The second game, involving coloured threads, is a metaphor for the pursuit of knighthoods by the members of the Whig party (on Swift's distrust of the Whigs, see Contextual Overview, pp. 15–18). Here, blue ribbons represent the Order of the Garter, the oldest British order of chivalry, including the monarch and twenty-five knights, whose emblem was a blue garter. The red ribbon stands for the Order of Bath, whose badges of honour were worn on a red ribbon, and the green ribbon stands for the Order of the Thistle, the highest honour in Scotland, whose emblems include a green sash.

THIS Diversion is only practised by those Persons, who are Candidates for great Employments, and high Favour, at Court. They are trained in this Art from their Youth, and are not always of noble Birth, or liberal Education. When a great Office is vacant, either by Death or Disgrace, (which often happens) five or six of those Candidates petition the Emperor to entertain his Majesty and the Court with a Dance on the Rope; and whoever jumps the highest without falling, succeeds in the Office. Very often the chief Ministers themselves are commanded to shew their Skill, and to convince the Emperor that they have not lost their Faculty. *Flimnap*, the Treasurer, is allowed to cut a Caper on the strait Rope, at least an Inch higher than any other Lord in the whole Empire. I have seen him do the Summerset[8] several times together, upon a Trencher[9] fixed on the Rope, which is no thicker than a common Packthread[10] in *England*. My Friend *Reldresal*,[11]

---

8  Somersault.
9  A wooden platter on which to serve or carve meat.
10  Strong, thick twine for tying bundles.
11  This may be Lord Townshend, Secretary of State and a chief ally of Walpole.

principal Secretary for private Affairs, is, in my Opinion, if I am not partial, the second after the Treasurer; the rest of the great Officers are much upon a Par. [. . .]

THERE is likewise another Diversion, which is only shewn before the Emperor and Empress, and first Minister, upon particular Occasions. The Emperor lays on a Table three fine silken Threads of six Inches long. One is Blue, the other Red, and the third Green. These Threads are proposed as Prizes, for those Persons whom the Emperor hath a mind to distinguish by a peculiar Mark of his Favour. The Ceremony is performed in his Majesty's great Chamber of State; where the Candidates are to undergo a Tryal of Dexterity very different from the former; and such as I have not observed the least Resemblance of in any other Country of the old or the new World. The Emperor holds a Stick in his Hands, both Ends parallel to the Horizon, while the Candidates advancing one by one, sometimes leap over the Stick, sometimes creep under it backwards and forwards several times, according as the Stick is advanced or depressed. Sometimes the Emperor holds one End of the Stick, and his first Minister the other; sometimes the Minister has it entirely to himself. Whoever performs his Part with most Agility, and holds out the longest in *leaping* and *creeping*, is rewarded with the Blue-coloured Silk; the Red is given to the next, and the Green to the third, which they all wear girt twice round about the Middle; and you see few great Persons about this Court, who are not adorned with one of these Girdles. (I, iii, pp. 31–3)

> Gradually, the Lilliputians lose their fear of Gulliver. Out of sticks and his hand-kerchief Gulliver makes a parade ground 2½ feet square and 2 feet above the ground where the Emperor's best horseman can perform military exercises. The Emperor is so pleased, he persuades the Empress to let Gulliver hold her in a 'close chair' within 2 yards of the stage. It is in this section of the *Travels* that Gulliver most resembles the giant Gargantua (see Contextual Overview, **pp. 6–7**). As part of these exercises, the Emperor marches his troops between Gulliver's legs with instructions to the troops not to look up at Gulliver's torn trousers, which reveal his (by Lilliputian standards) gigantic genitalia. Gulliver is so vain that he will take flattery wherever he can find it, and he is secretly pleased when the soldiers sneak peeks at his impressive anatomy. This is but one of the episodes in the *Travels* that contributes to Gulliver's reputation for pride (see Modern Criticism, **pp. 89–93**).

He desired I would stand like a *Colossus*, with my Legs as far asunder as I conveniently could. He then commanded his General (who was an old experienced Leader, and a great Patron of mine) to draw up the Troops in close Order, and march them under me; the Foot by Twenty-four in a Breast, and the Horse by Sixteen, with Drums beating, Colours flying, and Pikes advanced. This Body consisted of three Thousand Foot, and a Thousand Horse. His Majesty gave Orders, upon Pain of Death, that every Soldier in his March should observe the strictest Decency, with regard to my Person; which, however, could not prevent some of the younger Officers from turning up their Eyes as they passed under me. And, to confess the Truth, my Breeches were at that Time in so ill a Condition, that they afforded some Opportunities for Laughter and Admiration." (I, iii, p. 36)

## Chapter IV

Mildendo, *the Metropolis of* Lilliput, *described, together with the Emperor's Palace. A Conversation between the Author and a principal Secretary, concerning the Affairs of that Empire: The Author's Offer to serve the Emperor in his Wars.*

As the final condition of his freedom, Gulliver must swear to a series of articles including promises not to leave Lilliput without permission, not to enter the capital without permission, not to flatten crops by sleeping on them, not to harm the populace or take them into his hands without their consent, to survey the kingdom and to aid the Lilliputians in their war with Blefuscu by destroying their fleet. Once he is freed, Gulliver asks permission to see the capital city of Mildendo, which is an exact square 500 feet long by 500 feet wide divided by two main streets 5 feet wide, with smaller streets and alleyways no wider than 18 inches. The city is surrounded by a wall 2½ feet high and 11 inches broad, wide enough for a coach and horses to drive around it. Gulliver takes off his coat to avoid damaging the roofs with his coattails. The Emperor's palace presents greater difficulties since the gates are but 18 inches high and 7 inches wide. The building of the outer court is 5 feet high and 4 inches thick, too high for Gulliver to step over. The apparent precision of Gulliver's description first inspired the admiration of early readers, like Monboddo and Scott (see Early Critical Reception, **pp. 69–71**), but it also inspired the suspicion of modern critics like Frank Brady (see Modern Criticism, **pp. 81–4**), who interpret Gulliver's apparent accuracy as part of the joke.

... The Emperor had a great Desire that I should see the Magnificence of his Palace: But this I was not able to do till three Days after, which I spent in cutting down with my Knife some of the largest Trees in the Royal Park, about an Hundred Yards distant from the City. Of these Trees I made two Stools, each about three Foot high, and strong enough to bear my Weight. The People having received Notice a second time, I went again through the City to the Palace, with my two Stools in my Hands. When I came to the Side of the outer Court, I stood upon one Stool, and took the other in my Hand: This I lifted over the Roof, and gently set it down on the Space between the first and second Court, which was eight Foot wide. I then stept over the Buildings very conveniently from one Stool to the other, and drew up the first after me with a hooked Stick. By this Contrivance I got into the inmost Court; and lying down upon my Side, I applied my Face to the Windows of the middle Stories, which were left open on Purpose, and discovered the most splendid Apartments that can be imagined. There I saw the Empress, and the young Princes in their several Lodgings, with their chief Attendants about them. Her Imperial Majesty was pleased to smile very graciously upon me, and gave me out of the Window her Hand to kiss. (I, iv, p. 43)

Like other travel writers (see Contemporary Documents, **pp. 32–3**), Gulliver promises that more detailed descriptions of the palace can be found in a sequel 'containing a general Description of this Empire, from its first Erection, through a long Series of Princes, with a particular Account of their Wars and Politicks, Laws, Learning, and Religion; their Plants and Animals, their peculiar Manners and Customs, with other Matters very curious and useful' (I, iv, pp. 43–4). Reldresal, the Principal Secretary, visits Gulliver one day to outline the political situation in Lilliput (which stands for England) and to explain why the country needs Gulliver's help to defeat the Blefuscudian navy, which is preparing to attack them. The whole struggle between Lilliput and Blefuscu, described by Reldresal here, may be seen as an allegory of the hostilities between England and France, conducted first by William III and then by Queen Anne. Swift strongly supported the cessation of the War of the Spanish Succession (1702–13), a peace engineered by his friends Robert Harley and Lord Bolingbroke. This account of the High-Heels and Low-Heels, like the description provided by Rapin Thoyras (see Contemporary Documents, **pp. 38–9**), provides a caricature of the division between Tory and Whig that divided the nation. The references to Big-Endians and Little-Endians point to the distinctions between Catholic and Protestant which still divided the French and the English (see Downie's discussion in Modern Criticism, **pp. 106–11**).

For, *said he*, as flourishing a Condition as we appear to be in to Foreigners, we labour under two mighty Evils; a violent Faction at home, and the Danger of an Invasion by a most potent Enemy from abroad.[12] As to the first, you are to understand, that for above seventy Moons past, there have been two struggling Parties in this Empire, under the Names of *Tramecksan*, and *Slameck-san*, from the high and low Heels on their Shoes, by which they distinguish themselves.[13]

IT is alledged indeed, that the high Heels are most agreeable to our ancient Constitution: But however this be, his Majesty hath determined to make use of only low Heels in the Administration of the Government, and all Offices in the Gift of the Crown; as you cannot but observe; and particularly, that his Majesty's Imperial Heels are lower at least by a *Drurr* than any of his Court; *(Drurr* is a Measure about the fourteenth Part of an Inch.) The Animosities between these two Parties run so high, that they will neither eat nor drink, nor talk with each other. We compute the *Tramecksan*, or High-Heels, to exceed us in Number; but the Power is wholly on our Side. We apprehend his Imperial Highness, the Heir to the Crown, to have some Tendency towards the High-Heels; at least we can plainly discover one of his Heels higher than the other; which gives him a Hobble

---

12  James III, son of James II, the Roman Catholic king who had abdicated the throne of England in 1688, continued to rally support among French Catholics and English Jacobites (supporters of the Stuarts) for an invasion of England to reestablish the Stuarts on the throne.

13  *Trameckson* and *Slamecksan* are made-up names for Tory and Whig. Because the Tories tended to side with the most conservative faction within the Church of England (or High Church) their heels are said to be 'high'. Because the Whigs tended to be more sympathetic to more liberal (Low Church) policies of religious toleration and accommodation with the Presbyterian and Dissenters, their heels are said to be 'low'.

in his Gait.[14] Now, in the midst of these intestine Disquiets, we are threatened with an Invasion from the Island of *Blefuscu*, which is the other great Empire of the Universe, almost as large and powerful as this of his Majesty. For as, to what we have heard you affirm, that there are other Kingdoms and States in the World, inhabited by human Creatures as large as your self, our Philosophers are in much Doubt; and would rather conjecture that you dropt from the Moon, or one of the Stars; because it is certain, that an hundred Mortals of your Bulk, would, in a short Time, destroy all the Fruits and Cattle of his Majesty's Dominions. Besides, our Histories of six Thousand Moons make no Mention of any other Regions, than the two great Empires of *Lilliput* and *Blefuscu*. Which two mighty Powers have, as I was going to tell you, been engaged in a most obstinate War for six and thirty Moons past. It began upon the following Occasion. It is allowed on all Hands, that the primitive Way of breaking Eggs before we eat them, was upon the larger End: But his present Majesty's Grand-father, while he was a Boy, going to eat an Egg, and breaking it according to the ancient Practice, happened to cut one of his Fingers.[15] Whereupon the Emperor his Father, published an Edict, commanding all his Subjects, upon great Penalties, to break the smaller End of their Eggs. The People so highly resented this Law, that our Histories tells us, there have been six Rebellions raised on that Account; wherein one Emperor lost his Life, and another his Crown. These civil Commotions were constantly fomented by the Monarchs of *Blefuscu*; and when they were quelled, the Exiles always fled for Refuge to that Empire.[16] It is computed, that eleven Thousand Persons have, at several Times, suffered Death, rather than submit to break their Eggs at the smaller End. Many hundred large Volumes have been published upon this Controversy: But the Books of the *Big-Endians* have been long forbidden, and the whole Party rendred incapable by Law of holding Employments.[17] During the Course of these Troubles, the Emperors of *Blefuscu* did frequently expostulate by their Ambassadors, accusing us of making a Schism in Religion, by offending against a fundamental Doctrine of our great Prophet *Lustrog*, in the fifty-fourth Chapter of the *Brundrecal* (which is their Alcoran).[18] This, however, is thought to be a meer Strain upon the Text: For the Words are these; *That all true Believers shall break their Eggs at the convenient End*: and which is the convenient End, seems, in my humble Opinion, to be left to every Man's Conscience, or at least in the Power of the chief Magistrate to determine.[19] Now the *Big-Endian* Exiles have found so much Credit in the Emperor of *Blefuscu's* Court; and so much private Assistance and Encouragement from their Party here

14 Frederick, Prince of Wales, later George II, had friends in both the Whig and Tory camps, hence the hobble in his gait. But he was also seen to be an opponent of Walpole's government.
15 While this is not an exact allegory, Swift may refer to Henry VIII (who broke away from the Roman Catholic Church, thus rejecting the doctrine of transubstantiation, i.e. breaking the egg at the larger end), Charles I (who was executed, in part because he was suspected of Catholic sympathies) and James II (who was Roman Catholic and was forced to abdicate the throne).
16 Reference to the numbers of English Catholics who found refuge in France.
17 Reference to the Test Act, which prevented Catholics and Protestant Dissenters from holding offices of public trust unless they took the sacraments according to the rites of the Church of England.
18 Eighteenth-century spelling of the Koran.
19 Reference to Swift's endorsement of the belief, in works like *Sentiments of a Church of England Man* (1711), that because the Anglican Church was the Church 'by law established', it had the right to exclude the members of other religions from all positions of public trust.

at home, that a bloody War hath been carried on between the two Empires for six and thirty Moons with various Success; during which Time we have lost Forty Capital Ships, and a much greater Number of smaller Vessels, together with thirty thousand of our best Seamen and Soldiers; and the Damage received by the Enemy is reckoned to be somewhat greater than ours. However, they have now equipped a numerous Fleet, and are just preparing to make a Descent upon us: And his Imperial Majesty, placing great Confidence in your Valour and Strength, hath commanded me to lay this Account of his Affairs before you. (I, iv, pp. 44–7)

## Chapter V

*The* Author *by an extraordinary Strategem prevents an Invasion. A high Title of Honour is conferred upon him. Ambassadors arrive from the Emperor of* Blefuscu, *and sue for Peace. The Empress's Apartment on fire by an Accident; the Author instrumental in saving the rest of the Palace.*

Like England and France, Lilliput and Blefuscu are divided by a channel 'eight hundred yards wide'. In keeping with his promise to help defend Lilliput against Blefuscu (see **p. 129**), Gulliver describes how he captured the entire Blefuscudian fleet. First he twisted together three of the strongest cables, each 'about as thick as Packthread', and then he formed hooks out of iron bars, each the size of a knitting needle. He attached these to the Blefuscudian ships standing in the harbour and dragged the entire navy off to Lilliput. By this point Gulliver has come to see himself as a defender of the Lilliputian way of life and, as he pulls the Blefuscudian fleet into the harbour of Lilliput, he cries out in a 'loud Voice, Long live the most puissant Emperor of Lilliput!' The Emperor is so impressed that he creates Gulliver a *Nardac*, which is the 'highest Title of Honour among them' (I, v, p. 51). Gulliver is proud to be a Nardac and apparently willing to regard the Lilliputians at their own high evaluation of themselves. This is an example of that moral blindness and 'pride' that critics have condemned in Gulliver's character (see Monk's discussion in Modern Criticism, **pp. 89–93**). Gulliver is not prepared, therefore, for the ambition and bloodthirstiness expressed by the Emperor, whose desire to destroy Blefuscu may allude to the Whig opposition to the Treaty of Utrecht (1713) that ended the War of the Spanish Succession (1702–1713) and which the Whigs regarded as having given away too much to the French, thus leading to the impeachment of Swift's friends Robert Harley and Viscount Bolingbroke. This passage may also suggest Swift's resistance to the subjugation of Ireland by the policies of Walpole's government in England, arguments put forward in such pamphlets as the *Drapier's Letters* (1724) and *A Modest Proposal* (1729).

I trebled the Cable to make it stronger; and for the same Reason I twisted three of the Iron Bars together, binding the Extremities into a Hook. Having thus fixed fifty Hooks to as many Cables, I went back to the North-East Coast, and putting off my Coat, Shoes, and Stockings, walked into the Sea in my Leathern Jerken, about half an Hour before high Water. I waded with what Haste I could, and swam in the Middle about thirty Yards until I felt Ground: I arrived to the Fleet in less than half an Hour. The Enemy was so frighted when they saw me, that they leaped out of the Ships, and swam to Shore; where there could not be fewer than thirty thousand Souls. I then took my Tackling, and fastning a Hook to the Hole at the Prow of each, I tyed all the Cords together at the End. While I was thus employed, the Enemy discharged several Thousand Arrows, many of which stuck in my Hands and Face; and besides the excessive Smart, gave me much Disturbance in my Work. My greatest Apprehension was for mine Eyes, which I should have infallibly lost, if I had not suddenly thought of an Expedient. I kept, among other little Necessaries, a Pair of Spectacles in a private Pocket, which . . . had escaped the Emperor's Searchers. These I took out, and fastened as strongly as I could upon my Nose; and thus armed went on boldly with the Work in spight of the Enemy's Arrows; many of which struck against the Glasses of my Spectacles, but without any other Effect, further than a little to discompose them. I had now fastened all the Hooks, and taking the Knot in my Hand, began to pull; but not a Ship would stir, for they were all too fast held by their Anchors. . . . I therefore let go the Cord, and leaving the Hooks fixed to the Shops, I resolutely cut with my Knife the Cables that fastened the Anchors. . . Then I took up the knotted End of the Cables to which my Hooks were tyed; and with great Ease drew fifty of the Enemy's largest Men of War after me. (I, v, pp. 51–2)

[. . .] His Majesty desired I would take some other Opportunity of bringing all the rest of his Enemy's Ships into his Ports. And so unmeasurable is the Ambition of Princes, that he seemed to think of nothing less than reducing the whole Empire of Blefuscu into a Province, and governing it by a Viceroy; of destroying the *Big-Endian* Exiles, and compelling that People to break the smaller End of their Eggs; by which he would remain sole Monarch of the whole World. But I endeavoured to divert him from this Design, by many Arguments drawn from the Topicks of Policy as well as Justice: And I plainly protested, that I would never be an Instrument of bringing a free and brave People into Slavery. (I, v, pp. 51–2)

> Gulliver's refusal to exterminate the Blefuscudians angers the Emperor of Lilliput and sets in motion the effort to finally get rid of Gulliver, a determination reinforced by the Queen's outrage over Gulliver's attempt to extinguish a fire in the palace by urinating on the flames, an action said to have violated the compact he originally signed with the Lilliputians and one which provides another example of Swift's apparent preoccupation with excrement (see Critical History, **p. 50–1**). This passage is often thought to refer to the profanity of *A Tale of a Tub*, which is said to have so angered Queen Anne that she swore she would never approve Swift's elevation to the position of bishop, a rank he coveted.

I was alarmed at Midnight with the Cries of many Hundred People at my Door; by which being suddenly awaked, I was in some Kind of Terror. I heard the Word *Burglum* repeated incessantly; several of the Emperor's Court making their Way through the Croud, intreated me to come immediately to the Palace, where her Imperial Majesty's Apartment was on fire, by the Carelessness of a Maid of

Honour, who fell asleep while she was reading a Romance.[20] I got up in an Instant; and Orders being given to clear the Way before me; and it being likewise a Moon-shine Night, I made a shift to get to the Palace without trampling on any of the People. I found they had already applied Ladders to the Walls of the Apartment, and were well provided with Buckets, but the Water was at some Distance. These Buckets were about the Size of a large Thimble, and the poor People supplied me with them as fast as they could; but the Flame was so violent, that they did little Good. I might easily have stifled it with my Coat, which I unfortunately left behind me for haste, and came away only in my Leathern Jerkin. The Case seemed wholly desperate and deplorable; and this magnificent Palace would have infallibly been burnt down to the Ground, if, by a Presence of Mind, unusual to me, I had not suddenly thought of an Expedient. I had the Evening before drank plentifully of a most delicious Wine, called *Glimigrim* (the *Blefuscudians* call it *Flunec*, but ours is esteemed the better Sort) which is very diuretick.[21] By the luckiest Chance in the World, I had not discharged myself of any Part of it. The Heat I had contracted by coming very near the Flames, and by my labouring to quench them, made the Wine begin to operate by Urine; which I voided in such a Quantity, and applied so well to the proper Places, that in three Minutes the Fire was wholly extinguished; and the rest of that noble Pile, which had cost so many Ages in erecting, preserved from Destruction. (I, v, pp. 55–6)

## Chapter VI

*Of the Inhabitants of* Lilliput; *their Learning, Laws, and Customs. The Manner of Educating their Children. The Author's Way of living in that Country. His Vindication of a Great Lady.*

> Gulliver's final offence is perhaps his most improbable: he is accused of sexual improprieties with the wife of the Treasurer. Gulliver's laboured defence of his own innocence, one that completely ignores the obvious impossibility of physically consummating an affair with a woman scarcely as tall as his own phallus, provides a perfect example of Swift's delight in playing with his reader's expectations and in laughing at the whole question of perspective in the *Travels*. (On mathematical proportion as part of an elaborate joke, see Brady's discussion in Modern Criticism, **pp. 81–4**.)

I am here obliged to vindicate the Reputation of an excellent Lady, who was an innocent Sufferer upon my Account. The Treasurer took a Fancy to be jealous of his Wife, from the Malice of some evil Tongues, who informed him that her Grace had taken a violent Affection for my Person; and the Court-Scandal ran for some

---

20  Here Swift alludes to the belief that servant girls were being corrupted by reading the romances popular with their young mistresses.

21  By this point in the story Gulliver has come to identify himself completely with the Lilliputians. Here Gulliver is proud not only because Lilliputian wine is superior, but also because it is diuretic – that is, it causes you to urinate more than other sorts of wine.

Time that she once came privately to my Lodging. This I solemnly declare to be a most infamous Falshood, without any Grounds, farther than that her Grace was pleased to treat me with all innocent Marks of Freedom and Friendship. I own she came often to my House, but always publickly, never ever without three more in the Coach, who were usually her Sister, and young Daughter, and some particular Acquaintance; but this was common to many other Ladies of the Court. And I still appeal to my Servants round, whether they at any Time saw a Coach at my Door without knowing what Persons were in it. On those Occasions, when a Servant had given me Notice, my Custom was to go immediately to the Door; and after paying my Respects, to take up the Coach and two Horses very carefully in my Hands [. . .] and place them on a Table, where I had fixed a moveable Rim quite round, of five Inches high, to prevent Accidents. [. . .] I should not have dwelt so long upon this Particular, if it had not been a Point wherein the Reputation of a great Lady is so nearly concerned; to say nothing of my own; although I had the Honour to be a *Nardac*, which the Treasurer himself is not. (I, vi, pp. 69–71)

Gulliver discovers that the Council has secretly passed articles of impeachment against him charging him with making water in the precincts of the palace, refusing to exterminate the Blefuscudians, as well as other charges. It has been argued that these articles allegorically represent similar articles of impeachment brought by Walpole's administration against Swift's friends the Earl of Oxford and Viscount Bolingbroke (see Downie's discussion in Modern Criticism, **pp. 106–11**). Pretending that all is normal, Gulliver returns to Blefuscu on a diplomatic mission, and, while there, he discovers a boat. This he refits, stocks with provisions and puts to sea, where he is rescued by an English merchant vessel that eventually returns Gulliver to England.

# Part II: A Voyage to Brobdingnag

## Chapter I

*A great Storm described. The long Boat sent to fetch Water, the Author goes with it to discover the Country. He is left on Shoar, is seized by one of the Natives, and carried to a Farmer's House. His Reception there, with several Accidents that happened there. A Description of the Inhabitants.*

Gulliver remains at home for only two months before putting to sea again aboard the merchant ship *Adventure*, bound for Surat, a trading port on the western coast of India. After a storm at sea (the details of which Swift copied from a popular mariner's magazine (see Contemporary Documents, **pp. 32–3**), the *Adventure* drops anchor near 'a great Island or Continent', so that the crew can take on fresh water. The crew abandons Gulliver in order to avoid a giant who is chasing them. Gulliver also runs away and eventually finds himself in a field where the barley is 40 feet high and the hedges over 120 feet high. Looking through the hedge Gulliver sees a man coming towards him who appeared 'as Tall as an ordinary Spire-steeple' taking 10 yards at a stride. When the man speaks his voice is 'louder than a speaking Trumpet' (II, i, p. 97). Given the cruelty of the Lilliputians, Gulliver expects that these creatures will be proportionately more savage. He is surprised to discover, therefore, that the Brobdingnagians are actually generous and polite, far more polite than Gulliver himself. Book II owes the most visible debts to the tradition of the Philosophic Voyage, including works like Cyrano de Bergerac's *Comical History of the States and Empires of the Moon and Sun* or Gabriel de Foigny's *A New Discovery of Terra Incognita Australis, or the Southern World* (see Contemporary Documents, **p. 32**). In the Philosophic Voyage, a European is transported to an imaginary country where he engages in discussion with the natives, whose civilization is often more advanced than the European's and who teach him lessons he could not learn elsewhere. Here, as with the Philosophic Voyage in general, the logic depends entirely on comparison. Where the Lilliputians were small, vengeful versions of the English, the Brobdingnagians are large, generous and civilized. It is Gulliver who now represents the worst aspects of European civilization. The more forcefully he defends his native country, the more barbarous he appears.

Being quite dispirited with Toil, and wholly overcome by Grief and Despair, I lay down between two Ridges, and heartily wished I might there end my Days. I bemoaned my desolate Widow, and Fatherless Children:[1] I lamented my own Folly and Wilfulness in attempting a second Voyage against the Advice of all my Friends and Relations. In this terrible Agitation of Mind I could not forbear thinking of *Lilliput*, whose Inhabitants looked upon me as the greatest Prodigy that ever appeared in the World; where I was able to draw an Imperial Fleet in my Hand, and perform those other Actions which will be recorded for ever in the Chronicles of that Empire, while Posterity shall hardly believe them, although attested by Millions. I reflected what a Mortification it must prove to me to appear as inconsiderable in this Nation, as one single *Lilliputian* would be among us. But, this I conceived was to be the least of my Misfortunes: For, as human Creatures are observed to be more Savage and cruel in Proportion to their Bulk; what could I expect but to be a Morsel in the Mouth of the first among these enormous Barbarians who should happen to seize me? Undoubtedly Philosophers are in the Right when they tell us, that nothing is great or little otherwise than by Comparison: It might have pleased Fortune to let the *Lilliputians* find some Nation, where the People were as diminutive with respect to them, as they were to me. And who knows but that even this prodigious Race of Mortals might be equally overmatched in some distant Part of the World, whereof we have yet no Discovery? (II, i, pp. 98–9)

---

1    This is one of the few times that Gulliver even remembers that he has a family back in England.

Gulliver's assertion that nothing is 'great or little other than by comparison' links his experience in his *Travels* with the wider discussion of the place of human beings in the Great Chain of Being, a popular metaphor ascribing to every species in the Creation a place on an interconnected hierarchy of being, starting with angels at the top to microscopic creatures at the bottom. We see this ranking of species here in Book II where Gulliver is compared with giants and again in Book IV where his various capacities are measured against those of the rational Houyhnhnms and the bestial Yahoos (see Key Passages, p. 169). This whole discussion of the relative position of individual species within the Great Chain of Being was intensified by the improvement of microscopes and telescopes in the seventeenth century, which revealed a universe of microscopic life previously invisible to the eye and also excited speculation about the possibility of life on other planets. Throughout *Gulliver's Travels* one also detects the influence of such works as George Berkeley's *A New Theory of Vision* (1709), which speculates about questions of perception and relative size. There was general agreement that human beings deserved their place near the top of the Chain of Being because they can speak. In order to prevent one of these giants from stepping on him, Gulliver cries out at the top of his lungs. At various times in Book II the Brobdingnagians refer to Gulliver as an 'animal' of some sort, a form of expression even more intense in Book IV. This repeated suggestion that Gulliver is nothing more than another sort of creature is a strategy designed to raise the question of what it is essential about human identity and to serve as an ironic counterweight to Gulliver's enormous pride (see Contextual Overview, pp. 13–15).

He considered a while with the Caution of one who endeavours to lay hold on a small dangerous Animal in such a Manner that it shall not be able either to scratch or to bite him; as I my self have sometimes done with a *Weasel* in *England*. At length he ventured to take me up behind by the middle between his Fore-finger and Thumb, and brought me within three Yards of his Eyes, that he might behold my Shape more perfectly. I guessed his Meaning; and my good Fortune gave me so much Presence of Mind, that I resolved not to struggle in the least as he held me in the Air above sixty Foot from the Ground; although he grievously pinched my Sides, for fear I should slip through his Fingers. All I ventured was to raise mine Eyes towards the Sun, and place my Hands together in a supplicating Posture, and to speak some Words in an humble melancholy Tone, suitable to the Condition I then was in. For, I apprehended every Moment that he would dash me against the Ground, as we usually do any little hateful Animal which we have a Mind to destroy But my good Star would have it, that he appeared pleased with my Voice and Gestures, and began to look upon me as a Curiosity; much wondering to hear me pronounce articulate Words, although he could not understand them. (II, i, pp. 99–100)

The Farmer takes Gulliver home, but when Gulliver sits down to eat with the farm family, the dangers of his tiny size become immediately apparent. Here the proportions are reversed and all those objects Gulliver had used in Lilliput must now be recalibrated for size. For the first time, Gulliver recognizes the full extent of his human vulnerability in a land of giants.

When they were sat down, the Farmer placed me at some Distance from him on the Table, which was thirty Foot high from the floor. I was in a terrible Fright, and kept as far as I could from the Edge, for fear of falling. The Wife minced a bit of Meat, then crumbled some Bread on a Trencher, and placed it before me. I made her a low Bow, took out my Knife and Fork, and fell to eat; which gave them exceeding Delight. The Mistress sent her Maid for a small Dram-cup, which held about two Gallons; and filled it with Drink: I took up the Vessel with much difficulty in both Hands, and in a most respectful Manner drank to her Lady-ship's Health, expressing the Words as loud as I could in *English*; which made the Company laugh so heartily, that I was almost deafened with the Noise. This Liquor tasted like a small Cyder, and was not unpleasant. Then the Master made me a Sign to come to his Trencher side; but as I walked on the Table, being in great surprize all the time, as the indulgent Reader will easily conceive and excuse, I happened to stumble against a Crust, and fell flat on my Face, but received no hurt. I got up immediately, and observing the good People to be in much Concern, I took my Hat (which I held under my Arm out of good Manners) and waving it over my Head, made three Huzza's, to shew I had got no Mischief by the Fall. But advancing forwards toward my Master (as I shall henceforth call him) his young-est Son who sate next him, an arch Boy of about ten Years old, took me up by the Legs, and held me so high in the Air, that I trembled every Limb; but his Father snatched me from him; and at the same time gave him such a Box on the left Ear, as would have felled an *European* Troop of Horse to the Earth; ordering him to be taken from the Table. [. . .] IN the Midst of Dinner my Mistress's favourite Cat leapt into her Lap. I heard a Noise behind me like that of a Dozen Stocking-Weavers at work; and turning my Head, I found it proceeded from the Purring of this Animal, who seemed to be three Times larger than an Ox, as I computed by the View of her Head, and one of her Paws, while her Mistress was feeding and stroaking her.[2] The Fierceness of this Creature's Countenance altogether dis-composed me; although I stood at the further End of the Table, above fifty Foot off; and although my Mistress held her fast for fear she might give a Spring, and seize me in her Talons. But it happened there was no Danger; for the Cat took not the least Notice of me when my Master placed me within three Yards of her. [. . .] I had less Apprehension concerning the Dogs, whereof three or four came into the Room, as it is usual in Farmers Houses; one of which was a Mastiff equal in Bulk to four Elephants, and a Grey-hound somewhat taller than the Mastiff, but not so large. (II, i, pp. 102–4)

---

2    Here, Gulliver reveals (as he does so often) his own mathematical preoccupation, measuring and weighing everything. He thinks of himself as a scientist who thinks only in specific and demon-strable terms.

The following passage, frequently cited as evidence of Swift's misogyny (see Critical History, **pp. 50–2**), reveals Gulliver's horror at the sight of a Brobdingnagian breast (see Modern Criticism, **pp. 89–93**). Here, as in the preceding passage, Gulliver provides yet another example of the truth that nothing is actually large or small except by comparison. Gulliver realizes that had the Lilliputian ladies, whose skin seemed so perfect, been as large as the women of Brobdingnag, they would have seemed hideous as well. In keeping with the metaphor of the Great Chain of Being, philosophers taught that our senses were perfectly attuned to our place in the universe. We perceive exactly as much as we need to perceive. In his *Essay on Man*, Alexander Pope asks: 'Why has not Man a microscopic eye? / For this plain reason, Man is not a Fly' (Book I, ii, lines 193–4). But, as if confirming the King's assertion that he is but 'odious vermin', Gulliver does have a 'microscopic eye'. Throughout the second voyage Gulliver is plagued by the fact that he can see and hear things that others can't. He is harassed by the buzzing of flies and horrified at the slime they leave on his food – filth which is invisible to the 'Natives of that Country, whose large Opticks were not so acute as mine' (II, iii, p. 130). The following passage calls attention to the related topics of observation and optics that recur in the first two books of the *Travels*. Here the world is seen through a magnifying glass. And thus so tender a moment as the nursing of an infant becomes horrifying to Gulliver, for whom the mother's breast seems monstrous and disgusting.

WHEN Dinner was almost done, the Nurse came in with a Child of a Year old in her Arms; who immediately spyed me, and began a Squall that you might have heard from *London-Bridge* to *Chelsea*;[3] after the usual Oratory of Infants, to get me for a Play-thing. The Mother out of pure Indulgence took me up, and put me towards the Child, who presently seized me by the Middle, and got my Head in his Mouth, where I roared so loud that the Urchin was frighted, and let me drop; and I should infallibly have broke my Neck, if the Mother had not held her Apron under me. The Nurse to quiet her Babe made use of a Rattle, which was a Kind of hollow Vessel filled with great Stones, and fastned by a Cable to the Child's Waist: But all in vain, so that she was forced to apply the last Remedy by giving it suck. I must confess no Object ever disgusted me so much as the Sight of her monstrous Breast, which I cannot tell what to compare with, so as to give the curious Reader an Idea of its Bulk, Shape and Colour. It stood prominent six Foot, and could not be less than sixteen in Circumference. The Nipple was about half the Bigness of my Head, and the Hue both of that and the Dug so varified with Spots, Pimples and Freckles, that nothing could appear more nauseous: For I had a near Sight of her, she sitting down the more conveniently to give Suck, and I standing on the Table. This made me reflect upon the fair Skins of our *English* Ladies, who appear so beautiful to us, only because they are of our own Size, and their Defects not to be seen but through a magnifying Glass, where we

---

3   A distance of about five miles.

find by Experiment that the smoothest and whitest Skins look rough and coarse, and ill coloured.

I REMEMBER when I was at *Lilliput*, the Complexions of those diminutive People appeared to me the fairest in the World: And talking upon this Subject with a Person of Learning there, who was an intimate Friend of mine; he said, that my Face appeared much fairer and smoother when he looked on me from the Ground, than it did upon a nearer View when I took him up in my Hand, and brought him close; which he confessed was at first a very shocking Sight. He said, he could discover great Holes in my Skin; that the Stumps of my Beard were ten Times stronger than the Bristles of a Boar; and my Complexion made up of several Colours altogether disagreeable: Although I must beg Leave to say for my self, that I am as fair as most of my Sex and Country, and very little Sunburnt by all my Travels. On the other Side, discoursing of the Ladies in that Emperor's Court, he used to tell me, one had Freckles, another too wide a Mouth, a third too large a Nose; nothing of which I was able to distinguish. I confess this Reflection was obvious enough; which, however, I could not forbear, lest the Reader might think those vast Creatures were actually deformed: For I must do them Justice to say they are a comely Race of People; and particularly the Features of my Master's Countenance, although he were but a Farmer, when I beheld him from the Height of sixty Foot, appeared very well proportioned. (II, i, pp. 105–7)

## Chapter II

*A Description of the Farmer's Daughter. The* Author *carried to a Market-Town and then to the Metropolis. The Particulars of his Journey.*

The Brobdingnagian farmer takes Gulliver into town in order to exhibit him as a freakish curiosity, much in the fashion described by Dennis Todd (see Modern Criticism, pp. 76–9).

I WAS placed upon a Table in the largest Room of the Inn, which might be near three Hundred Foot square. My little Nurse stood on a low Stool close to the Table, to take care of me, and direct what I should do. My Master, to avoid a Crowd, would suffer only Thirty People at a Time to see me. I walked about on the Table as the Girl commanded; she asked me Questions as far as she knew my Understanding of the Language reached, and I answered them as loud as I could. I turned about several Times to the Company, paid my humble Respects, said they were welcome; and used some other Speeches I had been taught. I took up a Thimble filled with Liquor, which *Glumdalclitch* had given me for a Cup, and drank their Health. I drew out my Hanger,[4] and flourished with it after the Manner of Fencers in *England*. My Nurse gave me Part of a Straw, which I exercised as a Pike, having learned the Art in my Youth. I was that Day shewn to

---

4   Sword.

twelve Sets of Company; and as often forced to go over again with the same Fopperies, till I was half dead with Weariness and Vexation. For, those who had seen me, made such wonderful Reports, that the People were ready to break down the Doors to come in. (II, ii, pp. 114–15)

## Chapter III

*The Author sent for to Court. The Queen buys him of his Master the Farmer, and presents him to the King. He disputes with his Majesty's great Scholars. An Apartment at Court is provided for the Author. He is in high Favour with the Queen. He stands up for the Honour of his own Country. His Quarrels with the Queen's Dwarf.*

Fearing that Gulliver might die from overexertion, the Farmer sells him to the Queen and agrees that his daughter Glumdalclitch, who has served as Gulliver's nurse, can go with him. The Queen treats Gulliver as if he is some new form of pet: 'giving great Allowance for my Defectiveness in Speaking, was however surprised at so much Wit and good Sense in so diminutive an Animal' (II, iii, p. 121). The King makes a similar assumption, asking the Queen: 'How long it was since she grew fond of a *Splacknuck*; [an animal about the size of a man] for such it seems he took me to be' (II, iii, p. 121). Here we are introduced to the question of where in the Great Chain of Being from angels to amoebas we are intended to place human beings. Is Gulliver really nothing more than a *splacknuck*? This is the question that the King addresses to his wisest advisers who express bafflement as to where to 'place' Gulliver. Here Swift laughs at both Ancients and Moderns, suggesting that defining Gulliver as a 'freak of nature' is as meaningless as the old Aristotelian argument that objects fell down because they chose to do so (see Modern Criticism, **pp. 72–6**). At times Gulliver wonders where to place himself. 'Neither indeed could I forbear smiling at my self, when the Queen used to place me upon her Hand towards a Looking-Glass, by which both our Persons appeared before me in full View together; and there could nothing be more ridiculous than the Comparison: So that I really began to imagine my self dwindled many Degrees below my usual Size. (II, iii, p. 128)

THE King, although he be as learned a Person as any in his Dominions; and had been educated in the Study of Philosophy, and particularly Mathematicks; yet when he observed my Shape exactly, and saw me walk erect, before I began to speak, conceived I might be a piece of Clock-work, (which is in that Country arrived to a very great Perfection) contrived by some ingenious Artist.[5] But, when he heard my Voice, and found what I delivered to be regular and rational, he could not conceal his Astonishment. . . . His Majesty sent for three great Scholars

---

5   Swift's contemporaries were fascinated by clocks and also by various forms of automata which could move on their own. See Stuart Sherman, *Telling Time: Clocks, Diaries, and Diurnal Form* (Chicago, Ill.: University of Chicago Press, 1997), and John W. Yolton, *Thinking Matter: Materialism in Eighteenth-Century Britain* (Minneapolis, Minn.: University of Minnesota Press, 1983).

who were then in their weekly waiting (according to the Custom in that Country.) These Gentlemen, after they had a while examined my Shape with much Nicety, were of different Opinions concerning me. They all agreed that I could not be produced according to the regular Laws of Nature; because I was not framed with a Capacity of preserving my Life, either by Swiftness, or climbing of Trees, or digging Holes in the Earth. They observed by my Teeth, which they viewed with great Exactness, that I was a carnivorous Animal; yet most Quadrupeds being an Overmatch for me; and Field-Mice, with some others, too nimble, they could not imagine how I should be able to support my self, unless I fed upon Snails and other Insects; which they offered by many learned Arguments to evince that I could not possibly do. One of them seemed to think that I might be an Embrio, or abortive Birth.[6] But this Opinion was rejected by the other two, who observed my Limbs to be perfect and finished; and that I had lived several Years, as it was manifested from my Beard; the Stumps whereof they plainly discovered through a Magnifying-Glass. They would not allow me to be a Dwarf, because my Littleness was beyond all Degrees of Comparison; for the Queen's favourite Dwarf, the smallest ever known in that Kingdom, was near thirty Foot high. After much Debate, they concluded unanimously that I was only *Relplum Scalcath*, which is interpreted literally *Lusus Naturae*;[7] a Determination exactly agreeable to the Modern Philosophy of Europe: whose Professors, disdaining the old Evasion of occult Causes, whereby the Followers of Aristotle endeavour in vain to disguise their Ignorance; have invented this wonderful Solution of all Difficulties, to the unspeakable Advancement of human, Knowledge. (II, iii, pp. 121–3)

The King asks Gulliver a series of questions about the manners, religion, laws, government and learning in Europe. Gulliver answers him in language drawn from the world of false panegyric – that is, praise that is undeserved. Gulliver's description of England as 'the Arbitress of Europe, the Seat of Virtue', and so on, is as corrupt as the language he uses on several other occasions – as, for example, when he describes the Queen of Brobdingnag as the 'Ornament of Nature, the Darling of the World, the Delight of her subjects, the Phoenix of the Creation' (II, iii, p. 120), or when he describes the tiny Emperor of Lilliput as the 'Delight and Terror of the Universe, whose Dominions extend five Thousand Blustrugs (about twelve Miles in Circumference) to the Extremities of the Globe: Monarch of all Monarchs; Taller than the Sons of Men' (I, iii, p. 37). In the following passage, Swift combines moral satire on human pretensions to grandeur (see Modern Criticism, **pp. 89–93**) with Scriblerian satire on the abuses of language (see Contextual Overview, **pp. 10–12**).

6  The Scriblerians were fascinated by accounts of monstrous births like the report of Mary Tofts, who is said to have given birth to a number of baby rabbits. As Christopher Fox points out in 'Swift and the Spectacle of Science', *Reading Swift*, ed. Hermann J. Real and Helgard Stover-Leidig (Munich: Verlag, 1998), eighteenth-century observers were deeply interested in teratology or 'the study of monstrous living forms' (pp. 200 ff).
7  Literally, 'freak of nature', a definition that finally tells us nothing we didn't already know.

[The King's] Apprehension was so clear, and his Judgment so exact, that he made very wise Reflexions and Observations upon all I said. But, I confess, that after I had been a little too copious in talking of my own beloved Country; of our Trade, and Wars by Sea and Land, of our Schisms in Religion, and Parties in the State; the Prejudices of his Education prevailed so far, that he could not forbear taking me up in his right Hand, and stroaking me gently with the other; after an hearty Fit of laughing, asked me whether I were a *Whig* or a *Tory*. Then turning to his first Minister, who waited behind him with a white Staff, near as tall as the Main-mast of the Royal *Sovereign*;[8] he observed, how contemptible a Thing was human Grandeur, which could be mimicked by such diminutive Insects as I: And yet, said he, I dare engage, those Creatures have their Titles and Distinctions of Honour; they contrive little Nests and Burrows, that they call Houses and Cities; they make a Figure in Dress and Equipage; they love, they fight, they dispute, they cheat, they betray. And thus he continued on, while my Colour came and went several Times, with Indignation to hear our noble Country, the Mistress of Arts and Arms, the Scourge of *France*, the Arbitress of *Europe*, the Seat of Virtue, Piety, Honour and Truth, the Pride and Envy of the World, so contemptuously treated. (II, iii, pp. 126–7)

## Chapter V

*Several Adventures that happened to the Author. The Execution of a Criminal. The Author shews his Skill in Navigation.*

Throughout the second voyage, Gulliver's pride in his own person suffers one embarrassment after another. He nearly drowns when the Queen's dwarf (who is over 30 feet high) drops him head first into a bowl of cream; in bed he is attacked by rats; awake, he is set upon by wasps with stings an inch and a half long. He is nearly killed when apples 'near as large as a Bristol Barrel [see note 7 on p. 158] came tumbling about my Ears', and he is flattened by hailstones 'near Eighteen Hundred Times as large' as those in Europe (II, v, p. 140). The Queen's dwarf wedges Gulliver waist deep in a marrow bone; a monkey mistakes him for her offspring and tries to feed him; Gulliver falls down a mole hole, trips over a snail shell and, when attempting to demonstrate his own agility by jumping over a cowpat, falls up to his waist in fresh manure. In the following passage Gulliver recounts his struggles to protect himself against the birds.

I CANNOT tell whether I were more pleased or mortified to observe in those solitary Walks, that the smaller Birds did not appear to be at all afraid of me; but would hop about within a Yard Distance, looking for Worms, and other Food, with as much Indifference and Security as if no Creature at all were near them. I remember, a Thrush had the Confidence to snatch out of my Hand with his Bill, a Piece of Cake that *Glumdalclitch* had just given me for my Breakfast. When

---

8   A ship in the Royal Navy.

I attempted to catch any of these Birds, they would boldly turn against me, endeavouring to pick my Fingers, which I durst not venture within their Reach; and then they would hop back unconcerned to hunt for Worms or Snails, as they did before. But, one Day I took a thick Cudgel, and threw it with all my Strength so luckily at a Linnet, that I knocked him down, and seizing him by the Neck with both my Hands, ran with him in Triumph to my Nurse. However, the Bird who had only been stunned, recovering himself, gave me so many Boxes with his Wings on both Sides of my Head and Body, although I held him at Arms Length, and was out of the Reach of his Claws, that I was twenty Times thinking to let him go. But I was soon relieved by one of our Servants, who wrung off the Bird's Neck; and I had him next Day for Dinner by the Queen's Command. This Linnet, as near as I can remember, seemed to be somewhat larger than an *English* Swan.[9] (II, v, p. 142)

It is not just the wildlife that humiliates Gulliver, however. The Maids of Honour, the young women at court, also refuse to take him seriously, exposing themselves as if he is a creature of no consequence, the more playful among them going so far as to use Gulliver as a kind of sex toy. The following passage, like Gulliver's description of the enormous breast, has often been cited as evidence of Swift's hatred of the body, the female body in particular (see Critical History, **pp. 51–2**; Modern Criticism, **pp. 84–9**), but it also provides further evidence of that sense of human vulnerability that suffuses the Voyage to Brobdingnag. One also notes a kind of delight in magnifying the processes of excretion, since a hogshead holds 63 gallons and a wine cask, known as a 'tun', holds 252. Such heroic urination, like Gulliver's epic three-minute pee putting out the fire in Lilliput (see Key Passages, **pp. 133–4**), may owe something to the influence of Rabelais (see Contextual Overview, **pp. 6–7**).

THE Maids of Honour often invited *Glumdalclitch* to their Apartments, and desired she would bring me along with her, on Purpose to have the Pleasure of seeing and touching me. They would often strip me naked from Top to Toe, and lay me at full Length in their Bosoms; wherewith I was much disgusted; because, to say the Truth, a very offensive Smell came from their Skins; which I do not mention or intend to the Disadvantage of those excellent Ladies, for whom I have all Manner of Respect: But, I conceive, that my Sense was more acute in Proportion to my Littleness; and that those illustrious Persons were no more disagreeable to their Lovers, or to each other, than People of the same Quality are with us in *England*. And, after all, I found their natural Smell was much more supportable than when they used Perfumes, under which I immediately swooned away. I cannot forget, that an intimate Friend of mine in *Lilliput* took the Freedom in a warm Day, when I had used a good deal of Exercise, to complain of a strong Smell about me; although I am as little faulty that way as most of my Sex: But I suppose, his Faculty of Smelling was as nice with regard to me, as mine was to that of this

---

9 The best account of Gulliver's vulnerability is Paul Fussell, *The Rhetorical World of Augustan Humanism* (Oxford: Oxford University Press, 1965), pp. 127–32.

People. Upon this Point, I cannot forbear doing Justice to the Queen my Mistress, and *Glumdalclitch* my Nurse; whose Persons were as sweet as those of any Lady in *England*.

THAT which gave me most Uneasiness among these Maids of Honour, when my Nurse carried me to visit them, was to see them use me without any Manner of Ceremony, like a Creature who had no Sort of Consequence. For, they would strip themselves to the Skin, and put on their Smocks in my Presence, while I was placed on their Toylet[10] directly before their naked Bodies; which, I am sure, to me was very far from being a tempting Sight, or from giving me any other Motions than those of Horror and Disgust. Their Skins appeared so coarse and uneven, so variously coloured when I saw them near, with a Mole here and there as broad as a Trencher, and Hairs hanging from it thicker than Pack-threads; to say nothing further concerning the rest of their Persons. Neither did they at all scruple while I was by, to discharge what they had drunk, to the Quantity of at least two Hogsheads, in a Vessel that held above three Tuns. The handsomest among these Maids of Honour, a pleasant frolicksome Girl of sixteen, would sometimes set me astride upon one of her Nipples; with many other Tricks, wherein the Reader will excuse me for not being over particular. But, I was so much displeased, that I entreated *Glumdalclitch* to contrive some excuse for not seeing that young Lady any more. (II, v, pp. 143–4)

## Chapter VI

*Several Contrivances of the Author to please the King and Queen. He shews his Skill in Musick. The King enquires into the State of Europe, which the Author relates to him. The King's Observations thereon.*

In a series of conversations with the King, Gulliver describes his native country, including its parliament, courts and church. Gulliver's account raises more questions than it answers, however, and the King interrogates him about the various corruptions in political and genteel life that Gulliver has unwittingly described. (On Swift's satire on English politics see Modern Criticism, **pp. 106–11**.) The King's conclusion that human beings are a 'pernicious Race of little odious vermin' **(p. 146)** serves to link all the other images of Gulliver as a *splacknuck*, and an insect, and is perhaps the most damning indictment of human nature to be found in the *Travels*.

HE was perfectly astonished with the historical Account I gave him of our Affairs during the last Century; protesting it was only an Heap of Conspiracies, Rebellions, Murders, Massacres, Revolutions, Banishments; the very worst Effects that Avarice, Faction, Hypocrisy, Perfidiousness, Cruelty, Rage, Madness, Hatred, Envy, Lust, Malice, and Ambition could produce.

HIS Majesty in another Audience, was at the Pains to recapitulate the Sum of all I had spoken; compared the Questions he made, with the Answers I had given;

---

10 Dressing table.

then taking me into his Hands, and stroaking me gently, delivered himself in these Words, which I shall never forget, nor the Manner he spoke them in. My little Friend *Grildrig*; you have made a most admirable Panegyrick upon your Country. You have clearly proved that Ignorance, Idleness, and Vice are the proper Ingredients for qualifying a Legislator. That Laws are best explained, interpreted, and applied by those whose Interest and Abilities lie in perverting, confounding, and eluding them. I observe among you some Lines of an Institution, which in its Original might have been tolerable; but these half erased, and the rest wholly blurred and blotted by Corruptions. It doth not appear from all you have said, how any one Perfection is required towards the Procurement of any one Station among you; much less that Men are ennobled on Account of their Virtue, that Priests are advanced for their Piety or Learning, Soldiers for their Conduct or Valour, Judges for their Integrity, Senators for the Love of their Country, or Counsellors for their Wisdom. As for yourself (continued the King) who have spent the greatest Part of your Life in travelling; I am well disposed to hope you may hitherto have escaped many Vices of your Country. But, by what I have gathered from your own Relation, and the Answers I have with much Pains wringed and extorted from you; I cannot but conclude the Bulk of your Natives, to be the most pernicious Race of little odious Vermin that Nature ever suffered to crawl upon the Surface of the Earth. (II, vi, pp. 163–4)

## Chapter VII

*The Author's Love of his Country. He makes a Proposal of much Advantage to the King; which is rejected. The King's great Ignorance in Politicks. The Learning of that Country very imperfect and confined. Their Laws, and military Affairs, and Parties in the State.*

Gulliver is oblivious to the accuracy of the King's diagnosis. Rather than expressing sorrow at the corruptions and enormities he has just described, Gulliver blames the King for failing to understand the virtues of England. Swift loves to manipulate a cliché, and here he inverts the argument (sometimes made by Deists and freethinkers) that travel and exploration would reveal the parochialism of European attitudes. The King of Brobdingnag is among the most humane and civilized characters in any of the four voyages, and Gulliver's condescension to the King's presumed limitations is but one more example of the pride that blinds him to the significance of his own actions (see Modern Criticism, **pp. 89–93**).

NOTHING but an extreme Love of Truth could have hindred me from concealing this Part of my story. It was in vain to discover my Resentments, which were always turned into Ridicule: And I was forced to rest with Patience, while my noble and most beloved Country was so injuriously treated. I am heartily sorry as any of my Readers can possibly be, that such an Occasion was given: But this Prince happened to be so curious and inquisitive upon every Particular, that it could not consist either with Gratitude or good Manners to refuse giving him what Satisfaction I was able. Yet thus much I may be allowed to say in my own Vindication; that I artfully eluded many of his Questions; and gave to every Point a more favourable turn by many Degrees than the strictness of Truth would allow. For, I have always born that laudable Partiality to my own Country, which *Dionysius Halicarnassensis*[11] with so much Justice recommends to an Historian. I would hide the Frailties and Deformities of my Political Mother, and place her Virtues and Beauties in the most advantageous Light. This was my sincere Endeavour in those many Discourses I had with that Monarch, although it unfortunately failed of Success.

BUT, great Allowances should be given to a King who lives wholly secluded from the rest of the World, and must therefore be altogether unacquainted with the Manners and Customs that most prevail in other Nations: The want of which Knowledge will ever produce many *Prejudices*, and a certain *Narrowness of Thinking*; from which we and the politer Countries of *Europe* are wholly exempted. And it would be hard indeed, if so, remote a Prince's Notions of Virtue and Vice were to be offered as a Standard for all Mankind. (II, vii, pp. 165–6)

In order to show the King how limited his perspective truly is, Gulliver offers to share the secret of gunpowder, a technology that will give the King power he never dreamt of before. Swift may have intended Gulliver's defence of gunpowder to serve as an ironic commentary on the pretensions of the Moderns, who had praised the uses of gunpowder to expand colonial influence and extend the range of Christianity and trade, listing them among the most notable achievements of the Moderns. Once again, Gulliver is unprepared for the King's rejection of his barbarous proposal. In the course of Gulliver's enthusiastic description of the mayhem produced by gunpowder, Swift provides a series of vignettes drawn from the War of the Spanish Succession (1702–13) a bloody conflict that had sickened Swift. This is one of the most powerful passages in the *Travels*, dramatizing Swift's own hatred of warfare. This passage also dramatizes Swift's distrust of political science, a view he develops at greater length in his description of the 'School of Political Projectors' in Book III (not included here).

In hopes to ingratiate my self farther into his Majesty's Favour, I told him of an Invention discovered between three and four hundred Years ago, to make a certain Powder; into an heap of which the smallest Spark of Fire falling, would kindle the whole in a Moment, although it were as big as a Mountain; and make it all fly up in the Air together, with a Noise and Agitation greater than Thunder. That, a proper Quantity of this Powder rammed into an hollow Tube of Brass or Iron, according to its Bigness, would drive a Ball of Iron or Lead with such Violence and Speed, as nothing was able to sustain its Force. That, the largest Balls thus discharged, would not only Destroy whole Ranks of an Army at once; but batter the strongest Walls to the Ground; sink down Ships with a thousand Men in each, to the Bottom of the Sea; and when linked together by a Chain, would cut through Masts and

---

11 A historian and rhetorician in the age of Augustus whose great works included *Roman Antiquities* and the *Art of Rhetoric*.

Rigging; divide Hundreds of Bodies in the Middle, and lay all Waste before them. That we often put this Powder into large hollow Balls of Iron, and discharged them by an Engine into some City we were besieging; which would rip up the Pavement, tear the Houses to Pieces, burst and throw Splinters on every Side, dashing out the Brains of all who came near. That I knew the Ingredients very well, which were Cheap, and common; I understood the Manner of compounding them, and could direct his Workmen how to make those Tubes of a Size proportionable to all other Things in his Majesty's Kingdom; and the largest need not be above two hundred Foot long; twenty or thirty of which Tubes, charged with the proper Quantity of Powder and Balls, would batter down the Walls of the strongest Town in his Dominions in a few Hours; or destroy the whole Metropolis, if ever it should pretend to dispute his absolute Commands. This I humbly offered to his Majesty, as a small Tribute of Acknowledgment in return of so many Marks that I had received of his Royal Favour and Protection.

THE King was struck with Horror at the Description I had given of those terrible Engines, and the Proposal I had made. He was amazed how so impotent and groveling an Insect as I (these were his Expressions) could entertain such inhuman Ideas, and in so familiar a Manner as to appear wholly unmoved at all the Scenes of Blood and Desolation, which I had painted as the common Effects of those destructive Machines; whereof he said, some evil Genius, Enemy to Mankind, must have been the first Contriver. As for himself, he protested, that although few Things delighted him so much as new Discoveries in Art or in Nature; yet he would rather lose Half his Kingdom than be privy to such a Secret; which he commanded me, as I valued my Life, never to mention any more.

A Strange Effect of *narrow Principles* and *short Views!* that a Prince possessed of every Quality which procures Veneration, Love and Esteem; of strong Parts, great Wisdom and profound Learning; endued with admirable Talents for Government, and almost adored by his Subjects; should from a *nice unnecessary Scruple*, whereof in *Europe* we can have no Conception, let slip an Opportunity put Into his Hands, that would have made him absolute Master of the Lives, the Liberties, and the Fortunes of his People. [. . .] I take this Defect among them to have risen from their Ignorance; by not having hitherto reduced *Politicks* into a *Science*, as the more acute Wits of *Europe* have done. For, I remember very well, in a Discourse one Day with the King; when I happened to say, there were several thousand Books among us written upon the *Art of Government*; it gave him (directly contrary to my Intention) a very mean Opinion of our Understandings. He professed both to abominate and despise all *Mystery, Refinement*, and *Intrigue*, either in a Prince or a Minister. He could not tell what I meant by *Secrets of State*, where an Enemy or some Rival Nation were not in the Case. He confined the Knowledge of governing within very *narrow Bounds*; to common Sense and Reason, to Justice and Lenity, to the Speedy Determination of Civil and criminal Causes; with some other obvious Topicks which are not worth considering. And, he gave it for his Opinion; that whoever could make two Ears of Corn, or two Blades of Grass to grow upon a Spot of Ground where only one grew before; would deserve better of Mankind, and do more essential service to his Country, than the whole Race of Politicians put together. (II, vii, pp. 166–8).

## Chapter VIII

*The King and Queen make a Progress to the Fontiers. The Author attends them. The Manner in which he leves the Country very particularly related. He returns to England.*

Soon after this interview, the King travels out of his capital and, in the course of the journey, Gulliver's box, which has served him as a private chamber, is carried off by an eagle, who drops it into the sea where it floats until it is rescued by an English ship. Gulliver tells the captain of his adventures and to verify the truth of his narrative he shows the captain a series of rarities that he has collected, including a comb made from the stumps of the King's beard, a collection of pins and needles, each a foot to a yard and a half long, four wasp stings as big as carpenter's tacks, a corn as big as an apple cut from the toe of a maid of honour, and a gold ring given to him by the Queen which fits over his head like a collar. Some of these find their way into the collections of the Royal Society (see Contextual Overview, **pp. 12–13**). The captain, suitably impressed with Gulliver's tale, suggests that Gulliver ought to write a narrative of his travels, a chance for Gulliver, whose *Travels* we are reading, to complain that the age is already pestered with travel narratives, but if he were to write one it would be significantly differently from those which were currently popular. (On contemporary travel narratives, see Contemporary Documents, **pp. 32–3**.)

The Captain was very well satisfied with this plain Relation I had given him; and said, he hoped when we returned to *England*, I would oblige the World by putting it in Paper, and making it publick. My Answer was, that I thought we were already overstocked with Books of Travels: That nothing could now pass which was not extraordinary; wherein I doubted, some Authors less consulted Truth than their own Vanity or Interest, or the Diversion of ignorant Readers. That my Story could contain little besides common Events, without those ornamental Descriptions of strange Plants, Trees, Birds, and other Animals; or the barbarous Customs and Idolatry of savage People, with which most Writers abound. However, I thanked him for his good Opinion, and promised to take the Matter into my Thoughts. (II, viii, pp. 185–6)

# Part III: A Voyage to Laputa, Balnibarbi, Luggnagg, Glubbdubdrib and Japan

Part III (or Book III as it is generally known) was the last to be written, and it has often struck critics as the least unified of the four voyages. Here Gulliver encounters five different cultures, not just one, and the satiric focus is more widely diffused. Having learned nothing from his previous voyages about the values of staying at home with his wife and being made a financial offer he can't

**Figure 6 Map of Laputa and Balnibarbi.**

refuse, Gulliver sets sail once again as a ship's surgeon aboard the *Hopewell* bound for the East Indies. Gulliver is put in charge of a sloop filled with goods for traffic with the natives. The sloop is is captured by pirates who set Gulliver adrift in a canoe. After sailing for several days Gulliver reaches a substantial island where he is able to find food and water and a cave where he can rest. When he awakes and looks around, he discovers that a giant floating island is lowering itself over his head. Using his pocket telescope, he discovers that the island is populated by large numbers of people. Gulliver calls to the people above and they let down a chair and pull him up. This flying island may have been suggested by Lucian's *True Story* where we also find flying islands and by Cyrano de Bergerac's *Comical History of the States and Empires of the Worlds in the Moon and the Sun* (see Contemporary Documents, **p. 31**).

## Chapter II

*The Humours and Dispositions of the* Laputans *described. An Account of their Learning. Of the King and his Court. The Author's Reception there. The Inhabitants subject to Fears and Disquietudes. An Account of the Women.*

The people who inhabit this flying island are preoccupied with mathematics and music, disciplines that were frequently linked in the seventeenth and eighteenth centuries. Indeed, the Laputans are so abstracted that in order to get their attention, one must hit them in the ear or the mouth with a bag full of peas. These 'flappers' may serve to satirize the notions of Hobbes and Locke that all knowledge was initially derived from sense impression. Their metaphorical explanations of how images 'strike' the senses are here literalized as forms of physical contact.

Their Heads were all reclined either to the Right, or the Left; one of their Eyes turned inward, and the other directly up to the Zenith. Their outward Garments were adorned with the Figures of Suns, Moons, and Stars, interwoven with those of Fiddles, Flutes, Harps, Trumpets, Guittars, Harpsicords, and many more Instruments of Musick, unknown to us in *Europe*. I observed here and there many in the Habit of Servants, with a blown Bladder fastned like a Flail to the End of a short Stick, which they carried in their Hands. In each Bladder was a small Quantity of dried Pease, or little Pebbles (as I was afterwards informed). With these Bladders they now and then flapped the Mouths and Ears of those who stood near them, of which Practice I could not then conceive the Meaning. It seems, the Minds of these People are so taken up with intense Speculations, that they neither can speak, or attend to the Discourses of others, without being rouzed by some external Taction upon the Organs of Speech and Hearing; for which Reason, those Persons who are able to afford it, always keep a *Flapper* (the Original is *Climenole*) in their Family, as one of their Domesticks; nor ever walk abroad or make Visits without him. And the Business of this Officer is, when two or more

Persons are in Company, gently to strike with his Bladder the Mouth of him who is to speak, and the Right Ear of him or them to whom the Speaker addresseth himself. This *Flapper* is likewise employed diligently to attend his Master in his Walks, and upon Occasion to give him a soft Flap on his Eyes; because he is always so wrapped up in Cogitation, that he is in manifest Danger of falling down every Precipice, and bouncing his Head against every Post. (III, ii, pp. 198–9)

[. . .] Before the Throne, was a large Table filled with Globes and Spheres, and Mathematical Instruments of all Kinds. His Majesty took not the least Notice of us, although our Entrance were not without sufficient Noise, by the Concourse of all Persons belonging to the Court. But, he was then deep in a Problem, and we attended at least an Hour, before he could solve it. There stood by him on each Side, a young Page, with Flaps in their Hands; and when they saw he was at Leisure, one of them gently struck his Mouth, and the other his Right Ear; at which he started like one awaked on the sudden, and looking towards me, and the Company I was in, recollected the Occasion of our coming, whereof he had been informed before. He spoke some Words; whereupon immediately a young Man with a Flap came up to my Side, and flapt me gently on the Right Ear; but I made Signs as well as I could, that I had no Occasion for such an Instrument; which as I afterwards found, gave his Majesty and the whole Court a very mean Opinion of my Understanding. The King, as far as I could conjecture, asked me several Questions, and I addressed my self to him in all the Languages I had. When it was found, that I could neither understand nor be understood, I was conducted by his Order to an Apartment in his Palace (this Prince being distinguished above all his Predecessors for his Hospitality to Strangers), where two Servants were appointed to attend me. My Dinner was brought, and four Persons of Quality, whom I remembered to have seen very near the King's Person, did me the Honour to dine with me. We had two Courses, of three Dishes each. In the first Course, there was a Shoulder of Mutton, cut into an Equilateral Triangle; a Piece of Beef into a Rhomboides; and a Pudding into a Cycloid. The second Course was two Ducks, trussed up into the Form of Fiddles; Sausages and Puddings resembling Flutes and Haut-boys,[1] and a Breast of Veal in the Shape of a Harp. The Servants cut our Bread into Cones, Cylinders, Parallelograms, and several other Mathematical Figures. (III, ii, pp. 200–1)

> Throughout the *Travels*, but particularly in Book III, Swift laughs at all those who become so enamoured of their theories that they ignore the practical results. This foolish preoccupation with speculative music and mathematics is so severe and so literally distracting, that even if a wife dallies with a lover in front of her own husband, he is 'always so wrapped in Speculation, that the Mistress and Lover may proceed to the greatest Familiarities before his Face, if he be but provided with Paper and Implements and without the Flapper at his Side' (III, ii, p. 207). Although the Laputans are preoccupied with music, the music they actually produce with their instruments is discordant and deafening. When Gulliver asks what they are doing, he is told that 'the People of their Island had

---

1   Oboes.

their Ears adapted to hear the Musick of the Spheres' (III, ii, p. 204), an ironic reference to the notion popularized by Ptolemy, a first-century Greek mathematician, that as the planets turned in their spheres they produced music inaudible to the human ear. Not surprisingly, even the everyday language of the Laputans has been corrupted by their mathematical obsessions: 'Their Ideas are perpetually conversant in Lines and Figures. If they would, for Example, praise the Beauty of a Woman, or any other Animal, they describe it by Rhombs, Circles, Parallelograms, Ellipses, and other Geometrical Terms (III, ii, p. 204). The corruption of language is an important theme in the *Travels*. Everything we know about the countries Gulliver visits must be translated from what the residents tell him, which means there is always the danger that something will get lost in translation. Here Gulliver describes the process by which he acquires yet another strange tongue and provides a clear instance of Gulliver's preoccupation with the spoken word, a hobbyhorse he shares with Swift (see Modern Criticism, **pp. 102–6** and Critical History, **pp. 59–60**).

AFTER Dinner my Company withdrew, and a Person was sent to me by the King's Order, attended by a *Flapper*. He brought with him Pen, Ink, and Paper, and three or four Books; giving me to understand by Signs, that he was sent to teach me the Language. We sat together four Hours, in which Time I wrote down a great Number of Words in Columns, with the Translations over against them. I likewise made a Shift to learn several short Sentences. For my Tutor would order one of my Servants to fetch something, to turn about, to make a Bow, to sit, or stand, or walk, and the like. Then I took down the Sentence in Writing. He shewed me also in one of his Books, the Figures of the Sun, Moon, and Stars, the Zodiack, the Tropics, and Polar Circles, together with the Denominations of many Figures of Planes and Solids. He gave me the Names and Descriptions of all the Musical Instruments, and the general Terms of Art in playing on each of them. After he had left me, I placed all my Words with their Interpretations in alphabetical Order. And thus in a few Days, by the Help of a very faithful Memory, I got some Insight into their Language. (III, ii, pp. 201–2)

Every satire requires a positive standard, something against which follies and abuses can be measured. Throughout *Gulliver's Travels*, Swift praises those who produce practical improvements. He clearly approves the King of Brobdingnag's statement that a person who can make one ear of corn or one blade of grass grow is a more valuable citizen than all the politicians combined (see Key Passages, **p. 148**). Swift consistently ridicules those whose pretensions outrun their performance. Of all the creatures Gulliver encounters, the Laputans are perhaps the most foolish and inept.

THEIR Houses are very ill built, the Walls bevil,[2] without one right Angle in any Apartment; and this Defect ariseth from the Contempt they bear for

2  Bow outward.

practical Geometry; which they despise as vulgar and mechanick, those Instructions they give being too refined for the Intellectuals of their Workmen; which occasions perpetual Mistakes. And although they are dextrous enough upon a Piece of Paper in the Management of the Rule, the Pencil, and the Divider, yet in the common Actions and Behaviour of Life, I have not seen a more clumsy, awkward, and unhandy People, nor so slow and perplexed in their Conceptions upon all other Subjects, except those of Mathematicks and Musick. They are very bad Reasoners, and vehemently given to Opposition, unless when they happen to be of the right Opinion, which is seldom their Case. Imagination, Fancy, and Invention, they are wholly Strangers to, nor have any Words in their Language by which those Ideas can be expressed; the whole Compass of their Thoughts and Mind, being shut up within the two forementioned Sciences. (III, ii, pp. 204–5)

## Chapter III

*A Phoenomenon solved by modern Philosophy and Astronomy. The* Laputians *great Improvements in the latter. The King's Method of suppressing Insurrections.*

The Laputans can also be tyrannical, and Gulliver reports how the King ordered the Island to fly slowly over the mainland, letting down long threads to collect the petitions of the people. If the people grow restless or rebellious, however, the King orders the Island to hover causing drought or disease, and if necessary he will use the Island as a platform from which to bomb the mainland with heavy stones. Swift's emphasis on the Crown's ability to respond oppressively to the petitions of the people has been interpreted as a veiled allegory of Ireland's struggle to gain its own rights from England. This passage is seen as a fictionalized version of Ireland's rejection of an English scheme to allow an Englishman, William Wood, to mint a new currency for Ireland. Swift's *Drapier's Letters* (1724) served to galvanize public opinion against the new currency scheme, and the plan was withdrawn in 1725 – a clear victory for the Irish. In the process, Walpole's ministry offered a reward of £300 for the capture of the author of the *Drapier's Letters*, and it is a mark of Swift's popularity that no one turned him in, even though his identity as the author was widely known. This may be one of those episodes that Swift had in mind when he spoke of politicians in London taking offence (see Contemporary Documents, **pp. 26–8**). 'An allegorical passage added to later versions of the *Travels*, which was not included in either the 1726 or 1735 editions of Swift's works, describes a rebellion in Lindalino (Dublin), whose citizens (symbolizing the Irish) 'complained of great Oppressions' from the King of Lagado (England). The Lindalinians put large magnets on top of the city towers. When the King orders the Island to be lowered over Lindalino to intimidate the people, the force of the magnets pulls the Island down so fast that it threatens to destroy the Island, forcing the King to accede to their demands. To Swift's contemporaries this might have seemed like a veiled summons to rebellion and, hence, the passage was never included during Swift's lifetime.

IF any Town should engage in Rebellion or Mutiny, fall into violent Factions, or refuse to pay the usual Tribute; the King hath two Methods of reducing them to Obedience. The first and the mildest Course is by keeping the Island hovering over such a Town, and the Lands about it; whereby he can deprive them of the Benefit of the Sun and the Rain, and consequently afflict the Inhabitants with Dearth and Diseases.[3] And if the Crime deserve it, they are at the same time pelted from above with great Stones, against which they have no Defence, but by creeping into Cellars or Caves, while the Roofs of their Houses are beaten to Pieces. But if they still continue obstinate, or offer to raise Insurrections, he proceeds to the last Remedy, by letting the Island drop directly upon their Heads, which makes a universal Destruction both of Houses and Men. However, this is an Extremity to which the Prince is seldom driven, neither indeed is he willing to put it in Execution; nor dare his Ministers advise him to an Action, which as it would render them odious to the People, so it would be a great Damage to their own Estates that lie all below; for the Island is the King's Demesn.[4]

BUT there is still indeed a more weighty Reason, why the Kings of this Country have been always averse from executing so terrible an Action, unless upon the utmost Necessity. For if the Town intended to be destroyed should have in it any tall Rocks, as it generally falls out in the larger Cities; a Situation probably chosen at first with a View to prevent such a Catastrophe: Or if it abound in high Spires or Pillars of Stone, a sudden Fall might endanger the Bottom or under Surface of the Island, which although it consist as I have said, of one entire Adamant[5] two hundred Yards thick, might happen to crack by too great a Choque, or burst by approaching too near the Fires from the Houses below; as the Backs both of Iron and Stone will often do in our Chimneys. Of all this the People are well apprized, and understand how far to carry their Obstinacy, where their Liberty or Property is concerned. And the King, when he is highest provoked, and most determined to press a City to Rubbish, orders the Island to descend with great Gentleness, out of a Pretence of Tenderness to his People, but indeed for fear of breaking the Adamantine Bottom; in which Case it is the Opinion of all their Philosophers, that the Load-stone could no longer hold it up, and the whole Mass would fall to the Ground. (III, iii, pp. 215–17)

## Chapter IV

*The Author leaves* Laputa, *is conveyed to* Balnibarbi, *arrives at the Metropolis. A Description of the Metropolis and the Country adjoining. The Author hospitably received by a great Lord. His Conversation with that Lord.*

Eventually, Gulliver grows bored with his stay on the flying island of Laputa and persuades the King to let him visit the mainland below. Here he meets Lord Munodi, who takes him on a tour. As they travel through the countryside,

---

3 Possibly a reference to England's laws in restraint of Irish trade like the Woollen Act of 1699, which controlled what Ireland could export and in turn what it was required to import from England.
4 Territory.
5 A hard stone that is supposedly unbreakable.

Gulliver is astounded at the apparent foolishness and inefficiency of the rural population, and in Lagado, the capital city, Gulliver is shocked by the oddity of the people in the streets who 'walked fast, looked wild, their Eyes fixed, and were generally in rags' (III, iv, p. 220). The poverty and misery that Gulliver finds in Balnibarbi has much in common with the conditions of Ireland as they were described in *Drapier's Letters* and *A Modest Proposal*, as well as in a number of eighteenth-century pamphlets (see Contemporary Documents, **pp. 36–7**). Lord Munodi is a composite portrait modeled on Swift's friends Sir William Temple and Robert Harley. Unlike the other denizens of Laputa, who are besotted by mathematics and music, Munodi is an admirer of the Ancients and a beacon of good-humoured reason (see Freedman's discussion in Modern Criticism, **pp. 72–6**). Munodi's defence of Ancient principles calls to mind the arguments of Swift's great patron, Sir William Temple, whose *Essay Upon Ancient and Modern Learning* (1690) had provided inspiration for Swift's defence of Temple and Ancient learning in *The Battle of the Books* (1704).

I could not forbear admiring at these odd Appearances both in Town and Country; and I made bold to desire my Conductor, that he would be pleased to explain to me what could be meant by so many busy Heads, Hands and Faces, both in the Streets and the Fields, because I did not discover any good Effects they produced; but on the contrary, I never knew a Soil so unhappily cultivated, Houses so ill contrived and so ruinous, or a People whose Countenances and Habit expressed so much Misery and Want [. . .][6]

[. . .] During our Journey, he [Lord Munodi] made me observe the several Methods used by Farmers in managing their Lands; which to me were wholly unaccountable: For except in some very few Places, I could not discover one Ear of Corn, or Blade of Grass. But, in three Hours travelling, the Scene was wholly altered; we came into a most beautiful Country; Farmers Houses at small Distances, neatly built, the Fields enclosed, containing Vineyards, Corngrounds and Meadows. Neither do I remember to have seen a more delightful Prospect. His Excellency observed my Countenance to clear up; he told me with a Sigh, that there his Estate began, and would continue the same till we should come to his House. That his Countrymen ridiculed and despised him for managing his Affairs no better, and for setting so ill an Example to the Kingdom; which however was followed by very few, such as were old and wilful, and weak like himself.

WE came at length to the House, which was indeed a noble Structure, built according to the best Rules of ancient Architecture. The Fountains, Gardens, Walks, Avenues, and Groves were all disposed with exact Judgment and Taste. I gave due Praises to every Thing I saw, whereof his Excellency took not the least Notice till after Supper; when, there being no third Companion, he told me with a very melancholy Air, that he doubted he must throw down his Houses in Town and Country, to rebuild them after the present Mode; destroy all his Plantations,

---

6   On Irish landscape in the *Travels*, see Carole Fabricant, *Swift's Landscape* (Baltimore, Md.: Johns Hopkins University Press, 1982), Chapter 2.

and cast others into such a Form as modern Usage required; and give the same Directions to all his Tenants, unless he would submit to incur the Censure of Pride, Singularity, Affectation, Ignorance, Caprice; and perhaps; increase his Majesty's Displeasure. (III, iv, pp. 221–3)

## Chapter V

*The Author permitted to see the grand Academy of Lagado. The Academy largely described. The Arts wherein the Professors employ themselves.*

While visiting the capital city of Lagado, Gulliver is taken to visit the scientific academy, which is based on Gresham College, site of the meetings of the Royal Society of London for the Improving of Natural Knowledge. Chartered in 1662 by Charles II, the Royal Society was intended to encourage the pursuit of experimental science in England. Early members included Isaac Newton (England's greatest mathematician) and Christopher Wren, its greatest architect. Gulliver's description of the mad 'projectors' of the Academy of Lagado offers his most sustained attack on experimental science in early eighteenth-century England (see Modern Criticism, **pp. 72–6**). For Swift, 'projector' is a pejorative word implying impractical experimentation, utopian fantasy or political chicanery. The speaker in *A Modest Proposal* (1729), who recommends eating Irish infants, is a self-professed projector. All of the projectors in the Academy of Lagado are involved in ridiculous projects of one kind or another. The first man Gulliver meets 'had been Eight Years upon a Project for extracting Sun-Beams out of Cucumbers, which were to be put into Vials hermetically sealed, and let out to warm the Air in raw inclement Summers' (III, v, pp. 226–7). Another man, born blind, relies on touch and smell in an attempt to mix colours for painters; another is determined to extract gunpowder from ice; and, finally, one has found a new 'Device of plowing the Ground with Hogs, to save the Charges of Plows, Cattle, and Labour' (III, v, p. 228). Like the projector who seeks to propagate a breed of 'naked Sheep', this projector's solution creates more problems than it solves, since in order to make his plan work he must first bury at 6-inch intervals acorns, dates and chestnuts which the hogs will then root up with their snouts. Ever the optimist, though, Gulliver is not discouraged by the obvious disadvantages of this plan. And while he admits that the charge and trouble is very great, and they had 'little or no Crop', he expresses hope that 'this Invention may be capable of great Improvement' (III, v, pp. 228–9) (see Contemporary Documents, **pp. 34–6**).

I WENT into another Chamber, but was ready to hasten back, being almost overcome with a horrible Stink. My Conductor pressed me forward, conjuring me in a Whisper to give no Offence, which would be highly resented; and therefore I durst not so much as stop my Nose. The Projector of this Cell was the most ancient Student of the Academy. His Face and Beard were of a pale Yellow; his Hands and Clothes dawbed over with Filth. When I was presented to him, he gave me a very close Embrace, (a Compliment I could well have excused). His

Employment from his first coming into the Academy, was an Operation to reduce human Excrement to its original Food, by separating the several Parts, removing the Tincture which it receives from the Gall, making the Odour exhale, and scumming off the Saliva. He had a weekly Allowance from the Society, of a Vessel filled with human Ordure, about the Bigness of a *Bristol* Barrel. (III, v, p. 227)[7]

[. . .] I WENT into another Room, where the Walls and Ceiling were all hung round with Cobwebs, except a narrow Passage for the Artist to go in and out. At my Entrance he called aloud to me not to disturb his Webs. He lamented the fatal Mistake the World had been so long in of using Silk-Worms, while we had such plenty of domestick Insects, who infinitely excelled the former, because they understood how to weave as well as spin. And he proposed farther, that by employing Spiders, the Charge of dying Silks would be wholly saved; whereof I was fully convinced when he shewed me a vast Number of Flies most beautifully coloured, wherewith he fed his Spiders; assuring us, that the Webs would take a Tincture from them; and as he had them of all Hues, he hoped to fit every Body's Fancy, as soon as he could find proper Food for the Flies, of certain Gums, Oyls, and other glutinous Matter, to give a Strength and Consistence to the Threads. (III, v, p. 229)

> Combining two passages from the *Philosophical Transaction of the Royal Society*, Swift provides an account of the earliest versions of artificial respiration which makes the experiments seem ridiculous (see Contemporary Documents, **pp. 34–5** and Contextual Overview, **p. 5**).

I WAS complaining of a small Fit of the Cholick; upon which my Conductor led me into a Room, where a great Physician resided, who was famous for curing that Disease by contrary Operations from the same Instrument. He had a large Pair of Bellows, with a long slender Muzzle of Ivory. This he conveyed eight Inches up the Anus, and drawing in the Wind, he affirmed he could make the Guts as lank as a dried Bladder. But when the Disease was more stubborn and violent, he let in the Muzzle while the Bellows was full of Wind, which he discharged into the Body of the Patient; then withdrew the Instrument to replenish it, clapping his Thumb strongly against the Orifice of the Fundament; and this being repeated three or four Times, the adventitious Wind would rush out, bringing the noxious along with it (like Water put into a Pump) and the Patient recovers. I saw him try both Experiments upon a Dog, but could not discern any Effect from the former. After the latter, the Animal was ready to burst, and made so violent a Discharge, as was very offensive to me and my Companions. The Dog died on the Spot, and we left the Doctor endeavouring to recover him by the same Operation. (III, v, p. 230)

> Among the strangest of the scientists is one who is attempting to produce all literature and knowledge using a word machine. Here Swift reveals his contempt for the pretensions of all linguists, in particular Bishop John Wilkins

---

7    A barrel made in Bristol, England. It may be a commentary on Gulliver's penchant for precise measurement that he is careful to point out that the barrels of excrement in Lagado are exactly the same size as the apples in Brobdingnag (see Key Passages, p. 143).

(1614–72), a founder of the Royal Society of London, whose *Essay Towards a Real Character and a Philosophical Language* (1668) argued that a universal language scheme would 'reduce all things and notions into such a frame, as may express their natural order, dependence, and relations'.[8] It is just such a 'frame' that is depicted here, both in Gulliver's description and in the accompanying illustration (Figure 7).

THE first Professor I saw was in a very large Room, with Forty Pupils about him. After Salutation, observing me to look earnestly upon a Frame, which took up the greatest Part of both the Length and Breadth of the Room; he said, perhaps I might wonder to see him employed in a Project for improving speculative Knowledge by practical and mechanical Operations. But the World would soon be sensible of its Usefulness; and he flattered himself, that a more noble exalted Thought never sprang in any other Man's Head. Every one knew how laborious the usual Method is of attaining to Arts and Sciences; whereas by his Contrivance, the most ignorant Person at a reasonable Charge, and with a little bodily Labour, may write Books in Philosophy, Poetry, Politicks, Law, Mathematicks and Theology, without the least Assistance from Genius or Study. He then led me to the Frame, about the Sides whereof all his Pupils stood in Ranks. It was Twenty Foot square, placed in the Middle of the Room. The Superficies[9] was composed of several Bits of Wood, about the Bigness of a Dye,[10] but some larger than others. They were all linked together by slender Wires. These Bits of Wood were covered on every Square with Paper pasted on them; and on these Papers were written all the Words of their Language in their several Moods, Tenses, and Declensions, but without any Order. The Professor then desired me to observe, for he was going to set his Engine at work. The Pupils at his Command took each of them hold of an Iron Handle, whereof there were Forty fixed round the Edges of the Frame; and giving them a sudden Turn, the whole Disposition of the Words was entirely changed. He then commanded Six and Thirty of the Lads to read the several Lines softly as they appeared upon the Frame; and where they found three or four Words together that might make Part of a Sentence, they dictated to the four remaining Boys who were Scribes. This Work was repeated three or four Times, and at every Turn the Engine was so contrived, that the Words shifted into new Places, as the square Bits of Wood moved upside down.

Six Hours a-Day the young Students were employed in this Labour; and the Professor shewed me several Volumes in large Folio already collected, of broken Sentences, which he intended to piece together; and out of those rich Materials to give the World a compleat Body of all Arts and Sciences. (III, v, pp. 231–3)

---

8 John Wilkins, Essay Towards a Real Character and a Philosophical Language (London: Gallibrand, 1668) p. 1.
9 The outside surfaces.
10 A round piece of wood.

Plate.V.Part.III.

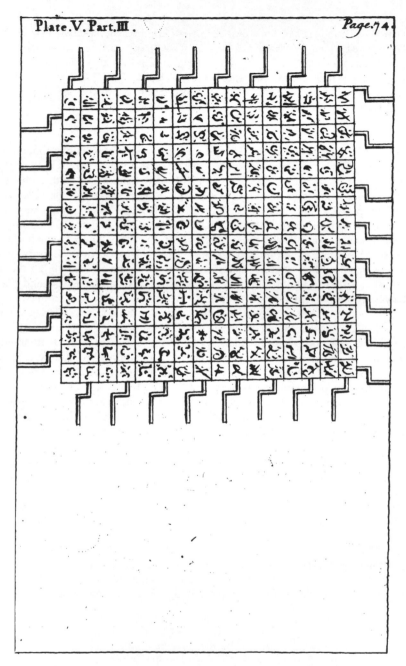

Figure 7 Word Frame of Lagado.

Gulliver next visits the School of Languages where the professors are seeking ways to improve the language of the country. Their first project is to cut all polysyllables into one and to leave out all verbs and participles, 'because in Reality all things imaginable are but Nouns'. This is a clear response to Thomas Sprat's recommendation that the Royal Society should aspire to express so many things in an equal number of words (see Contemporary Documents, **pp. 34–5**).

The other, was a Scheme for entirely abolishing all Words whatsoever. [. . .] An Expedient was therefore offered, that since Words are only Names for *Things*, it would be more convenient for all Men to carry about them, such *Things* as were necessary to express the particular Business they are to discourse on. And this Invention would certainly have taken Place, to the great Ease as well as Health of the Subject, if the Women in Conjunction with the Vulgar and Illiterate had not threatned to raise a Rebellion, unless they might be allowed the Liberty to speak with their Tongues, after the Manner of their Forefathers: Such constant irreconcileable Enemies to Science are the common People. However, many of the most Learned and Wise adhere to the new Scheme of expressing themselves by *Things*; which hath only this Inconvenience attending it; that if a Man's Business be very great, and of various Kinds, he must be obliged in Proportion to carry a greater Bundle of *Things* upon his Back, unless he can afford one or two strong Servants to attend him. I have often beheld two of those Sages almost sinking under the Weight of their Packs, like Pedlars among us; who when they met in the Streets would lay down their Loads, open their Sacks, and hold Conversation for an Hour together; then put up their Implements, help each other to resume their Burthens, and take their Leave.

BUT, for short Conversations a Man may carry Implements in his Pockets and under his Arms, enough to supply him, and in his House he cannot be at a Loss; therefore the Room where Company meet who practice this Art, is full of all *Things* ready at Hand, requisite to furnish Matter for this Kind of artificial Converse. (III, v, pp. 234–5)

## Chapter VII

*The Author leaves Lagado, arrives at* Maldonada. *No Ship ready. He takes a short Voyage to* Glubbdubdrib. *His Reception by the Governor.*

Tiring of Lagado and the island of Balnibarbi, Gulliver takes a side trip to the island of Glubbdubdrib, a land of magicians who have the power to summon up the dead, most of whom attempt to correct all the misinformation that has accumulated over the centuries. In what may be an imitation of Lucian's *True Story* (see Contemporary Documents, **pp. 29–30**), Alexander the Great tells Gulliver that 'he was not poisoned, but dyed of a Fever by excessive Drinking'. Gulliver sees Hannibal crossing the Alps who tells him that 'he had not a

Drop of Vinegar in his Camp' (III, vii, p. 249), an apparent rejection of Livy's account in Book XXI, Chapter 37, that when a large rock stopped the progress of Hannibal's army through the Italian Alps, his men heated the rock, then saturated it with vinegar so it could be more easily cut. Throughout the Glubb-dubdrib episode, Gulliver draws attention to the size, strength and virtue of the Ancients in contrast to the corruption that has afflicted the Moderns (see Modern Criticism, pp. 72–6).

I saw *Caesar* and *Pompey* at the Head of their Troops just ready to engage. I saw the former in his last great Triumph. I desired that the Senate of *Rome* might appear before me in one large Chamber, and a modern Representative, in Counterview, in another. The first seemed to be an Assembly of Heroes and Demy-Gods; the other a Knot of Pedlars, Pick-Pockets, Highwaymen and Bullies. (III, vii, pp. 249)

## Chapter VIII

*A further Account of Glubbdubdrib. Antient and Modern History Corrected.*

Swift also introduces more literary heroes, and in his description of the appearance and behaviour of Homer and Aristotle, he continues the assault on modern commentators and critics begun in *The Battle of the Books*. When the commentators are introduced to Homer and Aristotle, the Ancient heroes lose patience with modern expositors who had misrepresented their work and traduced their true genius. In the process of calling up various figures from history, Gulliver discovers how much the world has declined and how much of what passes for history is actually a tissue of lies (see Contemporary Documents, pp. 29–30 and Modern Criticism, pp. 72–6). In *A Tale of a Tub* (1704) Swift had referred to historians as 'mercenaries', and his 'disgust' with modern historians expressed here calls to mind Voltaire's remark that 'history is only a pack of lies we play on the dead'.[11]

I was chiefly disgusted with modern History. For having strictly examined all the Persons of greatest name in the Courts of Princes for an Hundred Years past, I found how the World had been misled by prostitute Writers, to ascribe the greatest Exploits in War to Cowards, the wisest Counsels to Fools, Sincerity to Flatterers, *Roman* Virtue to Betrayers of their Country, Piety to Atheists, Chastity to Sodomites, Truth to Informers.

How many innocent and excellent Persons had been condemned to Death or Banishment, by the practising of great Ministers upon the Corruption of Judges, and the Malice of Factions. How many Villains had been exalted to the highest

---

11  Louis Landa, *Gulliver's Travels and Other Writings* (Boston, Mass.: Riverside Houghton, 1960) pp. 513–14.

Places of Trust, Power, Dignity, and Profit: How great a Share in the Motions and Events of Courts, Councils, and Senates might be challenged by Bawds, Whores, Pimps, Parasites, and Buffoons: How low an Opinion I had of human Wisdom and Integrity, when I was truly informed of the Springs and Motives of great Enterprizes and Revolutions in the World, and of the contemptible Accidents to which they owed their Success. (III, viii, pp. 254–5)

## Chapter X

*The Luggnaggians commended. A particular Description of the Struldbruggs, with many Conversations between the Author and some Eminent Persons upon that Subject.*

Gulliver then travels to the Kingdom of Luggnagg, where he hears of strange creatures called Struldbruggs who live forever. Apparently having forgotten his outburst on the corruptions of the past, Gulliver cries out in rapture: 'Happy Nation, where every Child hath at least a Chance for being immortal!' (III, x, p. 265). As Gulliver's interpreter warns him, however, all is not what it seems, and those who wish for long lives suppose that they will always be young, healthy and vigorous. In his *Thoughts on Various Subjects* (PW, IV, p. 246), Swift had written that 'Every man desires to live long, but no man would be old', sentiments seemingly echoed by Gulliver's host, for whom the question is not whether 'a Man would chuse to be always in the Prime of Youth, attended with Prosperity and Health; but how he would pass a perpetual Life under all the usual Disadvantages which old Age brings along with it' (III, x, p. 270). This is the lesson enforced by the example of the Struldbruggs who cure Gulliver's desire for immortality, which contributed to charges that he was a misanthrope (see Critical History, **pp. 49–50** and Modern Criticism, **pp. 89–93**).

He said they commonly acted like Mortals, till about Thirty Years old, after which by Degrees they grew melancholy and dejected, increasing in both till they came to Fourscore. This he learned from their own Confession; for otherwise there not being above two or three of that Species born in an Age, they were too few to form a general Observation by. When they came to Fourscore Years, which is reckoned the Extremity of living in this Country, they had not only all the Follies and Infirmities of other old Men, but many more which arose from the dreadful Prospect of never dying. They were not only opinionative, peevish, covetous, morose, vain, talkative; but uncapable of Friendship, and dead to all natural Affection, which never descended below their Grand-children. Envy and impotent Desires, are their prevailing Passions. But those Objects against which their Envy seems principally directed, are the Vices of the younger Sort, and the Deaths of the old. By reflecting on the former, they find themselves cut off from all Possibility of Pleasure; and whenever they see a Funeral, they lament and repine that others are gone to an Harbour of Rest, to which they themselves never can hope to arrive. They have no Remembrance of any thing but what they learned and observed in their Youth and middle Age, and even that is very imperfect: And for the Truth or

Particulars of any Fact, it is safer to depend on common Traditions than upon their best Recollections. The least miserable among them, appear to be those who turn to Dotage, and entirely lose their Memories; these meet with more Pity and Assistance, because they want many bad Qualities; which abound in others.

[. . .] As soon as they have compleated the Term of Eighty Years, they are looked on as dead in Law; their Heirs immediately succeed to their Estates, only a small Pittance is reserved for their Support; and the poor ones are maintained at the publick Charge. After that Period they are held incapable of any Employment of Trust or Profit; they cannot purchase Lands, or take Leases, neither are they allowed to be Witnesses in any Cause, either Civil or Criminal, not even for the Decision of Meets and Bounds.

At Ninety they lose their Teeth and Hair; they have at that Age no Distinction of Taste, but eat and drink whatever they can get, without Relish or Appetite. The Diseases they were subject to, still continue without encreasing or diminishing. In talking they forget the common Appellation of Things, and the Names of Persons, even of those who are their nearest Friends and Relations. For the same Reason they never can amuse themselves with reading, because their Memory will not serve to carry them from the Beginning of a Sentence to the End; and by this Defect they are deprived of the only Entertainment whereof they might otherwise be capable.

The Language of this Country being always upon the Flux, the *Struldbruggs* of one Age do not understand those of another; neither are they able after two Hundred Years to hold any Conversation (farther than by a few general Words) with their Neighbours the Mortals; and thus they lye under the Disadvantage of living like Foreigners in their own Country.

[. . .] They were the most mortifying Sight I ever beheld; and the Women more horrible than the Men. [. . .] The Reader will easily believe, that from what I had heard and seen, my keen appetite for Perpetuity of Life was much abated. I grew heartily ashamed of the pleasing Visions I had formed; and thought no Tyrant could invent a Death into which I would not run with Pleasure from such a Life. (III, x, pp. 271–4)

> Gulliver soon leaves Luggnagg and sails to Japan, and from there to Amsterdam and then home.

# Part IV: A Voyage to the Country of the Houyhnhnms

> Gulliver stays at home with his family for five months. But after that time, he is tempted to go to sea once again, this time as the Captain of the *Adventure*, a merchant vessel. His crew having fallen ill, Gulliver lands in the Barbadoes to recruit new sailors. Unfortunately, most of these men are seasoned buccaneers who mutiny against Gulliver, hold him prisoner below decks and eventually set

him ashore on an unknown island. Once again, Gulliver determines to pacify the natives with 'some Bracelets, Glass Rings, and other Toys, which Sailors usually provide themselves with in those Voyages, and whereof I had some about me' (IV, i, p. 284). A bit like Robinson Crusoe who finds a footprint in the sand and knows that he is no longer alone on the island, Gulliver sees the tracks of human feet and those of horses. (On Swift and Defoe, see Contemporary Documents, **pp. 69–71** and Critical History, **pp. 54–5**.) Gulliver is surprised to discover that the human footprints have been made by the most noisome creatures he has ever seen (see Contemporary Documents, **pp. 37–8**).

## Chapter I

*The Author sets out as Captain of a Ship. His Men conspire against him, confine him a long Time to his Cabbin, set him on Shore in an unknown Land. He travels up into the Country. The* Yahoos, *a strange Sort of Animal, described. The Author meets two* Houyhnhnms.

Their Heads and Breasts were covered with a thick Hair, some frizzled and others lank; they had Beards like Goats and a Long Ridge of Hair down their Backs, and the fore Parts of their Legs and Feet; but the rest of their Bodies were bare, so that I might see their Skins, which were of a brown Buff Colour. They had no Tails, nor any Hair at all on their Buttocks, except about the *Anus*; which, I presume Nature had placed there to defend them as they sat on the Ground; for this Posture they used, as well as lying down, and often stood on their hind Feet. They climbed high Trees, as nimbly as a Squirrel, for they had strong extended Claws before and behind, terminating in sharp Points, and hooked. They would often spring, and bound, and leap with prodigious Agility. The Females were not so large as the Males; they had long lank Hair on their Heads, and only a Sort of Down on the rest of their Bodies, except about the *Anus* and *Pudenda*. Their Dugs hung between their fore Feet, and often reached almost to the Ground as they walked. The Hair of both Sexes was of several Colours, brown, red, black and yellow. Upon the whole, I never beheld in all my Travels so disagreeable an Animal, or one against which I naturally conceived so strong an Antipathy. (IV, i, pp. 284–5)

## Chapter II

*The Author conducted by a* Houyhnhnm *to his House. The House described. The Author's Reception. The Food of the* Houyhnhnms. *The Author in Distress for want of Meat, is at last relieved. His Manner of feeding in that Country.*

Gulliver's disgust with these creatures is not lessened when they all jump into the tree beneath which he is standing and 'discharge their Excrements' on his head. Gulliver is rescued by one of the horses he has seen standing in the field.

Thinking that this horse will lead to the masters of the island, from whom he can buy his freedom with the trinkets he has brought, Gulliver follows only to encounter more horses busily employed in 'domestick Business'. Gulliver is stunned to discover that these horses *are* the masters, and he is mortified to find that these creatures, called 'Houyhnhnms', assume that he himself is one of the 'Yahoos', from whom he had just been rescued. He is even more shocked when the Houyhnhnm mare places Gulliver side by side with one of 'those detestable Creatures, which I first met after my landing' (IV, ii, p. 203) in order to compare them. The description of the Yahoos that follows has much in common with descriptions of the Hottentots and Pygmies found in contemporary writings by Tyson and Buffon (see Contemporary Documents, **pp. 37–8**). This passage, and those that follow, also provide the most sustained exercise in cultural comparison that we encounter in the *Travels* (see also Gulliver's adventures in Brobdingnag, Key Passages, **p. 136**).

The Beast and I were brought close together; and our Countenances diligently compared, both by Master and Servant, who thereupon repeated several Times the Word *Yahoo*. My Horror and Astonishment are not to be described, when I observed, in this abominable Animal, a perfect human Figure; the Face of it indeed was flat and broad, the Nose depressed; the Lips large, and the Mouth wide: But these Differences are common to all savage Nations, where the Lineaments of the Countenance are distorted by the Natives suffering their Infants to lie grovelling on the Earth, or by carrying them on their Backs, nuzzling with their Face against the Mother's Shoulders. The Fore-feet of the *Yahoo* differed from my Hands in nothing else, but the Length of the Nails, the Coarseness and Brownness of the Palms, and the Hairiness on the Backs. . . . For as to those filthy Yahoos, although there were few greater Lovers of Mankind, at that time, than myself; yet I confess I never saw any sensitive Being so detestable on all Accounts; and the more I came near them, the more hateful they grew, while I stayed, in that Country. (IV, ii, p. 294–5)

### Chapter III

*The Author studious to learn the Language, the* Houyhnhnm *his Master assists in teaching him. The Language described. Several* Houyhnhnms *of Quality come out of Curiosity to see the Author. He gives his Master a short Account of his Voyage.*

Gulliver soon begins to admire the habits of the Houyhnhnms, who seem to be as civilized as the Yahoos are bestial, and he undertakes to learn the Houyhnhnm language which 'they produce through the nose and throat like High Dutch or German' (IV, iii, pp. 299–300). Once again, Swift directs our attention to the importance of the spoken word in the *Travels* (see also Key Passages, **pp. 153, 159–61** and Critical History, **pp. 58–9**). But as this passage also suggests, the absence of books or of literature may constitute a significant lacuna in this ideal Houyhnhnm society (see Modern Criticism, **pp. 102–6**). Swift may also suggest that the Houyhnhnms are less than perfect, since their language sounds like German, or 'High Dutch' as it was sometimes known – the language of George I and his courtiers, a language that was frequently ridiculed by Swift and his friends.

My principal Endeavour was to learn the Language, which my Master (for so I shall henceforth call him) and his Children, and every Servant of his House were desirous to teach me. For they looked upon it as a Prodigy, that a brute Animal should discover such Marks of a rational Creature. I pointed to every thing, and enquired the Name of it, which I wrote down in my *Journal Book*, when I was alone, and corrected my bad Accent, by desiring those of the Family to pronounce it often. [. . .]

In speaking, they pronounce through the Nose and Throat, and their Language approaches nearest to the *High Dutch* or *German*, of any I know in *Europe*; but is much more graceful, and more significant. The Emperor *Charles V.* made almost he same Observation, when he said, That if he were to speak to his Horse, it should be in *High Dutch*.

[. . .] To help my Memory, I formed all I learned into the *English* Alphabet, and writ the Words down with the Translations. This last, after some time, I ventured to do in my Master's Presence. It cost me much Trouble to explain to him what I was doing; for the Inhabitants have not the least Idea of Books or Literature. (IV, iii, p. 300)

The Houyhnhnms are confused by Gulliver's account of where he comes from and how he was cast ashore by a mutinous crew. Their opinion of his capacities is so low that they cannot imagine how such a species could build a boat or sail it. This is an important passage, because it suggests both the simplicity of the Houyhnhnms, who are quite mistaken about the capacities of human beings – Yahoos to them – and the simplicity of Gulliver, who takes at face value the Houyhnmhnms' claim that because they lack a word for lying, they are therefore incapable of falsehood. Critics have questioned just how seriously we are to take the Houyhnhnms' claims of perfection (see Modern Criticism, **pp. 89–93**), just as they have wondered how Swift intends for us to define human nature. Gulliver seemingly allows himself to be defined as one who has been 'taught to imitate a rational Creature; because the Yahoos whom he saw exactly resembled in my Head, Hands and Face, that were only visible) with some Appearance of Cunning, and the strongest Disposition to Mischief, were observed to be the most unteachable of all Brutes' (IV, iii, p. 301). Swift suggests a number of questions here: Is Gulliver rational? Is he merely feigning rationality, like the Yahoos? Or he is something else, '*rationis capax*' (capable of reason) as Swift had originally said? (see also Contextual Overview, **pp. 15–18**, Contemporary Documents, **p. 36**).

He replied, That I must needs be mistaken, or that I *said the thing which was not*. (For they have no Word in their Language to express Lying or Falshood.) He knew it was impossible that there could be a Country beyond the Sea, or that a Parcel of Brutes could move a wooden Vessel whither they pleased upon Water. He was sure no *Houyhnhnm* alive could make such a Vessel, or would trust *Yahoos* to manage it.

THE Word *Houyhnhnm*, in their Tongue, signifies a *Horse*; and in its Etymology, *the Perfection of Nature*. I told my Master, that I was at a Loss for Expression, but would improve as fast as I could; and hoped in a short time I should be able to tell him Wonders: He was pleased to direct his own Mare, his Colt and Fole, and the Servants of the Family to take all Opportunities of instructing me; and every Day for two or three Hours, he was at the same Pains himself: Several Horses and Mares of Quality in the Neighbourhood came often to our House, upon the Report spread of a wonderful *Yahoo*, that could speak like a *Houyhnhnm*, and seemed in his Words and Actions to discover some Glimmerings of Reason. (IV, iii, pp. 301–2)

> The fact that native populations frequently appear naked without any fear or embarrassment is a constant matter of interest to early travel reporters (see Foigny's account in Contemporary Documents, **pp. 3 1–2**). Nakedness becomes an important issue in *Gulliver's Travels* as well, for the Houyhnhnms are curious about Gulliver's strange skin that seems so different from the skin of the Yahoos. The Houyhnhnms have 'no conception' of clothing, and as long as they last, Gulliver's clothes preserve the illusion that he is fundamentally different than the Yahoos. However, Gulliver's secret is discovered when, during the night, the covers fall away to reveal that his skin is different to the clothes that cover it, 'that I was not the same Thing when I slept as I appeared to be at other times' (IV, iii, p. 302). Questions of exactly what sort of 'Thing' Gulliver might be are central to the discussion here.

I HAD hitherto concealed the Secret of my Dress, in order to distinguish myself as much as possible, from that cursed Race of *Yahoos*; but now I found it in vain to do so any longer. [. . .] I therefore told my Master, that in the Country from whence I came, those of my Kind always covered their Bodies with the Hairs of certain Animals prepared by Art, as well for Decency, as to avoid Inclemencies of Air both hot and cold; of which, as to my own Person I would give him immediate Conviction, if he pleased to command me; only desiring his Excuse, if I did not expose those Parts that Nature taught us to conceal. He said, my Discourse was all very strange, but especially the last Part; for he could not understand why Nature should teach us to conceal what Nature had given. That neither himself nor Family were ashamed of any Parts of their Bodies; but however I might do as I pleased. Whereupon, I first unbuttoned my Coat, and pulled it off. I did the same with my Wastecoat; I drew off my Shoes, Stockings and Breeches. I let my Shirt down to my Waste, and drew up the Bottom, fastening it like a Girdle about my Middle to hide my Nakedness.

My Master observed the whole Performance with great Signs of Curiosity and

Admiration. He took up all my Cloaths in his Pastern,[1] one Piece after another, and examined them diligently; he then stroaked my Body very gently, and looked round me several Times; after which he said, it was plain I must be a perfect *Yahoo*; but that I differed very much from the rest of my Species, in the Whiteness, and Smoothness of my Skin, my want of Hair in several Parts of my Body, the Shape and Shortness of my Claws behind and before, and my Affectation of walking continually on my two hinder Feet. He desired to see no more; and gave me leave to put on my Cloaths again. (IV, iii, pp. 303–4)

## Chapter IV

*The* Houyhnhnms *Notion of Truth and Falshood. The Author's Discourse disapproved by his Master. The Author gives a more particular Account of himself, and the Accidents of his Voyage.*

The Master Houyhnhnm questions Gulliver's assertion that Yahoos are the 'governing Animals' in England, and he is shocked at Gulliver's insistence that in Europe humans – that is, Yahoos – use Houyhnhnms as beasts of burden, going so far as to castrate horses to make them more tractable. Gulliver keeps talking and his Master tries desperately to 'place' him within a taxonomy that includes only Houyhnhnms and Yahoos. For critics who insist that Gulliver is meant to be seen neither as neither Yahoo nor Houyhnhnm, this simple dichotomy is interpreted as a weakness of Houyhnhnm reason (see Modern Criticism, **pp. 89–93**).

He said I differed indeed from other *Yahoos*, being much more cleanly, and not altogether so deformed; but in point of real Advantage, he thought I differed for the worse. That my Nails were of no Use either to my fore or hinder Feet: As to my fore Feet, he could not properly call them by that Name, for he never observed me to walk upon them; that they were too soft to bear the Ground; that I generally went with them uncovered, neither was the Covering I sometimes wore on them, of the same Shape, or so strong as that on my Feet behind. That I could not walk with any Security; for if either of my hinder Feet slipped, I must inevitably fall. He then began to find fault with other Parts of my Body; the Flatness of my Face, the Prominence of my Nose, mine Eyes placed directly in Front, so that I could not look on either Side without turning my Head: That I was not able to feed my self, without lifting one of my fore Feet to my Mouth: And therefore Nature had placed those Joints to answer that Necessity. He knew not what could be the Use of those several Clefts and Divisions in my Feet behind; that these were too soft to bear the Hardness and Sharpness of Stones without a Covering made from the Skin of some other Brute; that my whole Body wanted a Fence against Heat and Cold, which I was forced to put on and off every Day with Tediousness and Trouble. And lastly, that he observed every Animal in this Country naturally to abhor the *Yahoos*, whom the Weaker avoided, and the Stronger drove from them. So that

---

1  Part of the horse's hoof between the fetlock joint and the upper edge of the hoof.

supposing us to have the Gift of Reason, he could not see how it were possible to cure that natural Antipathy which every Creature discovered against us; nor consequently, how we could tame and render them serviceable. (IV, iv, pp. 310–11)

> The Houyhnhnm Master asks Gulliver to describe his native country, and the adventures that led him to Houyhnhnmland, but here, as in Brobdingnag, Gulliver has difficulty making his Master understand (see Key Passages, **pp. 146–7**). Once again we find Gulliver faced with the impossibility of finding language suitable to describe the corruption and brutality of the system he seeks to commend. It takes Gulliver several days and numerous circumlocutions to describe the whole notion of crime, which had forced Gulliver's fellow mariners to flee their native country in the first place.

He was wholly at a Loss to know what could be the Use or Necessity of practising those Vices. To clear up which I endeavoured to give him some Ideas of the Desire of Power and Riches; of the terrible Effects of Lust, Intemperance, Malice, and Envy. All this I was forced to define and describe by putting of Cases, and making Suppositions. After which, like one whose Imagination was struck with something never seen or heard of before, he would lift up his Eyes with Amazement and Indignation. Power, Government, War, Law, Punishment, and a Thousand other Things had no Terms, wherein that Language could express them; which made the Difficulty almost insuperable to give my Master any Conception of what I meant: But being of an excellent Understanding, much improved by Contemplation and Converse, he at last arrived at a competent Knowledge of what human Nature in our Parts of the World is capable to perform; and desired I would give him some particular Account of that Land, which we call *Europe*, especially, of my own Country. (IV, iv, pp. 313–14)

## Chapter V

*The Author at his Master's Commands informs him of the State of* England. *The Causes of War among the Princes of* Europe. *The Author begins to explain the* English *Constitution.*

> The Master Houyhnhnm spends hours listening as Gulliver describes the Glorious Revolution (1688) in which William of Orange was invited to assume the throne vacated by James II. He also describes the war with France, which William had begun in 1688, which had continued with occasional interruptions until 1713, and in which about 'a Million of Yahoos' had been killed. Gulliver tries once more to explain the differences between Protestants and Catholics that often lay at the heart of the political conflicts in Europe as a whole and in England in particular. Gulliver explains that these conflicts involved debates over transubstantiation, whether the bread and wine of the Eucharist were merely symbolic (the Anglican position) or whether they actually become the body and blood of Christ (Roman Catholic doctrine). Here, whistling alludes to the use of music in church services, kissing the post refers to the veneration of

> the crucifix and the coats to wearing clerical vestments – all 'indifferent' forms
> of liturgical ritual that had been rejected by Puritan reformers, whom Swift
> detested. (On Swift's hatred of Puritans and religious Nonconformists, see
> Contextual Overview, **p. 5**).

He asked me what were the usual Causes or Motives that made one Country go to
War with another. I answered, they were innumerable; but I should only mention
a few of the chief. Sometimes the Ambition of Princes, who never think they have
Land or People enough to govern: Sometimes the Corruption of Ministers, who
engage their Master in a War in order to stifle or divert the Clamour of the
Subjects against their evil Administration. Difference in Opinions hath cost many
Millions of Lives: For Instance, whether *Flesh* be *Bread*, or *Bread* be *Flesh*:
Whether the Juice of a certain *Berry* be *Blood* or *Wine*: Whether *Whistling* be a
Vice or a Virtue: Whether it be better to *kiss a Post*; or throw it into the Fire: What
is the best Colour for a *Coat*, whether *Black*, *White*, *Red* or *Grey*; and whether
it should be *long* or *short, narrow* or *wide, dirty* or *clean*; with many more,
Neither are any Wars so furious and bloody, or of so long Continuance, as those
occasioned by Difference in Opinion, especially if it be in things indifferent.
[. . .] If a Prince send Forces into a Nation, where the People are poor and ignorant, he may lawfully put half of them to Death, and make Slaves of the rest, in
order to civilize and reduce them from their barbarous Way of Living.[2] It is a very
kingly, honourable, and frequent Practice, when one Prince desires the Assistance
of another to secure him against an Invasion, that the Assistant, when he hath
driven out the Invader, should seize on the Dominions himself, and kill, imprison
or banish the Prince he came to relieve. Allyance by Blood or Marriage, is a
sufficient Cause of War between Princes; and the nearer the Kindred is, the greater
is their Disposition to quarrel: *Poor* Nations are *hungry*, and *rich* Nations are
*proud*; and Pride and Hunger will ever be at Variance. For these Reasons, the
Trade of a *Soldier* is held the most honourable of all others: Because a *Soldier* is a
*Yahoo* hired to kill in cold Blood as many of his own Species, who have never
offended him, as possibly he can. (IV, v, pp. 316–17)

> Gulliver's attempt to translate European action into terms the Houyhnhnms
> can understand serves to amplify the barbarism of the conflict Gulliver
> describes. Although the Houyhnhnm is horrified by Gulliver's account, since it
> provides evidence of the pernicious 'Effects of Reason you pretend to', he
> cannot believe that Yahoos could actually produce such mayhem, and 'therefore
> in recounting the Numbers of those who have been killed in Battle, I cannot but
> think that you have *Said the Thing which is not*' (IV, v, p. 318). Here, as in Brobding-
> nag, Gulliver misinterprets the generosity and horror of his interlocutors as a
> form of weakness or stupidity, and in the process he makes European behaviour,
> customs and institutions seem even more monstrous than they did when
> Gulliver first described them to the King of Brobdingnag in Book II (see Key
> Passages, **pp. 146–7**).

---

2    Another expression of Swift's hatred of colonialism.

I COULD not forbear shaking my Head and smiling a little at his Ignorance. And, being no Stranger to the Art of War, I gave him a Description of Cannons, Culverins, Muskets, Carabines, Pistols, Bullets, Powder, Swords, Bayonets, Sieges, Retreats, Attacks, Undermines, Countermines, Bombardments, Seafights; Ships sunk with a Thousand Men; twenty Thousand killed on each Side; dying Groans, Limbs flying in the Air: Smoak, Noise, Confusion, trampling to Death under Horses Feet: Flight, Pursuit, Victory; Fields strewed with Carcases left for Food to Dogs, and Wolves, and Birds of Prey; Plundering, Stripping, Ravishing, Burning and Destroying. And, to set forth the Valour of my own dear Countrymen, I assured him, that I had seen them blow up a Hundred Enemies at once in a Siege, and as many in a Ship; and beheld the dead Bodies drop down in Pieces from the Clouds, to the great Diversion of all the Spectators.

I WAS going on to more Particulars, when my Master commanded me Silence. He said [. . .] That, although he hated the *Yahoos* of this Country, yet he no more blamed them for their odious Qualities, than he did a *Gnnayh* (a Bird of Prey) for its Cruelty, or a sharp Stone for cutting his Hoof. But, when a Creature pretending to Reason, could be capable of such Enormities, he dreaded lest the Corruption of that Faculty might be worse than Brutality itself. He seemed therefore confident, that instead of Reason, we were only possessed of some Quality fitted to increase our natural Vices; as the Reflection from a troubled Stream returns the Image of an ill-shapen Body, not only *larger*, but more *distorted*. (IV, v, pp. 318–20)

## Chapter VI

*A Continuation of the State of* England, *under Queen* Anne. *The Character of a first Minister in the Courts of* Europe.

Gulliver attempts to make his Houyhnhnm Master understand the use of lawyers in England and the mechanics of lawsuits by which the worse cause always wins. Since lawsuits are the products of greed, Gulliver must also explain the uses of gold and the concept of poverty and wealth, and he can only do so by adopting the Houyhnhnm vocabulary. Here, Swift's satire against conspicuous consumption seems perfectly aligned with criticisms of British greed and mercantilism outlined in the *Drapier's Letters*, written almost simultaneously with the *Travels*. Swift had complained bitterly about the Irish import of luxuries, most notably tea, coffee and chocolate – a complaint unwittingly echoed in Gulliver's boast that 'this whole Globe of Earth must be at least three Times gone round, before one of our better Female Yahoos could get her Breakfast, or Cup to put it in' (IV, vi, p. 325). Although Gulliver seems to find no problem with what he is, one detects the voice of Swift the Irish patriot complaining of the effects of English mercantilism on the population of Ireland (see Contextual Overview, p. 16–17).

When a *Yahoo* had got a great Store of this precious Substance, he was able to purchase whatever he had a mind to; the finest Cloathing, the noblest Houses, great Tracts of Land, the most costly Meats and Drinks; and have his Choice of the most beautiful Females. Therefore since *Money* alone, was able to perform all these Feats, our Yahoos thought, they could never have enough of it to spend or to save, as they found themselves inclined from their natural Bent either to Profusion or Avarice. That, the rich Man enjoyed the Fruit of the Poor Man's Labour, and the latter were a Thousand to One in Proportion to the former. That the Bulk of our People was forced to live miserably, by labouring every Day for small Wages to make a few live plentifully. (IV, vi, pp. 324–5)

[. . .] In order to feed the Luxury and Intemperance of the Males, and the Vanity of the Females, we sent away the greatest Part of our necessary Things to other Countries, from whence in Return we brought the Materials of Diseases, Folly, and Vice, to spend among ourselves. Hence it follows of Necessity, that vast Numbers of our People are compelled to seek their Livelihood by Begging, Robbing, Stealing, Cheating, Pimping, Forswearing, Flattering, Suborning, Forging, Gaming, Lying, Fawning, Hectoring, Voting, Scribling, Stargazing, Poysoning, Whoring, Canting, Libelling, Free-thinking, and the like Occupations: Every one of which Terms, I was at much Pains to make him understand. (IV, vi, p. 326)

Much of the satire in *Gulliver's Travels* turns on the questions of language, of translating European culture into a foreign idiom and of translating foreign behaviour into familiar language we can understand. In the process, familiar institutions are defamiliarized, given new definitions and made to seem uniquely monstrous. Here Gulliver insists that if only he could make his Houyhnhnm Master 'understand', he too would accept the necessary connections of pimping, lying and stealing whose value seems self-evident to Gulliver, the representative spokesman for Western culture. Swift also exploits the satiric catalogue, a technique most fully articulated by Rabelais, a writer with whom Swift is frequently compared and whose influence is visible throughout the *Travels* (see Contextual Overview, **p. 7**). Not only is this list a long one, but also, by juxtaposing dissimilar offences – star-gazing and poisoning, for example – Swift systematically expands the scope of his satirical indictment and implies culpable relationships where none were seen to exist before. So, for example, even Gulliver's attempt to define medicine and the role of doctors in modern society turns into an unintentional indictment of modern gluttony and drunkenness and makes fun of Gulliver's pride in his own profession (medicine was a common butt of eighteenth-century satire).

I told him, we fed on a Thousand Things which operated contrary to each other; that we eat when we were not hungry, and drank without the Provocation of Thirst: That we sat whole Nights drinking strong Liquors without eating a Bit; which disposed us to Sloth, enflamed our Bodies, and precipitated or prevented Digestion. That, prostitute Female *Yahoos* acquired a certain Malady, which bred Rottenness in the Bones of those, who fell into their Embraces: That this and many other Diseases, were propagated from Father to Son; so that great Numbers come into the World with complicated Maladies upon them:[3] That, it would be endless to give him a Catalogue of all Diseases incident to human Bodies; for they could not be fewer than five or six Hundred, spread over every Limb, and Joynt: In short, every Part, external and intestine, having Diseases appropriated to each. (IV, vi, pp. 327–8)

## Chapter VII

*The Author's great Love of his Native Country. His Master's Observations upon the Constitution and Administration of* England, *as described by the Author, with parallel Cases and Comparisons. His Master's Observations upon human Nature.*

In the following passage, which calls to mind Apostle Paul's conversion on the road to Damascus, Gulliver accepts the Houyhnhnm indictment of the human species, confessing that his new-found love of truth will no longer allow him to defend the species to which he belongs or the culture he represents. Paul's conversion is an important model, because, like Gulliver, Paul changed his mind completely. Paul began as an early persecutor of the Christian Church, but he was miraculously felled from his horse on his way to Damascus, an event he interpreted as a sign from heaven that he should no longer persecute the Christians.

THE Reader may be disposed to wonder how I could prevail on my self to give so free a Representation of my own Species, among a Race of Mortals who were already too apt to conceive the vilest Opinion of Human Kind, from that entire Congruity bewixt me and their *Yahoos*.[4] But I must freely confess, that the many Virtues of those excellent *Quadrupeds* placed in opposite View to human Corruptions, had so far opened mine Eyes, and enlarged my Understanding, that I began to view the Actions and Passions of Man in a very different Light; and to think the Honour of my own Kind not worth managing; which, beside, it was impossible for me to do before a Person[5] of so acute a Judgment as my Master, who daily convinced me of a thousand Faults in my self, whereof I had not the least Perception before, and which with us would never be numbered even among human Infirmities. I had likewise learned from his Example an utter Detestation of all Falsehood or Disguise; and *Truth* appeared so amiable to me, that I determined upon sacrificing every thing to it. (IV, vii, pp. 334–5)

---

3  Syphilis and gonorrhea were at epidemic levels in parts of eighteenth-century London, and because there was no real cure they tended to be passed on to succeeding generations. Boswell's *London Journal* contains an extended account of just how easy it was to acquire 'signor gonorrhea' and just how difficult it was to get rid of it.

4  See Calhoun Winton, 'Conversion on the Road to Houyhnhnmland', *Sewanee Review* vol. 68 (1960), pp. 20–33.

5  It is one sign of Gulliver's transformation that he refers to the Houyhnhnms as 'persons'.

As Gulliver insists, only a complete dedication to truth could have compelled him to accurately transcribe his master's indictment of human behaviour, even human nature itself. In the following passage, which is central to the argument of Book IV, Gulliver's master insists on the sufficiency of reason, an assertion that calls to mind Swift's remark that he was preparing a treatise disproving that man is by definition *animal rationale* (rational animal), arguing instead that he is only *rationis capax* (capable of reason) (see Contextual Overview, **pp. 13–15**, Contemporary Documents, **p. 36** and Modern Criticism, **pp. 89–93**).

[He said] That he looked upon us as a Sort of Animals to whose Share, by what Accident he could not conjecture, some small Pittance of *Reason* had fallen, whereof we made no other Use than by its Assistance to aggravate our natural Corruptions, and to acquire new ones which Nature had not given us. [. . .] That, our Institutions of *Government* and *Law* were plainly owing to our gross Defects in *Reason*, and by consequence, in Virtue because *Reason* alone is sufficient to govern a Rational Creature; which was therefore a Character we had no Pretence to challenge, even from the Account I had given of my own People; although he manifestly perceived, that in order to favour them, I had concealed many Particulars, and often said the *Thing which was not*. (IV, vii, p. 336)

Following the logic of comparison which undergirds the structure of all four voyages, the Houyhnhnm Master describes Yahoo behaviour in terms that echo Gulliver's previous descriptions of human greed, drunkenness, even romance. Swift may also be thinking of the Yahoos in the terms popularly applied to the Irish in eighteenth-century pamphlets (see Contextual Overview, **p. 15** and Contemporary Documents, **pp. 36–7**).

He said, the *Yahoos* were known to hate one another more than they did any different Species of Animals; and the Reason usually assigned, was, the Odiousness of their own Shapes, which all could see in the rest, but not in themselves.[6] He had therefore begun to think it not unwise in us to *cover* our Bodies, and by that Invention, conceal many of our Deformities from each other, which would else be hardly supportable. But, he now found he had been mistaken; and that the Dissentions of those Brutes in his Country were owing to the same Cause with ours, as I had described them. For, if (said he) you throw among five *Yahoos* as much Food as would be sufficient for fifty, they will, instead of eating peaceably, fall together by the Ears, each single one impatient to *have all to it self*. [. . .] That, in some Fields of his Country, there are certain *shining Stones* of several Colours, whereof the *Yahoos* are violently fond; and when Part of these *Stones* are fixed in the Earth, as it sometimes happeneth, they will dig with their Claws for whole Days to get them out, and carry them away, and hide them by Heaps in their

---

6    There may be a suggestion here of Swift's comment in *The Battle of the Books* that satire is a looking glass in which a person sees everyone but himself.

Kennels; but still looking round with great Caution, for fear their Comrades should find out their Treasure. My Master said, he could never discover the Reason of this unnatural Appetite, or how these *Stones* could be of any Use to a *Yahoo*; but now he believed it might proceed from the same Principle of *Avarice*, which I had ascribed to Mankind. [. . .] There was also another Kind of Root very *juicy*, but something rare and difficult to be found, which the *Yahoos* sought for with much Eagerness, and would suck it with great Delight: It produced the same Effects that Wine hath upon us. It would make them sometimes hug, and sometimes tear one another; they would howl and grin, and chatter, and roul, and tumble, and then fall asleep in the Mud.

[. . .] His Honour had farther observed, that a Female *Yahoo* would often stand behind a Bank or a Bush, to gaze on the young Males passing by, and then appear, and hide, using many antick Gestures and Grimaces; at which time it was observed, that she had a most *offensive Smell*; and when any of the Males advanced, would slowly retire, looking often back, and with a counterfeit Shew of Fear, run off into some convenient Place where she knew the Male would follow her. (IV, vii, pp. 337–43)

## Chapter VIII

*The Author relateth several Particulars of the* Yahoos. *The great Virtues of the* Houyhnhnms. *The Education and Exercise of their Youth. Their general Assembly.*

> Yahoo females are sexually aggressive, as Gulliver discovers much to his horror. This is an important passage, because the fact that female Yahoos find him irresistible is but stronger proof, as if proof were needed, that he is a Yahoo.

BEING one Day abroad with my Protector the Sorrel Nag, and the Weather exceeding hot, I entreated him to let me bathe in a River that was near. He consented, and I immediately stripped myself stark naked, and went down softly into the Stream. It happened that a young Female *Yahoo* standing behind a Bank, saw the whole Proceeding; and inflamed by Desire, as the Nag and I conjectured, came running with all Speed, and leaped into the Water within five Yards of the Place where I bathed. I was never in my Life so terribly frighted; the Nag was grazing at some Distance, not suspecting any Harm: She embraced me after a most fulsome Manner; I roared as loud as I could, and the Nag came galloping towards me, whereupon she quitted her Grasp, with the utmost Reluctancy, and leaped upon the opposite Bank, where she stood gazing and howling all the time I was putting on my Cloaths.

THIS was Matter of Diversion to my Master and his Family, as well as of Mortification to my self. For now I could no longer deny, that I was a real *Yahoo*, in every Limb and Feature, since the Females had a natural Propensity to me as one of their own Species. (IV, viii, p. 347)

Having lived with the Houyhnhnms for three years, Gulliver remarks that his readers probably expect him to describe the manners and customs of the inhabitants of Houyhnhnmland. Here Gulliver describes Houyhnhnm reason that is cold and analytical, with no room for uncertainty or disagreement. The practical effects of Houyhnhnm reason are most visible in their mating habits and in their treatment of their foals. As the following passage suggests, while the Houyhnhnms may be 'rational', they also feel no emotion for their offspring, a fact that has led critics to suggest that Swift cannot possibly be recommending the Houyhnhnms as exemplars of reasonable behaviour if they are as coldly unfeeling as they seem. (On the critical debate over Swift's attitude towards the Houyhnhnm reason, see Critical History, **pp. 52–4**, and Modern Criticism, **pp. 89–93**.)

As these noble *Houyhnhnms* are endowed by Nature with a general Disposition to all Virtues, and have no Conceptions or Ideas of what is evil in a rational Creature; so their grand Maxim is, to cultivate Reason, and to be wholly governed by it. Neither is *Reason* among them a Point problematical as with us, where Men can argue with Plausibility on both Sides of a Question; but strikes you with immediate Conviction; as it must needs do where it is not mingled, obscured, or discoloured by Passion and Interest. I remember it was with extreme Difficulty that I could bring my Master to understand the Meaning of the word *Opinion*, or how a Point could be disputable; because Reason taught us to affirm or deny only where we are certain; and beyond our Knowledge we cannot do either. So that Controversies, Wranglings, Disputes . . . are Evils unknown among the *Houyhnhnms*. (IV, viii, p. 348)

[. . .] They have no Fondness for their Colts or Foles; but the Care they take in educating them proceedeth entirely from the Dictates of *Reason*. And, I observed my Master to shew the same Affection to his Neighbour's Issue that he had for his own. They will have it that *Nature* teaches them to love the whole Species, and it is *Reason* only that maketh a Distinction of Persons, where there is a superior Degree of Virtue.

When the Matron *Houyhnhnms* have produced one of each Sex, they no longer accompany with their Consorts, except they lose one of their Issue by some Casualty, which very seldom happens: But in such a Case they meet again; or when the like Accident befalls a Person, whose Wife is past bearing, some other Couple bestows on him one of their own Colts, and then go together a second Time, until the Mother be pregnant. This Caution is necessary to prevent the Country from being overburthened with Numbers. But the Race of inferior *Houyhnhnms* bred up to be Servants is not so strictly limited upon this Article; these are allowed to produce three of each Sex, to be Domesticks in the Noble Families.

In their Marriages they are exactly careful to chuse such Colours as will not make any disagreeable Mixture in the Breed. *Strength* is chiefly valued in the Male, and *Comeliness* in the Female; not upon the Account of Love, but to preserve the Race from degenerating: For, where a Female happens to excel in Strength, a Consort is chosen with regard to Comeliness. Courtships, Love, Presents, Joyntures, Settlements, have no Place in their Thoughts; or Terms whereby to express them in their Language. The young Couple meet and are joined, merely because it is the Determination of their Parents and Friends: It is what they see done every Day; and they look upon it as one of the necessary Actions in a reasonable Being. But the Violation of Marriage, or any other Unchastity, was never heard of: And the married Pair pass their Lives with the same Friendship, and mutual Benevolence that they bear to all others of the same species, who come in their Way; without Jealousy, Fondness, Quarrelling, or Discontent. (IV, viii, pp. 349–50)

## Chapter IX

*A grand Debate at the General Assembly of the* Houyhnhnms; *and how it was determined. The Learning of the* Houyhnhnms. *Their Buildings. Their Manner of Burials. The Defectiveness of their Language.*

The Houyhnhnms present other problems for critics seeking to hold them up as unqualified models. The Houyhnhnms have a traditional oral culture; they have no writing (see Modern Criticism, **pp. 102–6**). They have so little history that 'the historical Part is easily preserved without burthening their Memories' (IV, viii, p. 357). Swift fancied himself a historian, so it is not clear how we are supposed to view such assertive ahistoricism on the part of the Houyhnhnms. One might ask the same question regarding Gulliver's praise of Houyhnhnm poetry, which usually contains 'either some exalted Notions of Friendship and Benevolence, or the Praises of those who were Victors in Races' (IV, ix, p. 357), themes for which Swift had no apparent use in his own verse. One of the most vexing problems for critics seeking to elevate the Houyhnhnms as Swift's models is that they are not just emotionless, they are actually cruel. In a Grand Counsel called to debate the proposition whether 'the Yahoos should be exterminated from the face of the Earth', it is determined that Gulliver must leave because he is a partially reasonable, and therefore a more dangerous example to other Yahoos (IV, ix, p. 353). In this passage, several inconsistencies emerge, including the fact that creatures presumably moved only by the self-evidence of reason can actually debate anything, to say nothing of the fact that the Houyhnhnm counsel, ruled as it is by benevolence and reason, can so comfortably recommend the extermination of the Yahoos, who may have been the aboriginal inhabitants of the island who had then been subjugated by the Houyhnhnms. In a strange fashion, Gulliver himself is implicated in this genocidal fantasy when the Counsel entertains the possibility of castrating the Yahoos instead of killing them outright, a suggestion they took from Gulliver (see Critical History, **pp. 60–3**).

The Question to be debated was, Whether the *Yahoos* should be exterminated from the Face of the Earth. One of the *Members* for the Affirmative offered several Arguments of great Strength, and Weight; alledging, That, as the *Yahoos* were the most filthy, noisome, and deformed Animal which Nature ever produced, so they were the most restive and indocible, mischievous and malicious: They would privately suck the Teats of *Houyhnhnms* Cows; kill and devour their Cats, trample down their Oats and Grass, if they were not continually watched; and commit a Thousand other Extravagances. He took Notice of a general Tradition, that *Yahoos* had not been always in their Country: But, that many Ages ago, two of these Brutes appeared together upon a Mountain; whether produced by the Heat of the Sun upon corrupted Mud and Slime, or from the Ooze and Froth of the Sea, was never known. That these Yahoos engendered, and their Brood in a short time grew so numerous as to over-run and infest the whole Nation. That the *Houyhnhnms* to get rid of this Evil, made a general Hunting, and at last inclosed the whole Herd. . . . That there seemd to be much Truth in this Tradition, and that those Creatures could not be *Ylnhniamshy* (or *Aborigines* of the Land) because of the violent Hatred the Houyhnhnms as well as all other Animals, bore them. (IV, ix, pp. 353–4)

## Chapter X

*The Author's Oeconomy and happy Life among the* Houyhnhnms. *His great Improvement in Virtue, by conversing with them. Their Conversations. The Author hath Notice given him by his Master that he must depart from the Country. He falls into a Swoon for Grief, but submits. He contrives and finishes a Canoo, by the Help of a Fellow-Servant, and puts to Sea at a Venture.*

When we consider Gulliver's final transformation from doctor, captain and merchant seaman into a trotting, whinnying evangelist of Houyhnhnm virtue, it is hard to avoid the conclusion that Gulliver has been duped. Gulliver is 'Splendide Mendax', however, and as such critics as C. J. Rawson have argued, it is possible that as readers we are meant to be fooled as well (see Critical History, **pp. 55–8** and Modern Criticism, **pp. 93–8**).

WHEN I thought of my Family, my Friends, my Countrymen, of human Race in general, I considered them as they really were, *Yahoos* in Shape and Disposition, perhaps a little more civilized and qualified with the Gift of Speech; but making no other Use of Reason, than to improve and multiply those Vices, whereof their Brethren in this Country had only the Share that Nature allotted them. When I happened to behold the Reflection of my own Form in a Lake or Fountain, I turned away my Face in Horror and detestation of my self; and could better endure the Sight of a common *Yahoo*, than of my own Person, By conversing with the *Houyhnhnms*, and looking upon them with Delight, I fell to imitate their Gait and Gesture, which is now grown into a Habit; and my Friends often tell me in a blunt Way, that *I trot like a Horse*; which, however, I take for a great Compliment: Neither shall I disown, that in speaking I am apt to fall into the Voice and manner of the *Houyhnhnms*, and hear my self ridiculed on that Account without the least Mortification. (IV, x, p. 365)

## Chapter XI

*The Author's dangerous Voyage. He arrives at* New Holland, *hoping to settle there. Is wounded with an Arrow by one of the Natives. Is seized and carried by Force into a* Portugueze *Ship. The great Civilities of the Captain. The Author arrives at* England.

Gulliver builds a primitive canoe out of Yahoo skins(!), and casts off for a neighbouring island where he is attacked by natives. Fleeing once again, Gulliver is rescued by Portuguese sailors who are astounded at Gulliver's bizarre appearance and the fact that he neighs like a horse. Throughout the *Travels*, Gulliver has emphasized the importance of speech as proof of our humanity, but now Gulliver is horrified by the sound of human speech, which 'appeared to me as a monstrous as if a Dog or a Cow should speak in England, or a Yahoo in Houyhnhnm-Land' (IV, xi, p. 376). Despite the kindness of Captain de Mendez, a man described by Gulliver as a 'very courteous and generous Person' (IV, xi, p. 377), Gulliver treats him as if he is a Yahoo, attempting to jump overboard rather than consort with him. Treating Gulliver as if he has lost his mind, de Mendez carefully and generously carries him back to Lisbon. Over Gulliver's strenuous objections, de Mendez arranges for his return to England where Gulliver greets his wife and children as if they are all Yahoos. For those who follow the 'soft' school of interpretation (see Modern Criticism, **pp. 89–93**), de Mendez serves as a positive example of human virtue and benevolence and as an indicator that Swift does not mean to condemn all human beings in his portrait of the Yahoos. Gulliver's bizarre response to his family and the fact that he prefers the smell of horse manure to his wife's perfume suggest that we are intended to see him as the butt of Swift's satire, not as a spokesman for his misanthropy.

Our Voyage passed without any considerable Accident. In Gratitude to the Captain I sometimes sate with him at his earnest Request, and strove to conceal my Antipathy against human Kind, although it often broke out; which he suffered to pass without Observation. But the greatest Part of the Day, I confined myself to my Cabbin, to avoid seeing any of the Crew. The Captain had often intreated me to strip myself of my savage Dress, and offered to lend me the best Suit of Cloaths he had.

This I would not be prevailed on to accept, abhorring to cover myself with any thing that had been on the Back of a *Yahoo*. I only desired he would lend me two clean Shirts, which having been washed since he wore them, I believed would not so much defile me. These I changed every second Day, and washed them myself. (IV, xi, p. 379)

[. . .] My Wife and Family received me with great Surprize and Joy because they concluded me certainly dead; but I must freely confess the Sight of them filled me only with Hatred, Disgust and Contempt; and the more by reflecting on the near Alliance I had to them. For, although since my unfortunate Exile from the *Houyhnhnm* Country, I had compelled myself to tolerate the Sight of *Yahoos*, and to converse with *Don Pedro de Mendez*; yet my Memory and Imaginations were perpetually filled with the Virtues and Ideas of those exalted *Houyhnhnms*. And when I began to consider, that by copulating with one of the *Yahoo* Species, I had become a Parent of more; it struck me with the utmost Shame, Confusion and Horror.

As soon as I entered the House my Wife took me in her Arms, and kissed me; at which having not been used to the Touch of that odious Animal for so many Years I fell in a Swoon for almost an Hour. At the Time I am writing it is five Years since my last Return to *England*: During the first Year I could not endure my Wife or Children in my Presence, the very Smell of them was intolerable; much less could I suffer them to eat in the same Room. To this Hour they dare not presume to touch my Bread, or drink out of the same Cup; neither was I ever able to let one of them take me by the Hand. The first Money I laid out was to buy two young Stone-Horses, which I keep in a good Stable, and next to them the Groom is my greatest Favourite; for I feel my Spirits revived by the Smell he contracts in the Stable. My Horses understand me tolerably well; I converse with them at least four Hours every Day. They are Strangers to Bridle or Saddle; they live in great Amity with me, and Friendship to each other. (IV, xi, pp. 381–2)

## Chapter XII

*The Author's Veracity. His Design in publishing this Work. His Censure of those Travellers who swerve from the Truth. The Author clears himself from any sinister Ends in writing. An Objection answered. The Method of planting Colonies. His Native Country commended. The Right of the Crown to those Countries described by the Author, is justified. The Difficulty of conquering them. The Author takes his last Leave of the Reader; proposeth his Manner of Living for the futjre; gives good Advice, and concludeth.*

> The conclusion to *Gulliver's Travels* reasserts the truth of his narrative and insists on its differences from other travel accounts. At the same time, Swift offers the purest parody of other travel accounts that we find in the *Travels*, including promises of sequels to come. Once more, Swift calls attention to the truthfulness of contemporary travel accounts (see Contextual Overview, **pp. 9–10**, and Early Critical Reception, **pp. 69–71**).

THUS, gentle Reader, I have given thee a faithful History of my Travels for Sixteen Years, and above Seven Months; wherein I have not been so studious of Ornament as of Truth. I could perhaps like others have astonished thee with strange improbable Tales; but I rather chose to relate plain Matter of Fact in the simplest Manner and Style; because my principal Design was to inform, and not to amuse thee.

IT is easy for us who travel into remote Countries, which are seldom visited by *Englishmen* or other *Europeans*, to form Descriptions of wonderful Animals both at Sea and Land. Whereas, a Traveller's chief Aim should be to make Men wiser and better, and to improve their Minds by the bad, as well as good Example of what they deliver concerning foreign Places.

I COULD heartily wish a Law were enacted, that every Traveller, before he were permitted to publish his Voyages, should be obliged to make Oath before the *Lord High Chancellor*, that all he intended to print was absolutely true to the best of his Knowledge; for then the World would no longer be deceived as it usually is, while some Writers, to make their Works pass the better upon the Publick, impose the grossest Falsities on the unwary Reader. I have perused several Books of Travels with great Delight in my younger Days; but, having since gone over most Parts of the Globe, and been able to contradict many fabulous Accounts from my own Observation; it hath given me a great Disgust against this Part of Reading, and some Indignation to see the Credulity of Mankind so impudently abused. Therefore since my Acquaintance were pleased to think my poor Endeavours might not be unacceptable to my Country; I imposed on myself as a Maxim, never to be swerved from, that I would *strictly adhere to Truth*; neither indeed can I be ever under the least Temptation to vary from it, while I retain in my Mind the Lectures and Example of my noble Master, and the other illustrious *Houyhnhnms*, of whom I had so long the Honour to be an humble Hearer.

> – *Nec si miserum Fortuna Sinonem*
> *Finxit, vanum etiam, mendacemque improba finget.*[7]

[. . .] It is highly probable, that such Travellers who shall hereafter visit the Countries described in this Work of mine, may by detecting my Errors (if there be any) and adding many new Discoveries of their own, jostle me out of Vogue, and stand in my Place; making the World forget that ever I was an Author. This indeed would be too great a Mortification if I wrote for Fame: But, as my sole Intention was the PUBLICK GOOD, I cannot be altogether disappointed. (IV, xii, pp. 383–5)

In one final irony, Gulliver realizes that it is his duty to send a notice to the Secretary of State describing the lands he has found, 'because whatever lands are discovered by a Subject, belong to the Crown'. As Gulliver points out, however, these conquests might not be as easy as those of 'Ferdinando Cortez over the naked Americans' (IV, xii, pp. 386–7), or as Swift suggests in *Drapier's Letters* (1724) over the Irish. It is perhaps consistent with Swift's growing reputation as an Irish patriot that Gulliver ends his *Travels* with a darkly ironic account of colonial rapacity (see Critical History, **pp. 60–3**). Here, as in *A Modest Proposal*, Swift claims to exempt the English from his condemnation, claims undercut by Swift's long and public conflict with the 'vigilant and virtuous Governors' sent from London to deal with the Irish (see also Key Passages, **pp. 154–5**).

---

7   Virgil's *Aeneid*, Book II, pp. 79–80, 'Although vile Fortune has made Sinon wretched, she has not made him false and a liar', a speech in which Sinon convinces the Trojan leaders that the wooden horse is harmless and that they should bring it into the city. Like Sinon, Gulliver too is telling lies about horses. Indeed, one might argue that the *Travels* itself is a kind of Trojan horse, whose outside does not prepare us for what it contains.

BUT, I had another Reason which made me less forward to enlarge his Majesty's Dominions by my Discoveries: To say the Truth, I had conceived a few Scruples with relation to the distributive Justice of Princes upon those Occasions. For Instance, A Crew of Pyrates are driven by a Storm they know not whither; at length a Boy discovers Land from the Top-mast; they go on Shore to rob and plunder; they see an harmless People, are entertained with Kindness, they give the Country a new Name, they take formal Possession of it for the King, they set up a rotten Plank or a Stone for a Memorial, they murder two or three Dozen of the Natives, bring away a Couple more by Force for a Sample, return home, and get their Pardon. Here commences a new Dominion acquired with a Title by *Divine Right*. Ships are sent with the first Opportunity; the Natives driven out or destroyed, their Princes tortured to discover their Gold; a free Licence given to all Acts of Inhumanity and Lust; the Earth reeking with the Blood of its Inhabitants: And this execrable Crew of Butchers employed in so pious an Expedition, is a *modern Colony* sent to convert and civilize an idolatrous and barbarous People.

[ . . . ] BUT this Description, I confess, doth by no means affect the *British* Nation, who may be an Example to the whole World for their Wisdom, Care, and Justice in planting Colonies; the liberal Endowments for the Advancement of Religion and Learning; their Choice of devout and able Pastors to propagate *Christianity*; their Caution in stocking their Provinces with People of sober Lives and Conversations from this the Mother Kingdom; their strict Regard to the Distribution of Justice, in supplying the Civil Administration through all their Colonies with Officers of the greatest Abilities, utter Strangers to Corruption: And to crown all, by sending the most vigilant and virtuous Governors, who have no other Views than the Happiness of the People over whom they preside, and the Honour of the King their Master. (IV, xii, pp. 387–9)

Consistent with the the doubleness of perspective that we find throughout the *Travels*, however, Gulliver still wants to make sure that even though he may condemn the behaviour of colonial conquerors, he will get credit for having discovered these lands, should anyone actually decide to colonize them. He is 'ready to depose, when I shall be lawfully called, That no European did ever visit these Countries before me. I mean, if the Inhabitants ought to be believed' (IV, xii, p. 389). In the end, Gulliver learns nothing from his experience (see Tracy on plot, Modern Criticism, **pp. 79–81**). He retires to his garden where he thinks about how to apply those excellent Lessons of Virtue which I learned among the *Houyhnhnms*; to instruct the *Yahoos* of my own Family as far as I shall find them docible Animals; to behold my Figure often in a Glass, and thus if possible habituate my self by Time to tolerate the Sight of a human Creature. (IV, xii, p. 389)

I BEGAN last Week to permit my Wife to sit at Dinner with me, at the farthest End of a long Table; and to answer (but with the utmost Brevity) the few Questions I asked her. Yet the Smell of a *Yahoo* continuing very offensive, I always keep my Nose well stopt with Rue, Lavender, or Tobacco-Leaves. And although it be hard for a Man late in Life to remove old Habits; I am not altogether out of Hopes in some Time to suffer a Neighbour Yahoo in my Company, without the Apprehensions I am yet under of his Teeth or his Claws.

My Reconcilement to the *Yahoo*-kind in general might not be so difficult, if they would be content with those Vices and Follies only which Nature hath entitled them to. I am not in the least provoked at the Sight of a Lawyer, a Pick-pocket, a Colonel, a Fool, a Lord, a Gamester, a Politician, a Whoremunger, a Physician, an Evidence, a Suborner, an Attorney, a Traytor, or the like: This is all according to the due Course of Things: But, when I behold a Lump of Deformity, and Diseases both in Body and Mind, smitten with *Pride*, it immediately breaks all the Measures of my Patience; neither shall I be ever able to comprehend how such an Animal and such a Vice could tally together. The wise and virtuous *Houyhnhnms*, who abound in all Excellencies that can adorn a rational Creature, have no Name for this Vice in their Language, which hath no Terms to express any thing that is evil, except those whereby they describe the detestable Qualities of their *Yahoos*; among which they were not able to distinguish this of Pride, for want of thoroughly understanding Human Nature, as it sheweth it self in other Countries, where that Animal presides. But I, who had more Experience, could plainly observe some Rudiments of it among the wild *Yahoos*.

BUT the *Houyhnhnms*, who live under the Government of Reason, are no more proud of the good Qualities they possess, than I should be for not wanting a Leg or an Arm, which no Man in his Wits would boast of, although he must be miserable without them. I dwell the longer upon this Subject from the Desire I have to make the Society of an *English Yahoo* by any Means not insupportable; and therefore I here intreat those who have any Tincture of this absurd Vice, that they will not presume to appear in my Sight. (IV, xii, pp. 390–1)

# 4

# Further Reading

# Further Reading

This brief bibliography is not intended to provide an exhaustive listing of Swift criticism. Readers wishing to investigate the full range of commentary on *Gulliver's Travels* should consult James E. Tobin and Louis A. Landa, *Jonathan Swift: A List of Critical Studies Published from 1895 to 1945* (New York: Cosmopolitan Science and Art, 1945); James J. Stathis, *A Bibliography of Swift Studies, 1945–65* (Nashville, Tenn.: Vanderbilt University Press, 1967); and Richard H. Rodino, *Swift Studies 1965–1980: An Annotated Bibliography* (New York: Garland, 1984). For books and articles written over the past twenty-five years, readers should consult either the *MLA International Bibliography*, published annually, or *The Eighteenth Century: A Current Bibliography*, prepared annually by the American Society for Eighteenth-Century Studies. *The English Short Title Catalog, 1473–1800* (Detroit, Mich.: Thomson Gale, 2003) provides a complete bibliography of first editions available in microfilm and is available both on CD-ROM and online.

## Editions and Texts

The standard edition of Swift's letters is *The Correspondence of Jonathan Swift*, 5 vols, ed. Harold Willliams (Oxford: Clarendon Press, 1963–5). Students looking for a dependable, one-volume edition of the poems can do no better than *The Complete Poems*, ed. Pat Rogers (Harmondsworth: Penguin, 1983). For most scholars and critics of *Gulliver's Travels*, the standard text has been Volume XI in *The Prose Works of Jonathan Swift*, ed. Herbert Davis, 14 vols (Oxford: Blackwell, 1939–68), but the most recent attempt to establish a dependable text is *Gulliver's Travels: Based on the 1726 Text: Contexts, Criticism*, ed. Albert Rivero, Norton Critical Editions (New York: Norton, 2002). For the textual history of *Gulliver's Travels*, the reader should begin with Arthur E. Case, 'The Text of Gulliver's Travels' in *Four Essays on Gulliver's Travels* (Princeton, NJ: Princeton University Press, 1945), pp. 1–49; Harold H. Williams, *The Text of Gulliver's Travels* (Cambridge: Cambridge University Press, 1952); and F. P. Lock, 'The Text of Gulliver's Travels', *Modern Language Review*, vol. 76, no. 3 (July 1981), pp. 513–33.

## Biographies

Swift's early life is covered by A. C. Elias, *Swift at Moor Park: Problems in Biography and Criticism* (Philadelphia, Pa.: University of Pennsylvania Press, 1982). The best record of Swift's early years in London remains *Journal to Stella*, ed. Harold Williams (Oxford: Clarendon Press, 1948). Joseph McMinn, *Jonathan Swift* (Basingstoke: Macmillan, 1990) provides the most recent account of Swift's Irish experience. The best one-volume biography is David Nokes, *Jonathan Swift: a Hypocrite Reversed: a Critical Biography* (New York: Oxford University Press, 1985), and if there is a definitive version of Swift's life, it is Irvin Ehrenpreis, *Swift, the Man, His Works, and the Age*, 3 vols (Cambridge, Mass.: Harvard University Press, 1962–83).

## Essay Collections

Many of the standard essays on satire and *Gulliver's Travels* can be found in Frank Brady, ed., *Twentieth-Century Interpretations of 'Gulliver's Travels': A Collection of Essays* (Englewood Cliffs, NJ: Prentice-Hall, 1968); Ernest Lee Tuveson, ed., *Swift: A Collection of Critical Essays* (Englewood Cliffs, NJ: Prentice-Hall, 1964); and Claude Rawson, ed., *Jonathan Swift: A Collection of Critical Essays* (Englewood Cliffs, NJ: Prentice-Hall, 1995). More recent essays, some of them commissioned, can be found in Frank Palmeri, ed., *Critical Essays on Jonathan Swift* (New York: G. K. Hall, 1993), and Brian A. Connery, ed., *Representations of Jonathan Swift* (Newark, Del.: University of Delaware Press, 2002), which places special emphasis on Ireland, race and gender. Several anthologies of critical essays have been published to commemorate special Swift anniversaries: A. Norman Jeffares, ed., *Fair Liberty Was All His Cry: A Tercentenary Tribute to Jonathan Swift 1667–1967* (London: Macmillan, 1967); Roger McHugh and Philip Edwards, eds, *Jonathan Swift: A Dublin Tercentenary Tribute* (Dublin: Dolmen Press and Oxford University Press, 1967); Brian Vickers, ed., *The World of Jonathan Swift* (Cambridge, Mass.: Harvard University Press, 1968); and, most recently, Aileen Douglas, Patrick Kelley, and Ian Campbell Ross, eds, *Locating Swift: Essays from Dublin on the 250th Anniversary of the Death of Jonathan Swift, 1667–1745* (Dublin: Four Courts Press, 1998). More specialized collections include Christopher Fox and Brenda Tooley, eds, *Walking Naboth's Vineyard: New Studies of Swift* (Notre Dame, Ind.: University of Notre Dame Press, 1995), which focuses on Swift's experience in Ireland, and, finally, Herbert Davis, *Jonathan Swift: Essays on His Satire and Other Satires* (New York: Oxford University Press, 1964).

## Critical Histories and Casebooks

*Swift: The Critical Heritage*, ed. Kathleen Williams (London: Routledge; New York: Barnes & Noble, 1970) provides a sampling of eighteenth-century critical response to *Gulliver's Travels*. Milton Voigt, *Swift and the Twentieth Century*

(Detroit, Mich.: Wayne State University Press, 1964) offers a summary of Swift criticism as well as generous excerpts. Perhaps the two best casebooks on *Gulliver's Travels* are Milton P. Foster, *A Casebook on Gulliver among the Houyhnhnms*. (New York: Crowell, 1961), and Christopher Fox, ed., *Gulliver's Travels: Complete, Authoritative Text with Biographical and Historical Contexts, Critical History, and Essays from Five Contemporary Critical Perspectives* (Boston, Mass.: Bedford Books, 1995).

## Book-Length Studies and Individual Essays

In addition to the titles cited earlier in the annotations and headnotes, readers will also find these more specialized studies relevant to the analysis of *Gulliver's Travels*: Ellen Douglas Leyburn, *Satiric Allegory: Mirror for Man* (New Haven, Conn.: Yale University Press, 1956); Edward W. Rosenheim, Jr., *Swift and the Satirist's Art* (Chicago, Ill.: University of Chicago Press, 1963); Everett Zimmerman, *Swift's Narrative Satires: Author and Authority* (Ithaca, NY: Cornell University Press, 1983); Robert Phiddian, *Swift's Parody* (Cambridge: Cambridge University Press, 1995); and W. B. Carnochan, *Lemuel Gulliver's Mirror for Man* (Berkeley, Calif.: University of California Press, 1968). For a discussion of Gulliver as a Modern, see Patrick Reilly, *Jonathan Swift: The Brave Desponder* (Carbondale and Edwardsville, Ill: Southern Illinois University Press, 1982).

Perhaps the most useful introductory essay on *Gulliver's Travels* is Allan Bloom, 'An Outline of Gulliver's Travels', in *Ancients and Moderns*, ed. Joseph Cropsey (New York: Basic Books, 1962). Readers interested in Swift's use of sources should first consult Arthur E. Case, *Four Essays on Gulliver's Travels* (Princeton, NJ: Princeton University Press, 1945) and then look to T. O. Wedel, 'On the Philosophical Background of Gulliver's Travels', *Studies in Philology*, vol. 23 (1926), pp. 434–50. Together, these two studies lay out the main outlines for subsequent discussion of the historical and philosophical backgrounds of the *Travels*. Also useful are Jenny Mezciems, 'Swift's Praise of Gulliver: Some Renaissance Background to the Travels', in C. J. Rawson, ed., *The Character of Swift's Satire: A Revised Focus* (Newark, Del.: University of Delaware Press, 1983), pp. 245–81; Martin Kallich, *The Other End of the Egg: Religious Satire in 'Gulliver's Travels'* (Bridgeport, Conn.: Conference on British Studies at the University of Bridgeport, 1970); Louis A. Landa, 'Swift, the Mysteries and Deism', *Studies in English* (Austin, Tex.: University of Texas, 1944); Margaret Olofson Thickstun, 'The Puritan Origins of Gulliver's Religious Conversion in Houyhnhnmland', *SEL*, vol. 37, no. 3 (summer 1997), pp. 517–34; Anne Barbeau Gardiner, ' "Be ye as the horse!": Swift, Spinoza, and the Society of Virtuous Atheists', *Studies in Philology*, vol. 97, no. 2 (spring 2000), pp. 229–54; Sarah Wintle, 'If Houyhnhnms Were Horses: Thinking with Animals in Book IV of Gulliver's Travels', *The Critical Review*, vol. 34 (1994), pp. 3–21; Nicholas Hudson, 'Gulliver's Travels and Locke's Radical Nominalism', *1650–1850: Ideas, Aesthetics, and Inquiries in the Early Modern Era*, Vol. I (1994), pp. 247–66; and, finally, Leland D. Peterson, ' "Gulliver's Travels": Ancient and Modern History Corrected', *Swift Studies*, vol. 6 (1991), pp. 83–110.

Readers interested in Swift's uses of travel narrative in the *Travels* should consult Percy G. Adams, *Travel Literature and the Evolution of the Novel* (Lexington, Ky.: University of Kentucky Press, 1983; R. W. Frantz, *The English Traveler and the Movement of Ideas, 1660–1732* (Lincoln, Nebr.: University of Nebraska Press, 1934); Charles Batten, Jr., *Pleasurable Instruction: Form and Convention in Eighteenth-Century Travel Literature* (Berkeley, Calif.: University of California Press, 1978); Arthur Sherbo, 'Swift and Travel Literature', *Modern Language Studies*, vol. 9, no. 3 (fall 1979), pp. 114–27; and Maximillian E. Novak, 'Gulliver's Travels and the Picaresque Voyage: Some Reflections on the Hazards of Genre Criticism', in Frederik N. Smith, ed., *The Genres of Gulliver's Travel* (Newark, Del.: University of Delaware Press, 1990).

In addition to the studies cited above, other major discussions of politics in *Gulliver's Travels* include George Orwell, 'Politics vs. Literature: An Examination of Gulliver's Travels', in *Shooting an Elephant and Other Essays* (London: Secker & Warburg, 1950). All discussions of political allegory in *Gulliver's Travels* owe a debt to Charles H. Firth, 'The Political Significance of Gulliver's Travels', *Proceedings of the British Academy*, vol. 9 (1919–20), pp. 237–59. Many of the arguments put forward there are reinforced, modified or refuted by J. A. Downie, 'The Political Significance of Gulliver's Travels', *Swift and His Contexts*, ed. John Irwin Fischer, Hermann, J. Real and James Woolley (New York: AMS Press, 1989), pp. 1–9; Phillip Harth, 'The Problem of Political Allegory in Gulliver's Travels', *Modern Philology* vol. 73, pt. 2 (1975–6), pp. 540–7; F. P. Lock, *The Politics of 'Gulliver's Travels'* (Oxford: Clarendon Press, 1980); Bertrand Goldgar, *Walpole and the Wits: The Relation of Politics to Literature* (Lincoln, Nebr.: University of Nebraska Press, 1976); Ian Higgins, *Swift's Politics: A Study in Disaffection* (Cambridge: Cambridge University Press, 1994); David Bywaters, 'Gulliver's Travels and the Mode of Political Parallel During Walpole's Administration', *ELH (English Library History)*, vol. 54 (1987), pp. 717–40; and, finally, Edward W. Said, 'Swift's Tory Anarchy', *Eighteenth-Century Studies*, vol. 3 (1969), pp. 48–66.

Readers interested in feminist criticism may wish to consult Carol Houlihan Flynn, *The Body in Swift and Defoe* (Cambridge: Cambridge University Press, 1990); Felicity Nussbaum, *The Brink of All We Hate: English Satires on Women, 1660–1750* (Lexington, Ky.: University of Kentucky Press, 1984); Ellen Pollak, *The Poetics of Sexual Myth: Gender and Ideology in the Verse of Swift and Pope* (Chicago, Ill.: University of Chicago Press, 1985); and Susan Gubar, 'The Female Monster in Augustan Satire', *Signs: Journal of Women in Culture and Society*, vol. 3, no. 2 (winter 1977). Notable New Historicist approaches include Carole Fabricant, *Swift's Landscape* (Baltimore, Md.: Johns Hopkins University Press, 1982); Michael McKeon, 'Parables of the Younger Son (I): Swift and the Containment of Desire', in *The Origins of the English Novel 1660–1740* (Baltimore, Md.: Johns Hopkins University Press, 1987), pp. 338–56; and Edward Said, 'Swift as Intellectual', *The World, the Text, and the Critic* (Cambridge, Mass.: Harvard University Press, 1983), pp. 72–89.

Deconstructionist approaches to Swift include Grant Holly, 'Travel and Translation: Textuality in Gulliver's Travels', *Criticism*, vol. 21 (1979), pp. 134–52; Clive T. Probyn, 'Starting from the Margins: Teaching Swift in the Light of Post-structuralist Theories of Reading and Writing', *Critical Approaches to Teaching*

*Swift*, ed. Peter J. Schakel (New York: AMS Press, 1992), pp. 19–35. In addition to the works by Rawson and Rodino (cited above), reader-response discussions of the *Travels* include Janet E. Aikins, 'Reading "with conviction": Trial by Satire', in Smith, *Genres*, pp. 203–29; Louise K. Barnett, 'Deconstructing Gulliver's Travels: Modern Readers and the Problematic of Genre', in Smith, *Genres* (1990), pp. 230–45; Robert W. Uphaus, 'Swift and the Problematic Nature of Meaning,' in *The Impossible Observer* (Lexington, Ky.: University of Kentucky Press, 1979), pp. 9–27; and Loftus Jestin, 'Splendide Mendax: Purposeful Misprision, Determinant Irony, in Gulliver's Travels', *Swift Studies*, vol. 14 (1999), pp. 99–114. Students interested in psychoanalytic readings may also wish to consult John Traugott, 'The Yahoo in the Doll's House: *Gulliver's Travels* The Children's Classic', *English Satire and the Satiric Tradition*, ed. Claude Rawson (Oxford: Basil Blackwell, 1984), pp. 127–50; Ruth Salvaggio, 'Swift and Psychoanalysis, Language and Women', *Women's Studies*, vol. 15 (1988), pp. 417–34; and the review essay by Hermann Real, and Heinz J. Vienken, 'Psychoanalytic Criticism and Swift: The History of a Failure', *Eighteenth-Century Ireland*, Vol. I (1986), pp. 127–41.

# Index

NOTE: Page numbers in bold indicate an extract by an author or from a particular work. Page numbers followed by an n indicate information is found only in a footnote.

# Related series from Routledge

## THE NEW CRITICAL IDIOM
Series Editor: John Drakakis,
University of Stirling

*The New Critical Idiom* is an invaluable series of introductory guides to today's critical terminology. Each book:

- provides a handy, explanatory guide to the use (and abuse) of the term
- offers an original and distinctive overview by a leading literary and cultural critic
- relates the term to the larger field of cultural representation.

With a strong emphasis on clarity, lively debate and the widest possible breadth of examples, *The New Critical Idiom* is an indispensable approach to key topics in literary studies.

'Easily the most informative and wide-ranging series of its kind, so packed with bright ideas that it has become an indispensable resource for students of literature.' – *Terry Eagleton, University of Manchester*

**A selection of titles available in this series are:**

**The Author** by Andrew Bennett
**Comedy** by Andrew Stott
**Crime Fiction** by John Scaggs
**Genre** by John Frow
**Literature** by Peter Widdowson

**Myth** by Laurence Coupe
**Narrative** by Paul Cobley
**Realism** by Pam Morris
**Romanticism** by Aidan Day
**Science Fiction** by Adam Roberts

For further information on individual books
in the series and a full range of titles, visit:
**www.routledge.com/literature/nci**

# Related series from Routledge

## ROUTLEDGE CRITICAL THINKERS

Series Editor: Robert Eaglestone,
Royal Holloway, University of London

*Routledge Critical Thinkers* is a series of accessible introductions to key figures in contemporary critical thought.

'This series demystifies the demigods of theory.' – *Susan Bennett, University of Calgary, Canada*

**Titles in this series include:**

*Louis Althusser* by Luke Ferretter
*Roland Barthes* by Graham Allen
*Jean Baudrillard* by Richard J. Lane
*Simone de Beauvoir* by Ursula Tidd
*Homi K. Bhabha* by David Huddart
*Maurice Blanchot* by Ullrich Haase and William Large
*Judith Butler* by Sara Salih
*Gilles Deleuze* by Claire Colebrook
*Jacques Derrida* by Nicholas Royle
*Michel Foucault* by Sara Mills
*Sigmund Freud* by Pamela Thurschwell
*Stuart Hall* by James Procter

*Martin Heidegger* by Timothy Clark
*Fredric Jameson* by Adam Roberts
*Jean-François* Lyotard by Simon Malpas
*Jacques Lacan* by Sean Homer
*Julia Kristeva* by Noëlle McAfee
*Paul de Man* by Martin McQuillan
*Friedrich Nietzsche* by Lee Spinks
*Paul Ricoeur* by Karl Simms
*Edward Said* by Bill Ashcroft and Pal Ahluwalia
*Gayatri Chakravorty Spivak* by Stephen Morton
*Slavoj Žižek* by Tony Myers

For further information on individual books
in the series and a full range of titles, visit:
**www.routledge.com/literature/nci**

# Related titles from Routledge

## The Routledge Dictionary of Literary Terms

### Peter Childs and Roger Fowler

*The Routledge Dictionary of Literary Terms* is a twenty-first century update of Roger Fowler's seminal *Dictionary of Modern Critical Terms*. Bringing together original entries written by such celebrated theorists as Terry Eagleton and Malcolm Bradbury with new definitions of current terms and controversies, this is the essential reference book for students of literature at all levels. This book includes:

- New definitions of contemporary critical issues such as 'Cybercriticism' and 'Globalization'.
- An exhaustive range of entries, covering numerous aspects to such topics as genre, form, cultural theory and literary technique.
- Complete coverage of traditional and radical approaches to the study and production of literature.
- Thorough accounts of critical terminology and analysis of key academic debates.
- Full cross-referencing throughout and suggestions for further reading.

ISBN10: 0–415–36117–6 (hbk)
ISBN10: 0–415–34017–9 (pbk)

ISBN13: 978–0–415–36117–0 (hbk)
ISBN13: 978–0–415–34017–5 (pbk)

Available at all good bookshops
For ordering and further information please visit:
## www.routledge.com

# Related titles from Routledge

## The Routledge Companion
## to Critical Theory

### Simon Malpas and Paul Wake

*The Routledge Companion to Critical Theory* is an indispensable guide for anyone coming to this exciting field of study for the first time.

Exploring ideas from a diverse range of disciplines, this clearly presented text encourages the reader to develop a deeper understanding of how to approach the written word. Defining what is generically referred to as 'critical theory', *The Routledge Companion to Critical Theory* explores some of the most complex and fundamental concepts in the field, ranging from historicism to postmodernism, from psychoanalytic criticism to race and postcolonialism.

Key features include:

- clear and detailed introductory chapters written by experts in each area
- almost 200 fully cross-referenced dictionary entries
- a range of illustrations drawn from literature, film and contemporary culture, which illustrate complex theoretical ideas
- a dictionary of terms and thinkers that students are likely to encounter
- guidance on further reading to direct students towards crucial primary essays and introductory chapters on each concept.

Tailored to meet the needs of undergraduate students when they first encounter theory, as well as when their knowledge and experience develop and they want to know where to go next, this is the ideal resource for those studying this fascinating area.

ISBN10: 0–415–33295–8 (hbk)
ISBN10: 0–415–33296–6 (pbk)

ISBN13: 978–0–415–33295–8 (hbk)
ISBN13: 978–0–415–33296–5 (pbk)

Available at all good bookshops
For ordering and further information please visit:
**www.routledge.com**

# Related titles from Routledge

## Literary Theory: The Basics
### Hans Bertens

Part of the successful *Basics* series, this accessible guide provides the ideal first step in understanding literary theory. Hans Bertens:

- leads students through the major approaches to literature which are signalled by the term 'literary theory'
- places each critical movement in its historical (and often political) context
- illustrates theory in practice with examples from much-read texts
- suggests further reading for different critical approaches
- shows that theory can make sense and that it can radically change the way we read.

Covering the basics and much more, this is the ideal book for anyone interested in how we read and why that matters.

ISBN10: 0–415–35112–X (pbk)
ISBN13: 978–0–415–35112–6 (pbk)

Available at all good bookshops
For ordering and further information please visit:
## www.routledge.com

# Related titles from Routledge

## Doing English
### A Guide for Literature Students
Robert Eaglestone

'*Doing English* . . . is excellent: a thought-provoking and accessible argument exploring the changing character of English Literature as it has developed outside the school curriculum over the last half century.' – *The English and Media Magazine*

'If students read what Eaglestone has to say, they will certainly be more confident in confronting some of the challenges and contradictions which exist in literary studies in universities.' – *Dr Roy Johnson, Mantex.co.uk*

Aimed at students in the final year of secondary education or beginning degrees, this readable book provides the ideal introduction to studying English literature. *Doing English*:

- explains what 'doing English' really means
- introduces current ideas about literature, contexts and interpretations
- bridges the gap between 'traditional' and 'theoretical' approaches to literature, showing why English has had to change and what those changes mean for students of the subject.

Doing English deals with the exciting new ideas and contentious debates that make up English today, covering a broad range of issues from the history of literary studies and the canon to Shakespeare, politics and the future of English. The second edition has been revised throughout and includes a new chapter on narrative. Robert Eaglestone's refreshingly clear explanations and advice make this volume essential reading for all those planning to 'do English' at advanced or degree level.

ISBN10: 0–415–28422–8 (hbk)
ISBN10: 0–415–28423–6 (pbk)

ISBN13: 978–0–415–28422–6 (hbk)
ISBN13: 978–0–415–28423–3 (pbk)

Available at all good bookshops
For further information on our literature series, please visit:

## www.routledge.com/literature/series.asp
For ordering and further information please visit:

## www.routledge.com

# Related titles from Routledge

## Critical Practice (Second Edition)
### Catherine Belsey
### New Accents Series

'A fine assessment of recent work in literary theory and a suggestive account of new directions for criticism to take.' – *William E. Cain*

What is poststructuralist theory, and what difference does it make to literary criticism? Where do we find the meaning of the text: in the author's head? in the reader's? Or do we, instead, *make* the meaning in the practice of reading itself? If so, what part do our own values play in the process of interpretation? And what is the role of the text?

Catherine Belsey explains these and other questions concerning the relations between human beings and language, readers and texts, writing and cultural politics. The volume simply and lucidly explains the views of such key figures as Louis Althusser, Roland Barthes, Jacques Lacan and Jacques Derrida, and shows their theories at work in readings of familiar literary texts.

With a new chapter, updated guidance on further reading and revisions throughout, this second edition of *Critical Practice* is the ideal guide to the present and the future of literary studies.

ISBN10: 0–415–28005–2 (hbk)
ISBN10: 0–415–28006–0 (pbk)

ISBN13: 978–0–415–28005–1 (hbk)
ISBN13: 978–0–415–28006–0 (pbk)

Available at all good bookshops
For ordering and further information please visit:
### www.routledge.com

# Related titles from Routledge

## Culture and the Real
### Theorizing Cultural Criticism
Catherine Belsey
### New Accents Series

What makes us the people we are? Culture evidently plays a part, but how large a part? Is culture alone the source of our identities? Catherine Belsey calls for a more nuanced account of what it is to be human. In the light of a characteristically lucid account of their views, as well as their debt to Kant and Hegel, she takes issue with Jean-François Lyotard, Judith Butler, and Slavoj Zizek. Drawing examples from film and art, fiction and poetry, Professor Belsey builds on the insights of her influential Critical Practice to provide not only an accessible introduction to current debates, but a major new contribution to cultural criticism and theory.

ISBN10: 0–415–25288–1 (hbk)
ISBN10: 0–415–25289–X (pbk)

ISBN13: 978–0–415–25288–1 (hbk)
ISBN13: 978–0–415–252898 (pbk)

Available at all good bookshops
For ordering and further information please visit:
## www.routledge.com

# Related titles from Routledge

## The Singularity of Literature
Derek Attridge

'Wonderfully original and challenging.' – *J. Hillis Miller*

Literature and the literary have proved singularly resistant to definition. Derek Attridge argues that such resistance represents not a dead end, but a crucial starting point from which to explore anew the power and practices of Western art.

In this lively, original volume, the author:

- Considers the implications of regarding the literary work as an innovative cultural event
- Provides a rich new vocabulary for discussions of literature, rethinking such terms as invention, singularity, otherness, alterity, performance and form
- Argues the ethical importance of the literary institution to a culture
- Demonstrates how a new understanding of the literary might be put to work in a "responsible", creative mode of reading.

*The Singularity of Literature* is not only a major contribution to the theory of literature, but also a celebration of the extraordinary pleasure of the literary, for reader, writer, student or critic.

ISBN10: 0–415–33592–2 (hbk)
ISBN10: 0–415–33593–0 (pbk)

ISBN13: 978–0–415–33592–8 (hbk)
ISBN13: 978–0–415–33593–5 (pbk)

Available at all good bookshops
For ordering and further information please visit:
### www.routledge.com